An Auto-Instructional Text in

CORRECT WRITING

Form B

An Auto-Instructional Text in
CORRECT WRITING

Second Edition

Form B

Eugenia Butler
University of Georgia

Mary Ann Hickman
Gainesville Junior College

Lalla Overby
Brenau College

D.C. Heath and Company
Lexington, Massachusetts
Toronto

This work is a revision of *An Auto-Instructional Text in Correct Writing,* Forms I and II, by Edwin M. Everett, Marie Dumas, and Charles Wall, all late of the University of Georgia.

Published simultaneously in Canada.

Printed in the United States of America.

International Standard Book Number: 0-669-02484-8

To the Instructor

An Auto-Instructional Text in Correct Writing, Second Edition, Form B, is a revision and enlargement of earlier editions.

The authors have adopted a format which combines the best features of a handbook of grammar and composition and a workbook of exercises. Wherever possible, the exercises have been simplified in order to make them more than usually illustrative of the grammatical principles involved. The exposition of the various aspects of grammar and sentence structure is addressed to the student in as simple terms as possible and is more extensive than that in most other workbooks. The discussion of such subjects as parts of speech, diction, and vocabulary is not intended to be exhaustive, but rather to offer the instructor sufficient opportunity for more extensive discussion of these topics as the occasion arises. The greatly enlarged Glossary of Faulty Diction is an especially useful feature, and it is accompanied by exercises so that it may be used for reference and study.

Sentences used in the exercises of this text have been carefully formulated to reflect the sort of writing that is a part of everyday life. This characteristic should help the student see that correct and accurate usage is not for "formal" occasions only, but that it should extend into every aspect of one's daily communication.

The treatment of punctuation is a distinctive adjunct of this book, since it serves as a follow-up to the chapters in which the basic principles of sentence structure are discussed. When students reach the lesson on punctuation, they will already have learned most of the rules in that lesson, which can then serve as a review of the entire subject instead of a listing of arbitrary rules to be memorized. There are, however, numerous occasions when it seems appropriate simply to cite a rule without attempting theoretical explanations which would defeat the purpose of the text as an elementary handbook for grammar and composition. A rule governing punctuation, grammar, or sentence structure may be susceptible to modification or exception, but it is nonetheless useful for being arbitrarily stated. If students do not know that their sentences contain comma splices, they are hardly prepared at that stage of development to explore the subtleties of such a construction.

A central point which should emerge through a student's careful use of this text is that the study of grammar and of sentence elements is of value primarily as a means toward better communication and understanding.

To the Student

This book is a combination textbook, workbook, program, and reference. It contains a great deal of information in the various chapters that precede the exercises. It is a workbook in which you will be able to write your answers. It is programmed so that you may check each answer as soon as you have written it. When you have worked all the exercises as well as the Achievement and Review Tests, you will still have a convenient reference handbook in which you can check points of grammar, usage, punctuation, and mechanics whenever you need to.

You will need a piece of heavy paper or cardboard approximately two inches wide and six inches long for use as an answer mask while doing the exercises. After reading Chapter 1, place the answer mask on page 12 to cover the left-hand column. When you have read the instructions and written your answer to the first question, slide the mask down far enough to uncover the correct answer and compare this answer with yours. Place a check mark after your answer if it is correct. Then answer the second question and proceed in the same way to compare answers and make check marks. When you have finished an exercise, add the number of check marks and enter the total in the space labelled SCORE. Working conscientiously through the lessons and exercises will put you well on your way to a mastery of grammar and usage, which in turn will help you to write and speak accurately and effectively.

Contents

NAME ______________________________ SCORE ________

DIAGNOSTIC TEST

In the following sentences identify the part of speech of each *italicized* word by writing one of the following numbers in the space at the right:

1	if it is a noun,	5	if it is an adverb,
2	if it is a pronoun,	6	if it is a preposition,
3	if it is a verb,	7	if it is a conjunction,
4	if it is an adjective,	8	if it is an interjection.

1. I have *only* one question to ask. ________
2. How did you fall *down* the steps? ________
3. I know the girl *who* is standing by the escalator. ________
4. These are the *four* top students in the senior class. ________
5. The woman's dress *suggests* that she is a nurse. ________
6. The campers *were frightened* by the sound of footsteps. ________
7. Chaucer is *frequently* called the father of English literature. ________
8. My brother *and* his family are moving to Buffalo. ________
9. *Well*, I have decided that I cannot go. ________
10. Each of us hopes to attend the *art* exhibit. ________
11. Cult worship is as old as man *himself*. ________
12. Missy jumps rope *almost* every morning. ________
13. Ralph emphasized *that* he was open to suggestions. ________
14. Danny wants to be an *airline* pilot. ________
15. The light switch is *behind* the door. ________
16. A tuition *increase* for next year is under consideration. ________
17. It is courageous to attempt the *impossible*. ________
18. The new building *will house* research facilities. ________
19. *George's* feet are extremely large. ________
20. The coast of Maine is rugged *but* beautiful. ________
21. Procrastination is the fault *of* many. ________
22. *Gee*, did you see that pass? ________
23. Patrick *is* very much *intrigued* by science-fiction. ________
24. Mr. O'Neal is running for the *Senate* next year. ________
25. *While* I was eating breakfast, I listened to the news. ________

Each of the following sentences either contains an error in grammar or is correct. Indicate the error or the correctness by writing one of the following numbers in the space at the right:

- **1** if the case of the pronoun is incorrect,
- **2** if the subject and verb do not agree,
- **3** if a pronoun and its antecedent do not agree,
- **4** if an adjective or an adverb is used incorrectly,
- **5** if the sentence is correct.

26. Each of the rivals says that the victory is theirs. ______
27. Father says that Jeff is real smart. ______
28. I don't believe that he will mind you going with us. ______
29. It is she who will present the bouquet to the honor guest. ______
30. Neither the steak nor the potato salad were very good. ______
31. I understand that the final decision will be between you and he. ______
32. There is a bed, a chest, and a table in the guest room. ______
33. Just give the message to whoever answers the phone. ______
34. Each of the actors was given their own copy of the script. ______
35. Don't you think that the wedding ceremony was real brief? ______
36. Aunt Marie often invites Andy and I to her house for Sunday dinner. ______
37. The sub-committee has sent their report to Dr. Cook. ______
38. Our cat Rosa along with her kittens sleep in the garage. ______
39. Meg's biology grade is some higher than mine. ______
40. Neither of the desserts appeal to me. ______
41. Should us campers take coats as well as sweaters? ______
42. I am certain that five dollars is the price of the key chain. ______
43. Every clerk in the store received their training from Mrs. Doster. ______
44. My grandmother is one of those persons who is prepared for any emergency. ______
45. You may ask whomever is at the desk for the key to the room. ______
46. Both Phyllis and me want to become nurses. ______
47. Even with a houseful of guests Mother still appears calmly. ______
48. The scouting party has returned to its base camp. ______
49. Wilbur along with his coach were at Duffy's Diner for breakfast. ______
50. I do believe that it is her, not her sister, working at Rich's. ______

Each of the following sentences either contains an error in sentence structure or is correct. Indicate the error or correctness by writing one of the following numbers in the space at the right:

1 if the sentence contains a dangling modifier,
2 if the sentence contains a misplaced modifier,
3 if the sentence contains a faulty reference of a pronoun,
4 if the sentence contains faulty parallelism,
5 if the sentence is correct.

51. After gathering up the children, the van was ready to leave for Rockwell Park. ____

52. The man was short, round, and wore a plaid suit. ____

53. One never knows when you will need an extra car key. ____

54. Marvin is studying public relations and plans to make it a career. ____

55. Abe told his brother that he needed to trim his beard. ____

56. The novel was written by James Joyce lying on my desk. ____

57. Having completed the highway, it was easy to reach Montgomery in four hours. ____

58. Every morning O'Neill reads the paper during breakfast, which annoys his wife. ____

59. Last night I only read the first chapter of my book. ____

60. His parents hope to eventually move to an apartment. ____

61. When completed in August, we can reach the island by the bridge. ____

62. The paint bucket is nearly empty, but I will buy more of it on my way to work. ____

63. Dr. Harley plans to publish his book about Ontario in the spring. ____

64. We not only wanted to visit the waterfront but also to eat at Arthur's Oyster Bar. ____

65. She is an ambitious girl and who is willing to work. ____

66. To re-wire the house, much skill is needed. ____

67. In talking with Maurice, he told me that he is quitting the team. ____

68. The television critic pronounced the new space series to be contrived, unexciting, and it attempts to copy *Star Wars*. ____

69. Lucy told Jessie Mae that her breakfast was getting cold. ____

70. I only had two more problems to complete when the bell rang for us to stop working. ____

71. As a teen-ager my friends used to call me Shorty. ____

72. According to commercials, that red toothpaste can make me a hit with the opposite sex, which would be a miracle. ____

73. By adding a ruffle to the hem of the skirt, Sandra's dress was long enough for Mary. ____

74. When we had all boarded the bus, Tom began counting noses and to realize that four people were still missing. ____

75. The boy who was paddling skillfully guided the canoe down the treacherous rapids. ____

Each of the following sentences contains an error in punctuation or mechanics, or is correct. Indicate the error or the correctness by writing one of the following numbers in the space at the right:

1 if a comma has been omitted,
2 if a semicolon has been omitted,
3 if an apostrophe has been omitted,
4 if quotation marks have been omitted,
5 if the sentence is correct.

76. When I was only two years old my family lived in Paris. ______
77. My familys home was on the Left Bank near the Seine River. ______
78. Stringing macaroni onto a piece of yarn kept the children quiet about ten minutes it wasn't long before they were restless again. ______
79. Do you always cross your *t*s with fancy curlicues, Meg? ______
80. You must catch that plane, cried Virginia, if you expect to make it to Seattle by eleven o'clock. ______
81. Its been far too long since we saw our relatives who live in New Mexico. ______
82. While looking for my credit card I found my lost earring. ______
83. The radiant happy bridal couple ran to their car amid a shower of rice. ______
84. It is past time you must admit for you to learn my zip code. ______
85. The boy we used to call Little Ben now weighs two hundred pounds. ______
86. You look smart in your velvet slacks nevertheless, I think that a dress would be more appropriate for the wedding. ______
87. Matts guitar lessons have been a mixed blessing; I'll be glad when he finally learns those chords. ______
88. Our washing machine regulates its own water temperature automatically. ______
89. If you have never heard Pete Fountain's Just a Closer Walk with Thee, you are missing something. ______
90. Mrs. Van Astorbilt you are occupying my pew. ______
91. Wouldnt you like to be a fly on the wall at that confrontation? ______
92. Nellie wants to go out to the woods and find a cedar Christmas tree but Sam and Dorothy want to buy a hemlock. ______
93. The Jacobsons have bought an old mansion and intend to restore it. ______
94. The long frustrating search for the lost child had a happy ending. ______
95. My new shirt washes beautifully it is Dacron. ______
96. What poem is it that begins, Tell me not in mournful numbers/Life is but an empty dream? ______
97. Frankly Marion I cannot support your scheme to discredit Joe. ______
98. I am happy for the first time in years for I have fallen in love. ______
99. He knocked on the door but could get no response. ______
100. Time was running out he had to try a field goal now, or it would be too late. ______

An Auto-Instructional Text in

CORRECT WRITING

Form B

1
The Parts of Speech

Our own language is one of the most fascinating subjects that we can investigate, and those of us who speak and write English can find pleasure in seeking to understand its various aspects. The concern of this book is Standard English and its use in contemporary writing. The study and description of Standard English, based on the thoughtful use of language by educated people, provide standards for correct writing. Although the English language is flexible and continually changing, it is possible to follow certain principles and to observe certain characteristics of usage which can make grammar a relatively exact study and one which can widen the scope of the individual in a satisfying way.

An understanding of the accurate and effective use of English is important not only for communication but also as a vital element of creative thought. Because words are used in the formulation of conscious thought, precise grammatical usage promotes clear thinking and insures logical and systematic transmission of ideas.

Knowledge of Standard English and its acceptable forms is basic to the education of all college students. Learning grammatical terms is an essential first step toward understanding what is correct and what is incorrect in speech and writing. The best place to begin this learning of terms is with the various elements that make up a sentence, elements called **parts of speech.** Any word's identification as a part of speech depends upon its usage within a sentence. The names of the eight parts of speech are as follows:

noun	adverb
pronoun	preposition
adjective	conjunction
verb	interjection

1a Noun

A **noun** (from Latin *nomen*, name) is the name of a person, place, thing, or idea. All nouns are either proper nouns or common nouns. A **proper noun** is the name of a particular person, place, or thing and is spelled with a capital letter:

John F. Kennedy	London, England
California	The Washington Monument
The Vatican	O'Keefe Junior High School

A **common noun** is the name of a class of persons, places, things, or ideas, and is not capitalized:

girl	home	dog	disgust
teacher	park	automobile	friendship
student	street	honesty	poverty

Nouns may also be classified as **individual** or **collective. Collective** nouns name groups of persons, places, or things that function as units:

flock	dozen
jury	the rich
team	club

Finally, nouns may be classified as **concrete** or **abstract.** The **concrete** noun names a person, place, or thing which can be perceived by one of the five senses. It can be seen, felt, smelled, heard, or tasted. Here are some examples of concrete nouns:

door	woman	scream
dress	city	snow
tree	odor	museum

An **abstract** noun is the name of a quality, condition, action, or idea. The following are examples of abstract nouns:

beauty	truth	kindness
fear	loneliness	campaign
dismissal	hatred	courtesy

A noun is said to belong to the **nominative**, the **objective**, or the **possessive case**, depending upon its function within a sentence. Subjects are in the nominative case (The *truck* stopped), objects are in the objective case (He saw the *parade*), and nouns showing possession are in the possessive case (That car is *John's*). As you can see, there is no difference in form between nouns in the nominative and the objective cases. The possessive case, however, changes a noun's form. (See Chapter 11 for a thorough discussion of case.)

A noun may be **singular** or **plural**, forming its plural generally by the addition of *-s* or *-es* to the end of the singular form (*girl, girls; potato, potatoes*).

Nouns, together with pronouns and other words or expressions that function as nouns, are sometimes called **substantives.**

1b Pronoun

A **pronoun** (from Latin *pro,* for, and *nomen,* name) is a word used in place of a noun. A pronoun usually refers to a noun or other substantive already mentioned, which is called its **antecedent** (from Latin *ante,* before, and *cedere,* to go). Most pronouns have antecedents, but some do not.

Pronouns are divided into seven categories:

PERSONAL PRONOUNS: I, you, he, it, they, etc.

DEMONSTRATIVE PRONOUNS: this, that, these, those

INDEFINITE PRONOUNS: each, anyone, everyone, either, etc.

INTERROGATIVE PRONOUNS: who, which, what

RELATIVE PRONOUNS: who, which, that

REFLEXIVE PRONOUNS: myself, yourself, herself, themselves, etc.

INTENSIVE PRONOUNS: I *myself,* you *yourself,* she *herself,* they *themselves,* etc.

The personal pronouns have differing forms depending upon whether they are subjects (*I* will help Mr. Curtis) or objects (Gene told *him* a story) or show possession (The red coat is *hers*). These differences in form, which are seen only in the possessive case of nouns, occur in all three cases (*nominative, objective,* and *possessive*) of pronouns.

Personal pronouns, like nouns, are singular and plural, but their plurals are irregularly formed: I, *we*; she, *they*; it, *they*; etc. The following table shows the various forms of the personal pronouns:

SINGULAR

	Nominative	*Objective*	*Possessive*
1st person	I	me	my, mine
2nd person	you	you	your, yours
3rd person	he, she, it	him, her, it	his, her, hers, its

PLURAL

	Nominative	*Objective*	*Possessive*
1st person	we	us	our, ours
2nd person	you	you	your, yours
3rd person	they	them	their, theirs

1c Adjective

An **adjective** (from Latin *adjectivum,* something that is added) modifies, describes, limits, or adds to the meaning of a noun or pronoun (*strange, lovely, three, French, those*). In other words, adjectives modify substantives. The articles *the, a,* and *an* are adjectives. Nouns in the possessive case (*Martha's* book, the *cat's* whiskers) and some possessive forms of the personal pronouns are used as adjectives:

my	our
your	your
his, her, its	their

Many demonstrative, indefinite, and interrogative forms may be used as either pronouns or adjectives:

DEMONSTRATIVE: this, that, these, those

INDEFINITE: each, any, either, neither, some, all, both, every, many, most

INTERROGATIVE: which, what, whose

When one of these words appears before a noun or other substantive, describing it or adding to its meaning (*this* cake, *those* gloves, *any* person, *some* food, *which* dress), it is an adjective. When the word stands in the place of a noun (*Those* are pretty roses), it is, of course, a pronoun.

Adjectives formed from proper nouns are called **proper adjectives** and are spelled with a capital letter **(German, Christian, Biblical, Shakespearean).**

1d Verb

A **verb** (from Latin *verbum,* word) is a word used to state or ask something and usually expresses an action (*spoke, tells, ran, argued, fights*) or a state of being (*is, seemed, existed, appears*). As its Latin origin indicates, the verb is *the* word in the sentence, for every sentence must have a verb, either expressed or understood.

TRANSITIVE AND INTRANSITIVE VERBS

A verb is called **transitive** if its action is directed toward some receiver, which may be the object of the verb or even its subject. (*David flew the plane,* or *The plane was flown by David.* Whether *plane* is the subject or object of the verb, the fact remains that David flew the plane, making *plane* in both sentences the receiver of the verb's action.)

NOTE: The term *action* should not be misinterpreted as always involving physical activity. The so-called "action" of a verb may not refer to a physical action at all: Mr. Lee *considered* the plan, Amanda *believed* Frank's story, Louise *wants* a new car. The verbs *considered, believed,* and *wants* are transitive verbs; and their objects *plan, story,* and *car* are receivers of their "action," even though there is no physical action involved.

A verb is called **intransitive** if its action is not directed toward some receiver. (*Lightning strikes. Mother is ill.*) Most verbs may be either transitive or intransitive, simply depending on whether or not a receiver of the verb's action is present in the sentence: *Lightning strikes tall trees* (*strikes* is transitive because *trees* is its object). *Lightning strikes suddenly* (*strikes* is intransitive because no receiver of its action is present).

LINKING VERBS

There is a special group of intransitive verbs which make a statement not by expressing action but by indicating a state of being or a condition. These verbs are called **linking verbs** because their function is to link the subject of a sentence with a noun, pronoun, or other substantive that identifies it or with an adjective that describes it. A subject and a linking verb cannot function together as a complete sentence without the help of the substantive or adjective needed to complete the thought; for example, in the sentence *Dorothy is my sister* the word *sister* is necessary to complete the sentence, and it identifies *Dorothy,* the subject. In the sentence *Dorothy is vigorous* the word *vigorous* is necessary, and it describes the subject.

The most common linking verb is the verb *to be* in all its forms, but any verb that expresses a state of being and is followed by a noun or an adjective that identifies or describes the subject is a linking verb. Following is a list of some of the most commonly used linking verbs:

appear	grow	seem	taste*
become	look	smell	
feel	remain	sound	

You will notice that those verbs referring to states of being perceived through the five "senses" are included in the list: *look, feel, smell, sound,* and *taste.* (Sally *looks* happy, I *feel* chilly, The coffee *smells* good, The ticking of the clock *sounded* loud, The plum pudding *tastes* spicy.)

ACTIVE AND PASSIVE VOICE

Transitive verbs are said to be in the **active voice** or the **passive voice. Voice** is the form of a verb that indicates whether the subject of the sentence performs the action or is the receiver of the action of the verb. If the subject performs the action, the verb is in the *active voice* (*Andy ate soup for lunch today*). If the subject receives the action, the verb is in the *passive voice* (*Soup was eaten by Andy for lunch today*).

TENSE

Tense is the form a verb takes in order to express the time of an action or a state of being, as in these examples: *Helen walks* (**present tense**); *Helen walked* (**past tense**). These two tenses, present and past, change the verb's simple form to show the time of the verb's action. The other four of the six principal tenses found in English verbs are formed through the use of **auxiliary** (helping) verb forms like the following:

am	is	were	have	had
are	was	will	has	been

The use of these auxiliary verbs creates **verb phrases** (groups of related words that function as single parts of speech). These verb phrases enable the writer to express time and time relationships far beyond those found in the simple present and past forms: She *has gone* to the office; Maggie *will ride* with me; You *must finish* your dinner; He *had expected* to win the prize; I *am planning* a trip.

CONJUGATION OF VERBS

Showing all forms of a verb in all its tenses is called **conjugation.** Any verb may be conjugated if its **principal parts** are known. These are (1) the first person singular, present tense, (2) the first person singular, past tense, (3) the past participle. (The **participle** is a verbal form which must always be accompanied by an auxiliary verb when it is used to create one of the verb tenses.)

---

*These verbs are not exclusively linking verbs; they may also be used in an active sense, possibly having objects, as in the following:

The dog cautiously *smelled* the food in its bowl.
We *looked* everywhere for the lost key.
Sharon *felt* the warmth of the log fire across the room.
Nick *tasted* the chowder and then added salt.

The principal parts of the verb *to call* are (1) *call,* (2) *called,* (3) *called.* The first two of these provide the basic forms of the simple tenses; the third is used with the auxiliary verbs to form verb phrases for the other tenses. The conjugation in the **indicative mood** (that form used for declarative or interrogative sentences) of the verb *to call* is given below:

ACTIVE VOICE

Singular	*Plural*
Present Tense	
1. I call	We call
2. You call	You call
3. He, she, it calls	They call
Past Tense	
1. I called	We called
2. You called	You called
3. He, she, it called	They called
Future Tense	
1. I shall (will) call	We shall (will) call
2. You will call	You will call
3. He, she, it will call	They will call
Present Perfect Tense	
1. I have called	We have called
2. You have called	You have called
3. He, she, it has called	They have called
Past Perfect Tense	
1. I had called	We had called
2. You had called	You had called
3. He, she, it had called	They had called
Future Perfect Tense	
1. I shall (will) have called	We shall (will) have called
2. You will have called	You will have called
3. He, she, it will have called	They will have called

PASSIVE VOICE

Singular	*Plural*
Present Tense	
1. I am called	We are called
2. You are called	You are called
3. He, she, it is called	They are called
Past Tense	
1. I was called	We were called
2. You were called	You were called
3. He, she, it was called	They were called

Future Tense	
1. I shall (will) be called	We shall (will) be called
2. You will be called	You will be called
3. He, she, it will be called	They will be called

Present Perfect Tense	
1. I have been called	We have been called
2. You have been called	You have been called
3. He, she, it has been called	They have been called

Past Perfect Tense	
1. I had been called	We had been called
2. You had been called	You had been called
3. He, she, it had been called	They had been called

Future Perfect Tense	
1. I shall (will) have been called	We shall (will) have been called
2. You will have been called	You will have been called
3. He, she, it will have been called	They will have been called

NOTE: You have probably noticed that in the future and future perfect tenses the auxiliary verb *shall* is used in the first persons singular and plural. Traditionally, written English has required this usage, but contemporary grammarians now suggest that the distinction need be made only in formal written English and that *will* may usually be used throughout a conjugation. For emphasis, however, *shall* may occasionally be needed, especially to express strong determination or invitation:

We *shall* overcome!

Shall we dance?

PROGRESSIVE TENSES

To express an action or state in progress either at the time of speaking or at the time spoken of, forms of the auxiliary verb *to be* are combined with the present participle (See Chapter 4, Section C) as follows:

Progressive Present Tense	
1. I am calling	We are calling
2. You are calling	You are calling
3. He, she, it is calling	They are calling

Progressive Past Tense	
1. I was calling	We were calling
2. You were calling	You were calling
3. He, she, it was calling	They were calling

This process may be continued through the various tenses of the active voice, as indicated below:

PROGRESSIVE FUTURE TENSE: I shall (will) be calling, etc.

PROGRESSIVE PRESENT PERFECT TENSE: I have been calling, etc.

PROGRESSIVE PAST PERFECT TENSE: I had been calling, etc.

PROGRESSIVE FUTURE PERFECT TENSE: I shall (will) have been calling, etc.

In the passive voice, the progressive is generally used only in the simple present and past tenses:

PROGRESSIVE PRESENT TENSE: I am being called, etc.

PROGRESSIVE PAST TENSE: I was being called, etc.

In the remaining tenses of the passive voice, the progressive forms—though feasible—become awkward (I shall be being called, I have been being called, etc.).

AUXILIARY VERBS *TO BE* AND *TO HAVE*

As you have seen, the verbs *to be* and *to have* are used to form certain tenses of all verbs. Following are the conjugations of these two auxiliary verbs in the indicative mood, active voice:

The principal parts of *to be* are (1) *am,* (2) *was,* and (3) *been.*

	Present Tense	
	Singular	*Plural*
1.	I am	We are
2.	You are	You are
3.	He, she, it is	They are
	Past Tense	
1.	I was	We were
2.	You were	You were
3.	He, she, it was	They were
	Future Tense	
1.	I shall (will) be	We shall (will) be
2.	You will be	You will be
3.	He, she, it will be	They will be
	Present Perfect Tense	
1.	I have been	We have been
2.	You have been	You have been
3.	He, she, it has been	They have been
	Past Perfect Tense	
1.	I had been	We had been
2.	You had been	You had been
3.	He, she, it had been	They had been

Future Perfect Tense	
1. I shall (will) have been	We shall (will) have been
2. You will have been	You will have been
3. He, she, it will have been	They will have been

The principal parts of the verb *to have* are (1) *have,* (2) *had,* and (3) *had.*

Present Tense	
Singular	*Plural*
1. I have	We have
2. You have	You have
3. He, she, it has	They have
Past Tense	
1. I had	We had
2. You had	You had
3. He, she, it had	They had
Future Tense	
1. I shall (will) have	We shall (will) have
2. You will have	You will have
3. He, she, it will have	They will have
Present Perfect Tense	
1. I have had	We have had
2. You have had	You have had
3. He, she, it has had	They have had
Past Perfect Tense	
1. I had had	We had had
2. You had had	You had had
3. He, she, it had had	They had had
Future Perfect Tense	
1. I shall (will) have had	We shall (will) have had
2. You will have had	You will have had
3. He, she, it will have had	They will have had

MOOD

Mood is the form a verb may take to indicate whether it is intended to make a statement, to give a command, or to express a condition contrary to fact. Besides the **indicative** mood shown in the conjugations above, there are the **imperative** and the **subjunctive** moods.

The **imperative** mood is used in giving commands or making requests, as in *TAKE me out to the ball game.* Here *TAKE* is in the imperative mood. The subject of an imperative sentence is *you,* usually understood, but sometimes expressed for the sake of emphasis, as in *You get out of here!*

The **subjunctive** mood is most often used today to express a wish or a condition contrary to fact. In the sentences *I wish I WERE going* and *If I WERE you, I would not go,* the verbs in capitals are in the subjunctive mood.

1e Adverb

An **adverb** (from Latin *ad,* to or toward, and *verbum,* word) usually modifies or adds to the meaning of verbs, adjectives, and other adverbs. Sometimes, however, it may be used to modify or qualify a whole phrase or clause, adding to the meaning of an idea that the sentence expresses. The following sentences illustrate the variety of uses of the adverb:

He ran *fast.* [*Fast* modifies the verb *ran.*]

The judges considered the contestants *unusually* brilliant. [*Unusually* modifies the adjective *brilliant.*]

She sang *very* loudly. [*Very* modifies the adverb *loudly.*]

The doves were flying *just* outside gun range. [*Just* modifies either the preposition *outside* or the whole prepositional phrase *outside gun range.*]

He had driven carefully *ever* since he was injured. [*Ever* modifies either the conjunction *since* or the whole clause *since he was injured.*]

Unfortunately, she has encountered rejection everywhere. [*Unfortunately* modifies the whole idea expressed in the sentence and cannot logically be attached to a single word.]

1e Preposition

A **preposition** (from Latin *prae,* before, and *positum,* placed) is a word placed usually before a substantive, called the *object of the preposition,* to show relationship between that object and some other word in the sentence. The combination of a preposition, its object, and any modifiers of the object is called a **prepositional phrase** (*in the mood, on the porch, of human events, toward the beautiful green lake*). You will see how necessary prepositions are to our language when you realize how often you use most of the ones in the group below, which includes some of the most commonly used prepositions:

about	between	over
above	beyond	past
across	but (meaning *except*)	since
after	by	through
against	concerning	throughout
along	down	to
amid	during	toward
among	except	under
around	for	underneath
at	from	until
before	in	up
behind	into	upon
below	like	with
beneath	of	within
beside	off	without
besides	on	

Ordinarily a preposition precedes its object, as its name indicates. Although a sentence ending with a preposition is frequently unemphatic or clumsy, it is in no way contrary to English usage. *She asked what they were cooked in* is better English than *She asked in what they were cooked.*

1g Conjunction

A **conjunction** (from Latin *conjungere,* to join) is a word used to join words or groups of words. There are two kinds of conjunctions: **coordinating conjunctions** and **subordinating conjunctions.**

COORDINATING CONJUNCTIONS

Coordinating conjunctions join sentence elements of equal rank. In the sentence *She was poor but honest* the conjunction *but* joins the two adjectives *poor* and *honest.* In *She was poor, but she was honest* the conjunction *but* joins the two independent statements *She was poor* and *she was honest.* The common coordinating conjunctions are the following:

and but or nor for

Yet in the sense of *but,* and *so* in the sense of *therefore* are also coordinating conjunctions. **Correlative conjunctions,** which are used in pairs (*either . . . or . . . , neither . . . nor . . .*) are coordinating conjunctions also.

SUBORDINATING CONJUNCTIONS

Subordinating conjunctions introduce certain subordinate or dependent elements and join them to the main or independent part of the sentence. In *Jack has gone home because he was tired* the subordinating conjunction *because* subordinates the clause that it is part of and joins it to the main part of the sentence, *Jack has gone home. If, whether, while, unless, although, as, before, after,* and *until* are common examples of subordinating conjunctions.

NOTE: Words like *however, therefore, nevertheless, moreover, in fact, consequently, hence,* and *accordingly* are essentially adverbs, not conjunctions; they are sometimes called **conjunctive adverbs.**

1h Interjection

An **interjection** (from Latin *inter,* among or between, and *jectum,* thrown) is an exclamatory word like *oh, ouch, please, why, hey* thrown into a sentence or sometimes used alone. An interjection is always grammatically independent of the rest of the sentence. Adjectives, adverbs, and occasionally other parts of speech become interjections when used as independent exclamations (*good! horrible! fine! what! wait!*).

Exercise 1 NOUNS AND PRONOUNS

Write every noun and pronoun found among the *italicized* words. After each noun write **N**; after each pronoun write **P**.

EXAMPLE: Angie and *Robin* bought *themselves* new *school* clothes.

Robin (**N**), themselves (**P**)

Answers	Sentences
	1. *I* saw Mr. Lewis *this morning.*
1. I (P), morning (N)	2. Doug and *his* wife are moving to *Detroit*, Michigan, next *month.*
2. Detroit (N), month (N)	3. *Zack's* father and *I* witnessed the *automobile accident.*
3. I (P), accident (N)	4. The *past* two *days we* have had the hottest weather of the *summer.*
4. days (N), we (P), summer (N)	5. *We* will *visit* my sister in *Idaho* next summer.
5. We (P), Idaho (N)	6. *One* of our fastest *runners* sprained his ankle yesterday.
6. One (P), runners (N)	7. *Each* of the students must *present* an oral report this *semester.*

7. Each (P), semester (N)	8. The *tour guide* stayed with *us all* day.
8. guide (N), us (P)	9. *Our* new little *kittens* spend all *their time* eating or sleeping.
9. kittens (N), time (N)	10. *They plan* to have a *reception* on the *patio.*
10. They (P), reception (N), patio (N)	11. Have *you read* the *assignment*?
11. you (P), assignment (N)	12. It rained *every* day during our first *week* of vacation.
12. week (N)	13. *Burt* found *these while* walking through the *woods.*
13. Burt (N), these (P), woods (N)	14. *Some* of *you* will need to buy *your* own *equipment.*
14. Some (P), you (P), equipment (N)	15. No one can doubt *Kathy's interest* in *her work.*
15. interest (N), work (N)	16. *There* is no *logic* in *his* recent *decision* to leave.
16. logic (N), decision (N)	**SCORE** ______

Exercise 2 PRONOUNS

In the sentences below identify the *italicized* pronouns by writing one of the following abbreviations:

P for personal,	**Inter** for interrogative,
D for demonstrative,	**Inten** for intensive,
I for indefinite,	**Ref** for reflexive.
Rel for relative,	

EXAMPLE: *Who* will be willing to wash dishes today?

Inter

	1. Peaches will make a delicious dessert if we can find *them.*
1. P	2. *One* of our new rose bushes has a bud.
2. I	3. Jean says that she wants to cook dinner *herself* tonight.
3. Inten	4. The man *whom* I was talking with is the newly elected mayor.
4. Rel	5. Mother cut *herself* with the sharp new paring knife.
5. Ref	6. *Which* of these books do you want to read first?
6. Inter	7. *These* are my prettiest place mats.
7. D	8. Won't you walk with *us* over to the Edwards's house?

8. P	9. Here is the surprise *that* I promised you.
9. Rel	10. *Each* of the actors returned to the stage for a curtain call.
10. I	**SCORE** ______

Exercise 3

ADJECTIVES AND ADVERBS

In the following sentences underline once all adjectives and words used as adjectives except the articles **a**, **an**, and **the**. Underline all adverbs twice.

EXAMPLE: Horseback riding is very delightful.

Horseback riding is very delightful.

	1. Baylor University has established much higher admission standards this year.
1. Baylor University has established much higher admission standards this year.	2. The little girl intently watched every movement of the baby elephant.
2. The little girl intently watched every movement of the baby elephant.	3. Christy is a very imaginative and creative architect.
3. Christy is a very imaginative and creative architect.	4. He was desperate for an alibi for the night of the murder.
4. He was desperate for an alibi for the night of the murder.	5. Most artists need the approval of their peers.
5. Most artists need the approval of their peers.	6. We had originally planned a winter vacation in Vail, Colorado.
6. We had originally planned a winter vacation in Vail, Colorado.	7. The Highlander in Highlands, North Carolina, combines a quaint Southern atmosphere with very tasty food.
7. The Highlander in Highlands, North Carolina, combines a quaint Southern atmosphere with very tasty food.	8. An executive meeting is not necessary this week.

8. An executive meeting is not necessary this week.	9. The judge was rather impatient with the lengthy testimony.
9. The judge was rather impatient with the lengthy testimony.	10. Leslie has always been a lonely child.
10. Leslie has always been a lonely child.	11. We were the only couple on the beach last night.
11. We were the only couple on the beach last night.	12. I have recently read several of P. D. James's mystery novels.
12. I have recently read several of P. D. James's mystery novels.	13. The tall, slim girl moved beautifully across the room.
13. The tall, slim girl moved beautifully across the room.	14. Priscilla is the only student with a perfect score.
14. Priscilla is the only student with a perfect score.	15. I left immediately after the first curtain call.
15. I left immediately after the first curtain call.	SCORE ______

Exercise 4 VERBS

Write the verbs in the following sentences. Write **A-T** after every transitive verb in the active voice and **P-T** after every transitive verb in the passive voice. Mark all intransitive verbs **I**.

EXAMPLE: Walker Percy's characters cannot communicate adequately with those around them.

can communicate **(I)**

	1. He was reading *Foxfire* for the first time.
1. was reading (A-T)	2. Marie watched the children in the garden.
2. watched (A-T)	3. Bluegrass music is very popular today.
3. is (I)	4. Inexpensive bicycles are often heavier than the more expensive ones.
4. are (I)	5. Luncheon will be served on the deck.
5. will be served (P-T)	6. We struggle every day with the same problems.
6. struggle (I)	7. I love corn on the cob with plenty of butter.
7. love (A-T)	8. At the end of the book the hero regains his speech.

Answers	Questions
8. regains (A-T)	9. The old hound was defeated by the new leader of the pack.
9. was defeated (P-T)	10. Did you remain in the room?
10. Did remain (I)	11. The forest suddenly became quiet.
11. became (I)	12. Paul has ordered Peter Matthiessen's book *The Snow Leopard*.
12. has ordered (A-T)	13. The young boy was rewarded for his honesty.
13. was rewarded (P-T)	14. Quentin's haughty attitude made me furious.
14. made (A-T)	15. The moon controls the tides.
15. controls (A-T)	**SCORE** ______

Exercise 5 **PREPOSITIONS**

Write the preposition for each of the following sentences. After each preposition write its object.

EXAMPLE: He refused all assistance from the welfare department.

from—department

	1. Shakespeare will always be among the great writers.
1. among—writers	2. Between you and me I admire him greatly.
2. Between—you, me	3. Everyone was invited but Susan.
3. but—Susan	4. The coach has not been satisfied with the team's performance.
4. with—performance	5. Across the river the journey ends.
5. Across—river	6. Into the thick of battle the cavalry charged.
6. Into—thick of—battle	7. We prepared supper for the soccer team.
7. for—team	8. Behind the barn the cows grazed.

8. Behind–barn	9. Before the opera we will eat dinner at my house.
9. Before–opera at–house	10. The storm raged throughout the night.
10. throughout–night	11. The little dog hid under the porch.
11. under–porch	12. We parked the car behind the department store.
12. behind–store	13. The football team came running from the dressing room.
13. from–room	14. Tom and Linda walked along the shore together.
14. along–shore	15. My grandmother told us tales about her childhood.
15. about–childhood	16. Walter will meet us outside the theater.
16. outside–theater	17. *Gideon's Trumpet* is a story of one man's search for justice.

17. of–search for–justice	18. I will be there in ten minutes.
18. in–minutes	19. Meredith sat on the edge of her chair, carefully following Dan's remarks.
19. on–edge of–chair	20. By the time Zelda arrived, the food was gone.
20. By–time	**SCORE** ______

Exercise 6	CONJUNCTIONS

In the following sentences there are both coordinating and subordinating conjunctions. Write each conjunction, and after it write **C** if it joins sentence elements of equal rank or **S** if it joins unequal elements.

EXAMPLE: Tim and his brother are tennis players.

and (**C**)

	1. When the rain stops, we will leave.
1. When (S)	2. My sister was offered the job, but she decided not to take it.
2. but (C)	3. After you finish reading, please take out the garbage.
3. After (S)	4. If Sally told him to jump off a cliff, he would do so.
4. If (S)	5. We will all go to dinner, and afterwards Leon and Nan can go to the race.
5. and (C) and (C)	6. After the game was over, the whole stadium was in confusion.
6. After (S)	7. My father always enjoyed reading the morning paper while he ate his breakfast.

7. while (S)	8. Are you planning to fly to Philadelphia, or will you take the train?
8. or (C)	9. Because Carol has had a variety of experiences in the academic world, she will be an excellent college president.
9. Because (S)	10. Whereas Hercules is remembered for his strength, Ulysses is remembered for his cunning.
10. Whereas (S)	11. Professor Shane will attend our workshop, though she cannot stay the entire day.
11. though (S)	12. Mary Jane called to tell me that she is a grandmother.
12. that (S)	13. If you will put the groceries on the table, I will prepare dinner.
13. If (S)	14. We will not leave until the game is over.
14. until (S)	15. He does not want to buy a new house, nor does he want to renovate an old one.
15. nor (C)	**SCORE** ______

Exercise 7 REVIEW OF PARTS OF SPEECH

In the following sentences identify the part of speech of each *italicized* word by writing one of the the following abbreviations:

N	for noun,	**Adv**	for adverb,
V	for verb,	**Prep**	for preposition,
P	for pronoun,	**C**	for conjunction,
Adj	for adjective,	**I**	for interjection.

EXAMPLE: I went for a *ride* on my nephew's motorcycle.

N

	1. Betty Jo is a *very* pretty girl.
1. Adv	2. *Oh*, I almost forgot to tell you about my new car.
2. I	3. Starvation *and* fire are the greatest threats to wild animals.
3. C	4. *We* all went to the Michigan-Michigan State game.
4. P	5. *Behind* the shed you will find the hoe.
5. Prep	6. A stop on the freeway is *dangerous*.
6. Adj	7. This morning I saw a *snake* crossing the road.
7. N	8. *Have* you *decided* which college you will attend?
8. V	9. Those tomato plants are doing *well*.

9. Adv	10. Jim and his family are going to Myrtle Beach *for* the Labor Day weekend.
10. Prep	11. Do you think *that* Donna will be chosen Homecoming Queen?
11. C	12. Jimmy *is selling* his van to his sister.
12. V	13. Cary wants to teach us sign *language*.
13. N	14. I watched the fight on *color* television last night.
14. Adj	15. We will visit the Delaware Art Museum *early* in the afternoon.
15. Adv	16. What kind of flowers are *these*?
16. P	17. Professor Alexander *carefully* explained the assignment to the class.
17. Adv	18. *Gee*, I will never finish translating my Latin.
18. I	19. *Neither* Tom *nor* Barbara has my book.
19. C	20. A student's life is frequently *quite* hectic.
20. Adv	**SCORE** ______

Exercise 8 REVIEW OF PARTS OF SPEECH

In the following sentences identify the part of speech of each *italicized* word by writing one of the following abbreviations:

N	for noun,	**Adv**	for adverb,
V	for verb,	**Prep**	for preposition,
P	for pronoun,	**C**	for conjunction,
Adj	for adjective,	**I**	for interjection.

EXAMPLE: The puppies must stay *in* the barn.

Prep

	1. He was awakened in the middle of the night by a *screech* owl.
1. Adj	2. Nature may *not* be as systematic as we think.
2. Adv	3. I could not serve on the jury *because* I was sick.
3. C	4. Vivian *was selected* editor of her college newspaper.
4. V	5. Today *we* discussed the upcoming election.
5. P	6. *Wow!* When did you get that new sports car?
6. I	7. *Ursula* is an unusual name.
7. N	8. Mr. Perry *organized* the school's jogging club.
8. V	9. Will *you* pick up my coat at the dry cleaner's?

9. P	10. Evelyn's *best* friend will be her roommate next year.
10. Adj	11. My grandparents spoke German *fluently*.
11. Adv	12. The box office is holding *two* tickets for you.
12. Adj	13. *Inside* the closet you will find your tennis shoes.
13. Prep	14. On the bulletin board I saw your name *and* Harry's.
14. C	15. Gloria wastes *too* much time.
15. Adv	16. Jennie's mare will have a colt *in* February.
16. Prep	17. Ferris is running for president of the *student* government.
17. Adj	18. Mr. Jones is an *attorney* in Columbus, Georgia.
18. N	19. Mary Clare, my dressmaker, made *me* a suede cloth suit for fall.
19. P	20. We bought new furniture *after* we moved.
20. C	SCORE ______

2

Recognizing Subjects, Verbs, and Complements

2a The Sentence

A **sentence** is made up of single parts of speech combined into a pattern which expresses a complete thought. In other words, a sentence is a group of words that expresses a complete thought. In its simplest form this complete statement is an independent clause or a **simple sentence.**

2b Subject and Predicate

Every simple sentence must have two basic elements: (1) the thing we are talking about, and (2) what we say about it. The thing we are talking about is called the **subject**, and what we say about it is called the **predicate**. The subject is a noun, a pronoun, or some other word or group of words used as a noun. The essential part of the predicate is a verb—a word which tells something about the subject. It tells that the subject *does* something or that something *is true* of the subject. Therefore, a subject and a verb are the fundamental parts of every sentence. In fact, it is possible to express meaning with just these two elements:

Pilots fly.

Flowers bloom.

In each example the verb says that the subject does something. The sentences are about pilots and flowers. What does each do? The pilots fly; the flowers bloom.

2c Finding the Verb

Finding verbs and subjects of verbs in a sentence is the first step in determining whether or not a group of words expresses a complete thought. Therefore, look first for the verb, the most important word in the sentence, and then for its subject.

The verb may sometimes be difficult to find. It may come anywhere in the sentence; for instance, it may precede the subject, as in some interrogative sentences (*Where is my pencil*?). It may consist of a single word or a group of two or more words; it may have other words inserted within the verb phrase; it may be combined with the negative *not* or with a contraction of *not*. To find the verb, however, look for the word or group of words that expresses an action or a state of being. In the following sentences the verbs are in italics:

My friend *stood* by me. [The verb *stood* follows the subject *friend.*]

By me *stood* my friend. [The verb *stood* precedes the subject *friend.*]

My friend *was standing* by me. [The verb *was standing* consists of two words.]

My friend *can*not *stand* by me. [The auxiliary verb *can* is combined with the negative adverb *not*, which is not part of the verb.]

Did my friend *stand* by me? [The verb *did stand* is divided by the subject.]

2d Finding the Subject

Sometimes finding the subject may also be difficult, for, as we have just seen, the subject does not always come immediately before the verb. Often it comes after the verb; often it is separated from the verb by a modifying element. Always look for the noun or pronoun about which the verb asserts something and disregard intervening elements:

Many of the children *come* to the clinic. [A prepositional phrase comes between the subject and the verb.]

There *are flowers* on the table. [The subject comes after the verb. The word *there* is never a subject; in this sentence it is an *expletive,* an idiomatic introductory word.]

In the room *were* a *cot* and a *chair*. [The subject comes after the verb.]

In an imperative sentence, a sentence expressing a command or a request, the subject *you* is usually implied rather than expressed. Occasionally, however, the subject *you* is expressed:

Come in out of the rain.

Shut the door!

You play goalie.

Either the verb or the subject or both may be **compound**; that is, there may be more than one subject and more than one verb:

The *boy* and the *girl* played. [Two subjects.]

The boy *worked* and *played.* [Two verbs.]

The *boy* and the *girl worked* and *played.* [Two subjects and two verbs.]

In the first sentence the compound subject is *boy* and *girl.* In the second sentence there is a compound verb, *worked* and *played*. In the third sentence both the subject and the verb are compound.

2e Complements

Thus far we have discussed two functions of words: that of nouns and pronouns as subjects and that of verbs as predicates.

A third function of words which we must consider is that of completing the verb. Nouns, pronouns, and adjectives are used to complete verbs and are called **complements**. A complement may be a **direct object**, an **indirect object**, a **predicate noun** or **pronoun**, a **predicate adjective**, an **objective complement**, or a **retained object**.

A **direct object** is a noun or noun equivalent which completes the verb and receives the action expressed in the verb:

> The pilot flew the plane. [*Plane* is the direct object of *flew*. Just as the subject answers the question "*who*?" or "*what*?" before the verb (Who flew?), so the direct object answers the question "*whom*?" or "*what*?" after the verb (Flew what?).]

An **indirect object** is a word (or words) denoting the person or thing indirectly affected by the action of a transitive verb. It is the person or thing to which something is given or for which something is done. Such words as *give, offer, grant, lend, teach,* etc., represent the idea of something done for the indirect object:

> We gave *her* the book. [*Her* is the indirect object of *gave*. The indirect object answers the question "*to (for) whom or what*?" after the verb *gave* (Gave to whom?).]

Certain verbs that represent the idea of taking away or withholding something can also have indirect objects:

> The judge *denied him* the opportunity to speak in his own defense.
>
> Father *refused Frances* the use of the car.

A **predicate noun** (also called **predicate nominative**) is a noun or its equivalent which renames or identifies the subject and completes such verbs as *be, seem, become,* and *appear* (called linking verbs):

> The woman is a *doctor*. [The predicate noun *doctor* completes the intransitive verb *is* and renames the subject *woman*.]
>
> My best friends are *she* and her *sister*. [The predicate pronoun *she* and the predicate noun *sister* complete the intransitive verb *are* and rename the subject *friends*.]
>
> Mary has become a *pilot*. [The predicate noun *pilot* completes the intransitive verb *has become* and renames the subject *Mary*.]

A **predicate adjective** is an adjective which completes a linking verb and describes the subject:

> The man seems *angry*. [The predicate adjective *angry* completes the intransitive verb *seems* and describes the subject *man*.]

An **objective complement** is a noun or an adjective which completes the action expressed in the verb and refers to the direct object. If it is a noun, the objective complement is in a sense identical with the direct object; if it is an adjective, it describes or limits the direct object. It occurs commonly after such verbs as *think, call, find, make, consider, choose,* and *believe:*

> Jealousy made Othello a *murderer*. [The objective complement *murderer* completes the transitive verb *made* and renames the direct object *Othello*.]
>
> She thought the day very *disagreeable*. [The objective complement *disagreeable* is an adjective which describes the direct object *day*.]

A **retained object** is a noun or noun equivalent which remains as the object when a verb which has both a direct and an indirect object is put into the passive voice. The other object becomes the subject of such a verb. Although either object may become the subject, the indirect object more commonly takes that position, and the direct object is retained:

The board granted him a year's leave of absence.
He was granted a year's leave of absence.

[In the second sentence the verb has been put into the passive voice, the indirect object of the first sentence has become the subject of the second, and the direct object has been retained.]

The teacher asked the student a difficult question.
A difficult question was asked the student.

[In the second sentence the verb has been put into the passive voice, the direct object of the first sentence has become the subject of the second, and the indirect object has been retained.]

Exercise 9	SUBJECTS AND VERBS

In each of the following sentences underline the subject once and the verb twice. Then copy each subject and its verb.

EXAMPLE: I am listening to Vivaldi's "The Four Seasons."

I *am listening*

	1. Aunt Callie plays bridge every Thursday.
1. Aunt Callie *plays*	2. There are two extra sandwiches in the refrigerator.
2. sandwiches *are*	3. A group from our church will tour Jerusalem this spring.
3. group *will tour*	4. On the kitchen table is a pencil.
4. pencil *is*	5. Al and Wayne work in the attorney general's office.
5. Al, Wayne *work*	6. Most students study all day and play all night.
6. students *study, play*	7. Annie stuffed the papers into her pocketbook.
7. Annie *stuffed*	8. Did you return the book to the library?

8. you *did return*	9. The noise from the band room disturbed our class.
9. noise *disturbed*	10. Not everyone will arrive tomorrow.
10. everyone *will arrive*	11. Leave all the explanations to me.
11. (you) *leave*	12. Had you met Fred before?
12. you *Had met*	13. Today is a lovely day.
13. Today *is*	14. Mother and I will meet you at the country club for lunch.
14. Mother, I *will meet*	15. For many years we did not hear from Cousin Charles.
15. we *did hear*	16. The courtroom was filled with reporters.
16. courtroom *was filled*	17. The attorneys are very much aware of public opinion.

17. attorneys *are*	18. The real source of the confusion was not clear.
18. source *was*	19. Dennis will be leaving for the University of Arizona next week.
19. Dennis *will be leaving*	20. Have you ever seen a baobab tree?
20. you *Have seen*	21. Honey is a good substitute for sugar.
21. Honey *is*	22. I started an afghan three years ago and still have not finished it.
22. I *started, have finished*	23. Arabian horses are famous for their beauty and spirit.
23. horses *are*	24. The Okefenokee Swamp in southeast Georgia covers six hundred square miles.
24. Okefenokee Swamp *covers*	25. Neither you nor I can solve their differences.
25. you, I *can solve*	26. Because of the hurricane we cancelled our trip to Ponte Vedra.

26. we *cancelled*	27. There is a basket of peaches for you on the kitchen table.
27. basket *is*	28. Jackie's little league football team practices three times a week.
28. team *practices*	29. I have only recently discovered the detective stories of Amanda Cross.
29. I *have discovered*	30. The lights from the mountain lodge guided our steps.
30. lights *guided*	31. Chuck and Bob washed and waxed the van.
31. Chuck, Bob *washed, waxed*	32. Why didn't you deposit your check yesterday?
32. you *did deposit*	33. The traffic was terrible on the expressway.
33. traffic *was*	34. Of course, air pollution is always bad on freeways.
34. pollution *is*	35. The woman in the blue dress is my husband's sister.
35. woman *is*	SCORE ______

Exercise 10 SUBJECTS AND VERBS

In each of the following sentences underline the subject once and the verb twice. Then copy each subject and its verb.

EXAMPLE: Monroe has already memorized his part for the play.

Monroe *has memorized*

	1. Few people know T. H. White's detective novel *Darkness at Pemberley.*
1. people *know*	2. Kathryn Thomson was guest speaker at our annual banquet.
2. Kathryn Thomson *was*	3. The agenda for the meeting has been published.
3. agenda *has been published*	4. The San Diego Padres play the Atlanta Braves this week.
4. San Diego Padres *play*	5. His younger son, Tom, is head of the merchandising department.
5. son *is*	6. American diplomats are drafting a middle-of-the-road plan.
6. diplomats *are drafting*	7. From the balcony we watched the street dancers.

7. we *watched*	8. Despite her lack of experience, the new professor's lectures encouraged much discussion.
8. lectures *encouraged*	9. The audience applauded the guitarist's performance.
9. audience *applauded*	10. Some of the cabins were built before 1900.
10. some *were built*	11. Squirrels are becoming a nuisance to us.
11. squirrels *are becoming*	12. Are your children always this rowdy?
12. children *are*	13. Joyce plays the piano quite well.
13. Joyce *plays*	14. The President, as well as the members of Congress, is responsible to the people.
14. President *is*	15. Our community had a barn raising.
15. community *had*	16. The snow forced us to cancel our parade.

16. snow *forced*	17. Pat and Mary Jane are meeting for lunch.
17. Pat, Mary Jane *are meeting*	18. Richard cooked our dinner and then entertained us with stories.
18. Richard *cooked, entertained*	19. The little dog was wet and hungry.
19. dog *was*	20. The airplane from Los Angeles will be one hour late.
20. airplane *will be*	21. The food at Deacon Burton's is delicious.
21. food *is*	22. Everyone in the community was taking part in the festival.
22. Everyone *was taking*	23. The old Mississippi steamboat is used as a restaurant.
23. steamboat *is used*	**SCORE** ______

Exercise 11 DIRECT OBJECTS AND PREDICATE NOUNS

Write the complement in each of the following sentences. Write **DO** if the complement is a direct object and **PN** if it is a predicate noun.

EXAMPLE: Our new neighbors have five children.

children **DO**

	1. She took the wrong expressway exit.
1. exit DO	2. Mr. Storm, the auditor, called you yesterday.
2. you DO	3. Were you a member of the 4-H Club?
3. member PN	4. I heard the train in the distance.
4. train DO	5. Do you have change for a quarter?
5. change DO	6. The blind boy by the door is president of the student body.
6. president PN	7. Ruth ordered pancakes and sausage for her breakfast.
7. pancakes, sausage DO	8. The thief stole her wallet from her open purse and ran down the hall.

8. wallet DO	9. The back door needs a new lock.
9. lock DO	10. My father was a naval officer.
10. officer PN	11. She enjoyed the crisp, fresh mountain air.
11. air DO	12. Josephine Tey is an exceptional mystery writer.
12. writer PN	13. Sally is a person with excellent taste in clothes.
13. person PN	14. Please sharpen all of these pencils for me.
14. all DO	15. The printer made a mistake in my order.
15. mistake DO	16. Lightning causes many deaths each year.
16. deaths DO	17. Monday was an overcast day.
17. day PN	18. We watched the tennis tournament on television.

18. tournament DO	19. Ralph became department head after Cameron's resignation.
19. head PN	20. Everyone loves a circus.
20. circus DO	21. Clifford's obsession with money was a well-known fact.
21. fact PN	22. During the evening the rain became sleet.
22. sleet PN	23. Our Latin professor has assigned twenty pages for tomorrow.
23. pages DO	24. A good book is good company.
24. company PN	25. Is this a shark's tooth?
25. tooth PN	SCORE ______

Exercise 12 INDIRECT OBJECTS AND OBJECTIVE COMPLEMENTS

In the following sentences identify the *italicized* complement by writing **IO** if it is an indirect object and **OC** if it is an objective complement.

EXAMPLE: We offered *them* a special program.

IO

	1. Steve cooked *us* a quiche for lunch.
1. IO	2. The team elected Liz *captain.*
2. OC	3. I offered the *auctioneer* twenty dollars for the vase.
3. IO	4. The class thought Joel's argument *illogical.*
4. OC	5. The faculty considered the dean a *bore.*
5. OC	6. Did you bring *me* a bag of potato chips?
6. IO	7. He painted his car *yellow.*
7. OC	8. Did you consider the course *worthwhile*?
8. OC	9. My aunt bought *me* a blouse for my birthday.
9. IO	10. We found Bob's excuse very *imaginative.*

10. OC	11. Tom and Molly consider backpacking a great *sport.*
11. OC	12. Winning the golf tournament made him *happy.*
12. OC	13. I will write your *brother* a letter tomorrow.
13. IO	14. Frances and George have been showing *us* their wedding pictures.
14. IO	15. Didn't you think John *rude*?
15. OC	16. I promised the *children* a surprise.
16. IO	17. The company provided *me* a new car.
17. IO	18. She wanted her hair *short.*
18. OC	19. At one time we thought her *pretty.*
19. OC	20. Their parents gave *them* a clothes allowance.
20. IO	**SCORE** ______

Exercise 13 COMPLEMENTS

In each of the following sentences identify the *italicized* word by writing

PN if it is a predicate noun,
PA if it is a predicate adjective,
DO if it is a direct object,
IO if it is an indirect object,
OC if it is an objective complement.

EXAMPLE: The class elected Robert its social committee *chairman.*

OC

	1. My little sister cannot drink *milk.*
1. DO	2. Elsie typed Tom's *report.*
2. DO	3. His niece sold *him* three raffle tickets.
3. IO	4. Can we paint the barn bright *red*?
4. OC	5. Yesterday's earthquake caused very little *damage.*
5. DO	6. That old house is an architectural *disaster.*
6. PN	7. Fred is not only *handsome* but also *smart.*
7. PA, PA	8. Henry offered *us* two tickets to the World Series.
8. IO	9. The room suddenly became strangely *quiet.*
9. PA	10. New England is *beautiful* in the fall.

10. PA	11. Dr. West asked *us* only three discussion questions on the final examination.
11. IO	12. Order *Gus* a hamburger and French fries.
12. IO	13. Dan became an excellent *golfer.*
13. PN	14. Dr. Edwards sent *me* a postcard from London.
14. IO	15. We were *happy* about Kay's promotion.
15. PA	16. The pretty little girl bought three *pieces* of candy.
16. DO	17. My aunt is a history *teacher*.
17. PN	18. The professor considered Larry very *intelligent.*
18. OC	19. Jim Gray sold *me* an original painting.
19. IO	20. His parents named him *Marlowe.*
20. OC	21. Grandmother always makes *spoonbread* when I visit her.
21. DO	22. They had no other *place* to go.

22. DO	23. Mr. James is a *man* of substance.
23. PN	24. Jim sends *her* flowers every day.
24. IO	25. The trees obstructed our *view* of the lake.
25. DO	26. Shaker furniture is *simple* and *solid.*
26. PA, PA	27. Peter bought *Rita* a hair dryer for her birthday.
27. IO	28. I cannot make a good chocolate *mousse.*
28. DO	29. The wind blew the *napkins* off the picnic table.
29. DO	30. The school board appointed Bob *principal*.
30. OC	31. We are stocking our *pond* with catfish.
31. DO	SCORE ______

3
The Sentence Fragment

3a Grammatical Fragments

If you are not careful to have both a subject and a predicate in your sentences, you will write sentence fragments instead of complete sentences. Observe, for example, the following:

> A tall, distinguished-looking gentleman standing on the corner in a pouring rain.
>
> Standing on the corner in a pouring rain and shielding himself from the deluge with a a large umbrella.

The first of these groups of words is no more than the subject of a sentence or the object of a verb or preposition. It may be part of such a sentence, for example, as *We noticed a tall, distinguished-looking gentleman standing on the corner in a pouring rain.* The second group is probably a modifier of some kind, the modifier of a subject, for instance: *Standing on the corner in a pouring rain and shielding himself from the deluge with a large umbrella, a tall, distinguished-looking gentleman was waiting for a cab.*

Another type of fragment is seen in the following illustrations:

> Because I had heard all that I wanted to hear and did not intend to be bored any longer.
>
> Who was the outstanding athlete of her class and also the best scholar.
>
> Although he had been well recommended by his former employers.

Each of these groups of words actually has a subject and a predicate, but each is still a fragment because the first word of each is a subordinating element and clearly indicates that the thought is incomplete, that the thought expressed depends upon some other thought. Such fragments are subordinate parts of longer sentences like the following:

> I left the hall because I had heard all that I wanted to hear and did not intend to be bored any longer.

The valedictorian was Alice Snodgrass, who was the outstanding athlete of her class and also the best scholar.

He did not get the job although he was well recommended by his former employers.

3b Permissible Fragments

A sentence fragment is usually the result of ignorance or carelessness. It is the sign of an immature writer. But, on the other hand, much correct spoken and written English contains perfectly proper fragments of sentences. The words *yes* and *no* may stand alone, as may other words and phrases in dialogue; there is nothing wrong, for example, in such fragments as the following:

The sooner, the better.

Anything but that.

Same as before.

Interjections and exclamatory phrases may also stand alone as independent elements. The following fragments are correct:

Ouch!

Tickets, please!

Not so!

3c Stylistic Fragments

There is another kind of fragment of rather common occurrence in the writing of some of the best authors. It is the phrase used for realistic or impressionistic effect, the piling up of words or phrases without any effort to organize them into sentences: "The blue haze of evening was upon the field. Lines of forest with long purple shadows. One cloud along the western sky partly smothering the red." This kind of writing, if it is to be good, is very difficult. Like free verse, it may best be left to the experienced writer. Students should learn to recognize a sentence fragment when they see one. They should use this form sparingly in their own writing. And they should remember two things: first, that the legitimacy of the sentence fragment depends upon whether it is used intentionally or not, and second, that in an elementary course in composition most instructors assume that a sentence fragment is unintended.

Study carefully the following sentence fragments and the accompanying comments:

A large woman of rather determined attitude who says that she wishes to see you to discuss a matter of great importance. [This is a typical fragment unintended by the writer, who seems to have felt that it is a complete sentence because there are a subject and a predicate in each subordinate clause.]

He finally decided to leave school. Because he was utterly bored with his work and was failing all his courses. [Here the second group of words is an unjustifiable fragment. It is a subordinate clause and should be attached to the main clause without a break of any kind.]

There were books everywhere. Books in the living room, books in the bedroom, books even in the kitchen. [The second group of words is a fragment, but it may be defended on grounds of emphasis. Many writers, however, would have used a comma or colon after *everywhere* and made a single sentence.]

Exercise 14 THE SENTENCE FRAGMENT

Indicate whether the following groups of words are complete sentences (**C**) or fragments of sentences (**F**).

EXAMPLE: Having read Silverstein's *Where the Sidewalk Ends.*

F

	1. Although they had not planned their vacation.
1. F	2. Ned deliberately forgot his dentist appointment.
2. C	3. The salesperson who sells wood stoves.
3. F	4. For the next few years Jack, who loves to sleep late.
4. F	5. During early October our publisher, who lives in Virginia.
5. F	6. Have you ever considered buying a log cabin?
6. C	7. This pottery, which is made by a Japanese technique.
7. F	8. If we start the project tomorrow.
8. F	9. I hope we don't miss the polo games this year.
9. C	10. Although we went farther up the river.

10. F	11. Tourists who visit the Grand Canyon.
11. F	12. After many hours of searching for the missing bracelet.
12. F	13. Are you familiar with the little poem "I Won't Hatch!"?
13. C	14. Directly across the road from us.
14. F	15. The florist delivered the flowers to the wrong house.
15. C	16. Americans' concern with accumulating things.
16. F	17. Yvette, who is returning to France next week.
17. F	18. That bay mare, whose name is Nora.
18. F	19. The fortune teller looked into her crystal ball but saw nothing.
19. C	20. Most of us do not take criticism well.
20. C	21. San Francisco is host city for our convention this year.

21. C	22. Tennis, which requires great concentration.
22. F	23. The summer heat, which was often unbearable, is now over.
23. C	24. The fire alarm having sounded.
24. F	SCORE ______

Exercise 15 THE SENTENCE FRAGMENT

Some of the following groups of words are fragments; some are sentences; some are fragments and sentences. Rewrite in such a way as to leave no fragments. Write **C** if the sentence is correct.

EXAMPLE: We will go fishing this weekend. If this beautiful weather continues.

We will go fishing this weekend if this beautiful weather continues.

	1. She helped her sister pack their china. Before the movers came.
1. She helped her sister pack their china before the movers came.	2. We can catch the express bus if you will hurry.
2. C	3. Carter Paul called. While you were out.
3. While you were out, Carter Paul called.	4. She left her attaché case in her car. Because she was in a hurry.
4. She left her attaché case in her car because she was in a hurry.	5. When I had difficulty reading the road signs. I realized that I needed new glasses.
5. When I had difficulty reading the road signs, I realized that I needed new glasses.	6. He will wash the dishes. While you put the baby to bed.

6. He will wash the dishes while you put the baby to bed.	7. Spending all his spare time washing and waxing his new car.
7. Dan was spending all his spare time washing and waxing his new car.	8. As I drive to work, listening for the traffic report on my radio.
8. As I drive to work, I listen for the traffic report on my radio.	9. Joe and Betty missed thc football game. Because the baby sitter did not come.
9. Joe and Betty missed the football game because the baby sitter did not come.	10. The lecture had ended, and hurrying to the student center for lunch.
10. The lecture having ended, we went hurrying to the student center for lunch.	11. Cape Cod, which is a beautiful resort area. I vacation there every fall.
11. I vacation every fall at Cape Cod, which is a beautiful resort area.	12. Taking care of horses requires time and knowledge.
12. C	13. A cluster of bats flew around us. Just as we entered the cave.

13. A cluster of bats flew around us just as we entered the cave.	14. Cameron doesn't want to spend all her money on car payments. Though she does want a new car.
14. Cameron doesn't want to spend all her money on car payments, though she does want a new car.	15. *In This Sign*, a fictional account of the life of a deaf girl, whose author is Joanne Greenberg.
15. *In This Sign*, a fictional account of the life of a deaf girl, was written by Joanne Greenberg.	SCORE ______

Exercise 16 THE SENTENCE FRAGMENT

Complete or revise the following sentence fragments in such a way as to make complete sentences.

EXAMPLE: Almost everyone who has the opportunity to read Dickens.

Almost everyone who has the opportunity to read Dickens can learn about nineteenth-century life in England.

	1. Success, which is valued by our society.
1. Success, which is valued by our society, has many definitions.	2. Failing the course but having to admit that he had learned a great deal.
2. Although he failed the course, he had to admit that he had learned a great deal.	3. Being completely misunderstood in the point I was trying to make.
3. I was completely misunderstood in the point I was trying to make.	4. Having spent the summer traveling and ready now to begin school.
4. Having spent the summer traveling and ready now to begin school, the boys had many tales to tell their classmates.	5. I, who am usually quite shy.
5. I, who am usually quite shy, was the life of the party.	6. If you cannot find your way to Demorest.

6. If you cannot find your way to Demorest, call us to come and get you.	7. While waiting in the beauty parlor and reading the fashion magazines.
7. While waiting in the beauty parlor, I read the fashion magazines.	8. When spending a day in the mountains and relaxing in a hammock.
8. When spending a day in the mountains, I often like to relax in a hammock.	9. The fact that you overslept and consequently missed the test.
9. The fact that you overslept and consequently missed the test is no excuse.	10. Danny's great joy at catching his first fish.
10. Danny's great joy at catching his first fish was a pleasure to see.	11. If you call me early Saturday morning and we work on your garden together.
11. If you call me early Saturday morning and we work on your garden together, we should be through with the planting by noon.	12. The huge silver lamp, being in the shape of a dolphin.
12. The huge silver lamp was in the shape of a dolphin.	13. The old clockmaker, saying that my recent purchase was a valuable antique.

13. The old clockmaker said that my recent purchase was a valuable antique.	14. Time and again, the heavy surf, knocking the little boy over and making him swallow the sea water.
14. Time and again, the heavy surf knocked the little boy over and made him swallow the sea water.	15. Sharpening my pencils and getting out a stack of fresh paper.
15. Sharpening my pencils and getting out a stack of fresh paper, I prepared to write a letter to the President of the United States.	16. With blankets piled high on the bed and with a roaring fire in the fireplace.
16. With blankets piled high on the bed and with a roaring fire in the fireplace, they kept warm in spite of the cold weather outside.	17. The boy who came to our back door and asked to borrow our weed cutter.
17. The boy who came to our back door and asked to borrow our weed cutter lives next door to Aunt Melissa.	SCORE ______

4
Verbals

Difficulty in recognizing verbs is often encountered because certain verb forms which function partly as verbs and partly as other parts of speech are confused with sentence verbs. (The *sentence verb* is the verb that states something about the subject and is capable of completing a statement.) These other verb forms are made from verbs but also perform the function of nouns, adjectives, or adverbs. In other words, they constitute a sort of half-verb. They are called **verbals.** The three verbal forms are the **gerund**, the **participle**, and the **infinitive**.

4a Verbals and Sentence Verbs

It is important that you distinguish between the use of a particular verb form as a verbal and its use as a main verb in a sentence. An illustration of the different uses of the verb form *running* will help you to make this distinction:

> *Running* every day is good exercise. [*Running* is a **gerund** and is the subject of the verb *is.*]
>
> *Running* swiftly, he caught the bandit. [*Running* is a **participle** and modifies the pronoun *he.*]
>
> The boy *is running* down the street. [*Is running* is the **sentence verb.** It is formed by using the present participle with the auxiliary verb *is.*]

It must be emphasized that *a verbal cannot take the place of a sentence verb* and that *any group of words containing a verbal but no sentence verb is a sentence fragment:*

> The boy *running* [A sentence fragment.]
>
> *To face* an audience [A sentence fragment.]
>
> The boy *running* up the steps is Charles. [A complete sentence.]
>
> *To face* an audience was a great effort for me. [A complete sentence.]

The following table shows the tenses and voices in which verbals appear:

GERUNDS AND PARTICIPLES

Tense	*Active Voice*	*Passive Voice*
Present	doing	being done
Past		done (This form applies only to participles.)
Present Perfect	having done	having been done
Progressive Present Perfect	having been doing	

INFINITIVES

Tense	*Active Voice*	*Passive Voice*
Present	to do	to be done
Present Perfect	to have done	to have been done
Progressive Present	to be doing	
Progressive Present Perfect	to have been doing	

4b The Gerund

A **gerund** is a verbal used as a noun and in its present tense always ends in *-ing*. Like a noun, a gerund is used as a subject, a complement, an object of a preposition, or an appositive. Do not confuse the gerund with the present participle, which has the same form but is used as an adjective:

> *Planning* the work carefully required a great deal of time. [*Planning* is a gerund used as subject of the sentence.]
>
> She was not to blame for *breaking* the vase. [*Breaking* is a gerund used as object of the preposition *for*.]
>
> I appreciated your *taking* time to help me. [*Taking* is a gerund used as direct object of *appreciated*.]
>
> His unselfish act, *giving* Marty his coat, plainly showed Ed's generosity. [*Giving* is a gerund used as the appositive of *act*.]

In the sentences above you will note examples of gerunds functioning as nouns but also taking objects as verbs do. In the first sentence the gerund *planning* is used as the subject of the verb *required*. *Planning* itself, however, is completed by the object *work* and is modified by the adverb *carefully*. This dual functioning of the gerund is apparent in the other three sentences as well.

It is important to remember a rule concerning the modification of gerunds: Always use the possessive form of a noun or pronoun before a gerund. Because gerunds are nouns, their modifiers, other than the adverbial ones just mentioned, must be adjectival; therefore, the possessive form, which has adjectival function, is the correct modifier:

Mr. Bridges was surprised at *Doug's* offering him the motorboat.

NOT

Mr. Bridges was surprised at Doug offering him the motorboat.

4c The Participle

A **participle** is a verbal used as an adjective. The present participle is formed by adding *-ing* to the verb: *do – doing.* Again, remember not to confuse the gerund and the present participle, which have the same form but do not function similarly. The past participle is formed in various ways. It may end in *-ed, -d, -t,* or *-n: talk – talked, hear – heard, feel – felt, know – known.* It may also be formed by a change of vowel: *sing – sung.*

The baby, *wailing* pitifully, refused to be comforted. [*Wailing* is a present participle. It modifies *baby.*]

The *broken* doll can be mended. [*Broken* is a past participle, passive voice. It modifies *doll.*]

An old coat, *faded* and *torn*, was her only possession. [*Faded* and *torn* are past participles, passive voice, modifying *coat.*]

Having been warned, the man was sent on his way. [*Having been warned* is the present perfect participle, passive voice. It modifies *man.*]

Like the gerund, the participle may have a complement and adverbial modifiers. In the sentence *Wildly waving a red flag, he ran down the track,* the participle *waving* has the object *flag* and the adverbial modifier *wildly.*

4d The Infinitive

An **infinitive** is a verbal consisting of the simple form of the verb preceded by *to* and used as a noun, an adjective, or an adverb:

To err is human. [*To err* is used as a noun, the subject of *is.*]

He wanted *to go* tomorrow. [*To go* is used as a noun, the object of the verb *wanted.*]

He had few books *to read.* [*To read* is used as an adjective to modify the noun *books.*]

Frank seemed eager *to go.* [*To go* is used as an adverb to modify the adjective *eager.*]

She rode fast *to escape* her pursuers. [*To escape* is used as an adverb to modify the verb *rode.*]

Sometimes the word *to* is omitted:

Susan helped *carry* the packages. [*To* is understood before the verb *carry.* (*To*) *carry* is used as an adverb to modify the verb *helped.*]

NOTE: An adverbial infinitive can frequently be identified if the phrase "in order" can be placed before it, as in *Katy paid ten dollars* (in order) *to get good seats at the play.*

Like the gerund and the participle, the infinitive may have a complement and adverbial modifiers:

He did not want *to cut the grass yesterday.* [The infinitive *to cut* has the object *grass* and the adverbial modifier *yesterday.*]

Exercise 17 VERBS AND VERBALS

In the following sentences identify each *italicized* expression by writing

V	if it is a verb,	**Part**	if it is a participle,
Ger	if it is a gerund,	**Inf**	if it is an infinitive.

EXAMPLE: *To avoid* the city traffic, *take* the bypass.

Inf, V

Answers	Sentences
	1. Labor Day always *falls* on a Monday.
1. V	2. Please water my *potted* plants while I *am visiting* my parents.
2. Part, V	3. He was confident that *insulating* his house would cut his *heating* bill by twenty-five percent.
3. Ger, Part	4. That shade of brown *is* very handsome on you.
4. V	5. The cookie jar needs *refilling.*
5. Ger	6. The dog waited patiently *to be fed.*
6. Inf	7. She enjoyed *listening* to her son play the piano.
7. Ger	8. The tomatoes are ready for *picking.*
8. Ger	9. If you *are planning to use* my car, put some gasoline in it.

9. V, Inf	10. The best time *to begin* planning next year's Christmas *shopping* is now.
10. Inf, Ger	11. *Driving* fast is always dangerous.
11. Ger	12. After *feeding* the horses, we were ready *to ride.*
12. Ger, Inf	13. The handsome young man *standing* by the piano will sing a tenor solo.
13. Part	14. Mountain *climbing* is difficult and *challenging.*
14. Ger, Part	15. She did not know how *to revive* the *wilting* plant.
15. Inf, Part	16. *To write* well, one must be able *to think* clearly.
16. Inf, Inf	17. The *winding* dirt road was covered with pine straw.
17. Part	18. Were you surprised *to see* Byron at the party?
18. Inf	19. I quit *smoking* two years ago.
19. Ger	20. The train *arrived* on time.
20. V	21. Will you clean up the *broken* glass?

21. Part	22. I hurriedly *read* this morning's paper.
22. V	23. I forgot *to bring* my office keys.
23. Inf	24. The *crowded* bus did not stop for me.
24. Part	25. Don't forget *to get* the bread at the grocery store.
25. Inf	26. *Boiled* peanuts are popular in Georgia.
26. Part	27. She could not remember the combination *to open* her locker.
27. Inf	28. *Watching* television has become the favorite American pastime.
28. Ger	29. Have you ever seen an *X-rated* movie?
29. Part	30. Jeff is a *dedicated* hockey player.
30. Part	SCORE ______

Exercise 18 **GERUNDS**

In the following sentences underline each gerund, then copy the gerund and after it write

S if the gerund is the subject of the verb,
PN if the gerund is the predicate nominative (noun),
DO if the gerund is the direct object of the verb,
OP if the gerund is the object of a preposition.

EXAMPLE: After hearing Jamie's new tape of country music, I bought one for myself.

hearing **OP**

	1. Last summer I took horseback riding.
1. riding DO	2. Greg enjoys reading science-fiction.
2. reading DO	3. Swimming is excellent exercise.
3. Swimming S	4. Gloria and Marcus dread moving away from Dayton.
4. moving DO	5. The little boy's cheeks were rosy from playing outside.
5. playing OP	6. Finding a parking space on campus after ten o'clock is nearly impossible.
6. Finding S	7. Harvey's main interest in life is hunting.

7. hunting PN	8. After exercising regularly for a month, I had lost six pounds.
8. exercising OP	9. Kathy's method of losing weight is dieting.
9. losing OP dieting PN	10. I embarrassed myself by blushing.
10. blushing OP	11. Creating a good impression was his number one goal.
11. Creating S	12. The alumni resented the coach's making excuses.
12. making DO	13. Irma will be responsible for planning the tour.
13. planning OP	14. Emptying the garbage was one of my chores.
14. Emptying S	15. A pleasant spectator sport is ice-skating.
15. ice-skating PN	16. Trying to correct my blunder only made it worse.
16. Trying S	17. Warren gets most of his information on sports by watching television.

17. <u>watching</u> OP	18. For some foolish, whimsical reason, Wes began singing in the middle of the test.
18. <u>singing</u> DO	19. Fumbling the ball cost the Rams the game.
19. <u>Fumbling</u> S	20. You will be responsible for collecting the money.
20. <u>collecting</u> OP	21. Listening to Eudora Welty read her stories is a pleasant experience.
21. <u>Listening</u> S	22. Cattle rustling still occurs in some parts of this country.
22. <u>rustling</u> S	23. Marty loved playing tennis even though she was not a good player.
23. <u>playing</u> DO	24. Willie's tooth finally stopped hurting.
24. <u>hurting</u> DO	25. Looking directly at the sun during an eclipse can injure one's eyes.
25. <u>Looking</u> S	26. The doctor recommended bicycling to strengthen Paul's leg muscles.

26. bicycling DO	27. Stephen, like most of us, enjoys winning.
27. winning DO	28. His arms were sore from rowing.
28. rowing OP	29. Walt's writing has improved.
29. writing S	30. The heel on one of her shoes needs replacing.
30. replacing DO	SCORE ______

Exercise 19 PARTICIPLES

Underline the participle in each sentence and then write the word it modifies.

EXAMPLE: Startled by the noise, Sarah turned on the light.

Startled *Sarah*

	1. Last summer's thickly overgrown garden had to be plowed under.
1. overgrown *garden*	2. A woman traveling alone is no longer an unusual sight.
2. traveling *woman*	3. Having made an idiot of myself, I hurriedly left the room.
3. Having made *I*	4. Shutting his eyes for a moment, Danny was soon asleep.
4. Shutting *Danny*	5. Did you repair Johnny's broken model plane?
5. broken *plane*	6. Stunned by Alice's answer, the class remained silent.
6. Stunned *class*	7. Can you remember your most embarrassing moment?

7. embarrassing *moment*	8. Bruce, having decided to quit school, began looking for a job.
8. having decided *Bruce*	9. Last spring Katie found a snakeskin lying in a pile of leaves.
9. lying *snakeskin*	10. When I visited Ellen, her dog watched me, sniffing cautiously at my shoes.
10. sniffing *dog*	11. The city council, expecting an assortment of conflicting opinions, convened early.
11. expecting *council* conflicting *opinions*	12. Preparing his new course, Dr. Peeples spent many hours in the library.
12. Preparing *Dr. Peeples*	13. Did you see that child darting into the street?
13. darting *child*	14. She heard the murderer walking slowly down the hall toward her door.
14. walking *murderer*	15. Refreshed after a shower, Ernie began preparing his supper.

15. Refreshed *Ernie*	16. The dishwasher has overflowed, flooding the kitchen.
16. flooding *dishwasher*	17. Mrs. Proudie has an exalted opinion of herself.
17. exalted *opinion*	18. Cissy looked out the window and saw her cat sitting on top of the car.
18. sitting *cat*	19. Nancy returned from a weekend trip to the mountains, raving about the beauty of the autumn leaves.
19. raving *Nancy*	20. I resent recorded telephone messages.
20. recorded *messages*	21. The flowered wallpaper made the room seem small.
21. flowered *wallpaper*	22. The attached letters should be kept confidential.
22. attached *letters*	23. Returning home late, she went straight to bed.
23. Returning *she*	24. My dinner last night was fried chicken.

24. fried *chicken*	25. Byron Herbert Reece was a well-known Georgia poet.
25. well-known *poet*	**SCORE** ______

Exercise 20 INFINITIVES

Underline the infinitive(s) in each of the following sentences, and then write **N** if it functions as a noun, **Adj** as an adjective, or **Adv** as an adverb.

EXAMPLE: To survive in the future, we will need to practice self-reliance.

To survive **Adv**
to practice **N**

	1. She has promised to bring ice cream and cake to the party.
1. to bring N	2. To think logically requires self-discipline.
2. To think N	3. Our professor assigned us Strunk and White's *The Elements of Style* to read.
3. to read Adj	4. To drain the pond in December was the height of folly.
4. To drain N	5. Joan forgot to close the windows last night.
5. to close N	6. My sister flew to California to visit her son and his family.
6. to visit Adv	7. I want to invite the Smiths to our open house.
7. to invite N	8. I am afraid to leave my car in the parking lot on Halloween.
8. to leave Adv	9. Love is easy to recognize but difficult to define.

9. to recognize Adv to define Adv	10. I was anxious to read Michener's new book.
10. to read Adv	11. Last winter I forgot to put antifreeze in my truck.
11. to put N	12. To find the missing heir took several years.
12. To find N	13. We arrived early to get good seats.
13. to get Adv	14. Sam's grammatical errors were too numerous to mention.
14. to mention Adv	15. The purpose of our meeting is to plan our spring workshop.
15. to plan N	16. Sally and Howard bought an old house to renovate.
16. to renovate Adj	17. Do you want to have dinner early?
17. to have N	18. The old man folded his hands and began to speak slowly.
18. to speak N	19. Did the student want to see the Dean?
19. to see N	20. I am planning to build a barn next summer.
20. to build N	21. The team played hard to win.

21. to win Adv	22. We will take a statewide poll to determine public opinion on this issue.
22. to determine Adv	23. A good student will set aside time to study.
23. to study Adj	24. Children are usually eager to discover their world.
24. to discover Adv	25. Juanita was anxious to study animal husbandry.
25. to study Adv	26. To talk to him is a waste of time.
26. To talk N	27. *The Book of Merlyn* is an exciting book to read.
27. to read Adj	28. The introductory course is designed to teach the student basic principles of physics.
28. to teach Adv	29. I don't pretend to understand his reasoning.
29. to understand N	30. Eager to meet the poet, Robert arrived early.
30. to meet Adv	31. I came prepared to stay for the semi-finals.
31. to stay Adv	32. How many tickets do we need to sell?
32. to sell N	33. Frank will never learn to swim, I fear.

33. to swim N	34. Ed wanted to go to the last game of the season.
34. to go N	35. I went to the library to finish my report.
35. to finish Adv	SCORE ______

Exercise 21 VERBALS

Underline the verbal in each of the following sentences. Then, identify it by writing

Ger for gerund,
Part for participle,
Inf for infinitive.

Finally, indicate the verbals by writing

Adj	for adjective,	**PN**	for predicate nominative,
Adv	for adverb,	**DO**	for direct object,
S	for subject,	**OP**	for object of a preposition.

EXAMPLE: Harry tried hard to be an artist.

Inf DO

Answers	Sentences
	1. I spent the morning searching for seashells.
1. searching Part Adj	2. Regina has two good books to read during the Christmas holidays.
2. to read Inf Adj	3. Children today spend too much time watching television.
3. watching Part Adj	4. I decided to take the job in Cleveland.
4. to take Inf DO	5. After examining the problem, will you help us with the solution?
5. examining Ger OP	6. A wounded animal can be dangerous.

6. wounded Part Adj	7. The President has difficult decisions to make.
7. to make Inf Adj	8. Listening attentively is an art.
8. Listening Ger S	9. Kirk has an overpowering personality.
9. overpowering Part Adj	10. Chipmunks and rabbits are amusing to watch.
10. amusing Part Adj to watch Inf Adv	11. Are you taking swimming this semester?
11. swimming Ger DO	12. Owning a house can be expensive.
12. Owning Ger S	13. The Old North Church, established in 1723, is the oldest church in Boston.
13. established Part Adj	14. The garbage men are coming today to move the debris.
14. to move Inf Adv	15. We borrowed money in order to pay our income taxes.

15. to pay Inf Adv	16. Having cut the firewood and kindling, Hank laid a fire.
16. Having cut Part Adj	17. Wasting time is Fred's worst fault.
17. Wasting Ger S	18. To save evergy, Ken rode his bicycle to work.
18. To save Inf Adv	19. During the winter remember to put out food for the birds.
19. to put Inf DO	20. *Blind Date* is a fascinating novel.
20. fascinating Part Adj	21. Susan went downstairs to eat a bowl of cereal.
21. to eat Inf Adv	22. Attaching the trailer to the rear of the truck, we headed for the beach.
22. Attaching Part Adj	23. Finding a good Mexican restaurant was the highlight of our evening.
23. Finding Ger S	24. Pat's responsibility was mowing the lawn.

24. mowing Ger PN	25. Those letters are ready for filing.
25. filing Ger OP	**SCORE** ______

5
Recognizing Phrases

A **phrase** is a group of related words, generally having neither subject nor predicate and used as though it were a single word. It cannot make a statement and is therefore not a clause.

A knowledge of the phrase and how it is used will suggest to you ways of diversifying and enlivening your sentences. Variety in using sentences will remedy the monotonous "subject first" habit. For instance, the use of the participial phrase will add life and movement to your style, because the participle is an action word, having the strength of its verbal nature in addition to its function as a modifier.

We classify phrases as **gerund**, **participial**, **infinitive**, **absolute**, **prepositional**, and **appositive**. The following sentences will show how the same idea may be expressed differently by the use of different kinds of phrases:

Sue swam daily. She hoped to improve her backstroke. ["Subject first" sentences.]

By *swimming daily*, Sue hoped to improve her backstroke. [Gerund phrase.]

Swimming daily, Sue hoped to improve her backstroke. [Participial phrase.]

Sue's only hope of improving her backstroke was *to swim daily*. [Infinitive phrase.]

With a daily swim Sue hoped to improve her backstroke. [Prepositional phrase.]

5a The Gerund Phrase

A **gerund phrase** consists of a gerund and any complement or modifiers it may have. The function of the gerund phrase is always that of a noun:

Being late for breakfast is Joe's worst fault. [The gerund phrase is used as the subject of the verb *is*.]

She finally succeeded in *opening the camera*. [The gerund phrase is the object of the preposition *in*.]

Bill hated *driving his golf balls into the lake.* [The gerund phrase is the object of the verb *hated.*]

His hobby, *making furniture,* is enjoyable and useful. [The gerund phrase is an appositive.]

5b The Participial Phrase

A **participial phrase** consists of a participle and any complement or modifiers it may have. It functions as an adjective:

Disappointed by his best friend, Roger refused to speak to him. [The participial phrase modifies the proper noun *Roger.*]

Having written the letter, Julie set out for the Post Office. [The participial phrase modifies the proper noun *Julie.*]

The boy *standing in the doorway* is the one who asked to borrow our rake. [The participial phrase modifies the noun *boy.*]

PUNCTUATION: Introductory participial phrases are set off by commas. Other participial phrases are also set off by commas unless they are essential to the meaning of the sentence. (See Chapter 19, Section b.)

5c The Infinitive Phrase

An **infinitive phrase** consists of an infinitive and any complement or modifiers it may have. Infinitives function as adjectives, adverbs, or nouns:

She had a plane *to catch at eight o'clock.* [The infinitive phrase modifies the noun *plane.*]

To be in Mr. Foster's class was *to learn the meaning of discipline.* [The first infinitive phrase is the subject of the verb *was.* The second infinitive phrase is the predicate nominative after the verb *was.*]

Millie left early *to avoid the heavy traffic.* [The infinitive phrase modifies the verb *left.*]

After the night outdoors we were happy *to be warm and dry again.* [The infinitive phrase modifies the adjective *happy.*]

Ted has no plans except *to watch television.* [The infinitive phrase is the object of the preposition *except.*]

We decided *to go for a long walk.* [The infinitive phrase is the direct object of the verb *decided.*]

Her fiancé seems *to be very pleasant.* [The infinitive phrase is the predicate adjective after the verb *seems.*]

PUNCTUATION: Introductory infinitive phrases used as modifiers are set off by commas. (See Chapter 19, Section b.)

5d The Absolute Phrase

A noun followed by a participle may form a construction grammatically independent of the rest of the sentence. This construction is called an **absolute phrase.** It is never a subject, nor does it modify any word in the sentence, but it is used *absolutely* or independently:

> *The bus having stopped,* the tourists filed out.
>
> *The theater being nearby,* I decided to walk.
>
> I shall do as I please, *all things considered.*

PUNCTUATION: An absolute phrase is always separated from the rest of the sentence by a comma. (See Chapter 19, Section b.)

5e The Prepositional Phrase

A **prepositional phrase** consists of a preposition followed by a noun or pronoun used as its object, together with any modifiers the noun or pronoun may have. The prepositional phrase functions usually as an adjective or an adverb:

> The plan *of the house* is very simple. [The prepositional phrase modifies the noun *plan.*]
>
> The river runs *through rich farmland.* [The prepositional phrase modifies the verb *runs.*]

PUNCTUATION: An introductory prepositional phrase, unless unusually long, is not set off by a comma. (See Chapter 19, Section b.)

5f The Appositive Phrase

An **appositive** is a word or phrase which follows another word and means the same thing. An appositive may be a noun phrase (that is, a noun and its modifiers), a gerund phrase, an infinitive phrase, or a prepositional phrase:

> This book, *a long novel about politics,* will never be a best seller. [Noun phrase used as an appositive.]
>
> Jean knew a way out of her difficulty: *telling the truth.* [Gerund phrase used as an appositive.]
>
> His greatest ambition, *to make a million dollars,* was doomed from the start. [Infinitive phrase used as an appositive.]
>
> The rustler's hideout, *in the old cave by the river,* was discovered by the posse. [Prepositional phrase used as an appositive.]

An appositive may be **essential** (sometimes called **fused**) or **nonessential**; it is essential if it positively identities that which it renames, frequently by use of a proper noun. Examples of both essential and nonessential appositives occur in the sentences below:

> The Victorian poets *Tennyson and Browning* were outstanding literary spokesmen of their day. [The appositive, *Tennyson and Browning,* identifies *poets* and thus is essential.]
>
> Tennyson and Browning, *two Victorian poets,* were outstanding literary spokesmen of their day. [The appositive, *two Victorian poets,* is nonessential because the poets are already identified by their names.]

PUNCTUATION: An appositive phrase is enclosed with commas unless it is essential. (See Chapter 19, Section b.)

Exercise 22 PHRASES

In each of the following sentences identify the *italicized* phrase by writing

Prep if it is a prepositional phrase,
Part if it is a participial phrase,
Ger if it is a gerund phrase,
Inf if it is an infinitive phrase,
App if it is an appositive phrase,
Abs if it is an absolute phrase.

(Since an absolute phrase must of necessity contain an expressed or understood participle, mark such a phrase only as absolute.)

EXAMPLE: *Behind the barn* you will find the tractor.

Prep

	1. *Having too many clothes* creates too many decisions.
1. Ger	2. Lady Macbeth was soon destroyed *by her own ambition.*
2. Prep	3. *The rain having started*, we sought shelter in an old cabin.
3. Abs	4. The poet spends many hours *observing nature.*
4. Part	5. Sophocles, *a Greek dramatist*, wrote that wisdom comes after suffering.
5. App	6. *During the summer months* we spend the weekends in the country.
6. Prep	7. The University of Michigan plans *to offer a variety of adult courses.*

7. Inf	8. We spent the afternoon *visiting art galleries.*
8. Part	9. *To select the right house plan* requires time and perseverance.
9. Inf	10. Red River, *an old frontier mining town*, is a popular New Mexico ski resort.
10. App	11. Roger rummaged *through the old trunk* and recalled his days as a boy.
11. Prep	12. I enjoy *watching the children next door.*
12. Ger	13. The stadium was dark and silent, *the spectators having gone.*
13. Abs	14. *Watching the merry-go-round*, I suddenly wanted to hop on.
14. Part	15. *Walking briskly* is good exercise.
15. Ger	16. *To be a successful student*, one must study daily.
16. Inf	17. In assembling its freshman class, Brown University strives *for diversity*.
17. Prep	18. Polly, *having read all of Galsworthy's novels*, now wants to read those of Henry James.

18. Part	19. *The court having recessed*, the reporters rushed to the telephones.
19. Abs	20. The sisters, *identical twins*, enjoy confusing their professors.
20. App	**SCORE** ______

Exercise 23	PHRASES

The sentences in the following exercise contain prepositional, verbal, and appositive phrases. Underline each phrase and show its use by writing **Adj** for adjective, **Adv** for adverb, or **N** for noun.

EXAMPLE: Stephen enjoys watching his father's softball games.
N

	1. Building a house is my next project.
1. Building a house N	2. The president of our college is a woman.
2. of our college Adj	3. Sally's plane will arrive at midnight.
3. at midnight Adv	4. Having created a mess, I left the house immediately.
4. Having created a mess Adj	5. The quarterback lost five important yards behind the line of scrimmage.
5. behind the line of scrimmage Adv	6. We will try to see the exhibit tomorrow.
6. to see the exhibit tomorrow N	7. Cold chicken for supper always pleases Father.
7. for supper Adj	8. Dr. McNabb, my English professor, recently retired.

8. my English professor N	9. Amy ordered several books to read this summer.
9. to read this summer Adj	10. The Alliance Theater sent the necessary information to us.
10. to us Adv	11. Dr. Thomas enjoyed advising students.
11. advising students N	12. During the last three months John has grown two inches.
12. During the last three months Adv	13. The apples were beginning to ripen.
13. to ripen N	14. The stadium was in an uproar after the game.
14. in an uproar Adj after the game Adv	15. Our sorority worked all night finishing our homecoming display.
15. finishing our homecoming display Adj	16. You will find the cookies in the cabinet.
16. in the cabinet Adv	17. *Aida* and *La Traviata*, two operas by Giuseppe Verdi, are his most popular works.

17. two operas by Giuseppe Verdi N

18. The cool breeze, refreshing us all, blew in from the sea.

18. refreshing us all Adj
from the sea Adv

19. Being a lighthouse keeper would be a lonely life.

19. Being a lighthouse keeper N

20. The light in the kitchen meant that Jake had arrived.

20. in the kitchen Adj

SCORE ______

Exercise 24 PHRASES

In each of the following sentences underline the phrase. Indicate its function by writing **Adj**, **Adv**, or **N**. Then write

Prep	for prepositional phrase,	**Inf**	for infinitive phrase,
Part	for participial phrase,	**App**	for appositive phrase.
Ger	for gerund phrase,		

EXAMPLE: Martin's house was filled with Sallie Middleton's bird prints.

Adv Prep

Answers	Sentences
	1. By noon I was starving.
1. By noon Adv Prep	2. Dr. Appleby spent a long time preparing her lectures.
2. preparing her lectures Adj Part	3. Did you understand the author's refusing the prize?
3. the author's refusing the prize N Ger	4. The full meaning of his thesis will probably escape you.
4. of his thesis Adj Prep	5. Her problem is that she cannot help eating too much.
5. eating too much N Ger	6. Martin Harris, a university law professor, is a former Rhodes scholar.

6. a university law professor N App	7. Having rested a few minutes, we continued our climb.
7. Having rested a few minutes Adj Part	8. To like Jill is not always easy.
8. To like Jill N Inf	9. Laura, my younger sister, will enter medical school next year.
9. my younger sister N App	10. To make things easier, I will make the beds.
10. To make things easier Adv Inf	11. Barry's constant complaining makes him tiresome.
11. Barry's constant complaining N Ger	12. Driving carefully, I avoided an accident.
12. Driving carefully Adj Part	13. Alice was worried about the baby's cough.
13. about the baby's cough Adv Prep	14. David hates practicing football, but he loves winning.
14. practicing football N Ger winning N Ger	15. Neither Chuck nor Don can afford to miss another class.

15. to miss another class N Inf	16. The children enjoyed learning the rhythmical nursery songs.
16. learning the rhythmical nursery songs N Ger	17. Having cleaned the pantry, Mary Ellen made herself some tea.
17. Having cleaned the pantry Adj Part	18. This winter you may want to read Tolkien's *The Hobbit.*
18. to read Tolkien's *The Hobbit* N Inf	19. Good literature offers the reader a broad perspective on life.
19. on life Adj Prep	20. Each of the riders must provide her own horse.
20. of the riders Adj Prep	SCORE ______

Exercise 25 PHRASES

A. Combine the following pairs of sentences, making one sentence a participial phrase. Be sure to punctuate each sentence properly.

EXAMPLE: The young woman hurried into the room. She was carrying an attaché case.

Carrying an attaché case, the young woman hurried into the room.

	1. Seventeenth-century churchmen were highly educated. They generally captivated their audiences.
1. Being highly educated, seventeenth-century churchmen generally captivated their audiences.	2. The checks are lying on the desk. They must be signed by the treasurer.
2. The checks lying on the desk must be signed by the treasurer.	3. Paula is determined to graduate first in her law class. She studies all the time.
3. Determined to graduate first in her law class, Paula studies all the time.	4. I washed my clothes at the laundromat last night. I met an old friend there.
4. Washing my clothes at the laundromat last night, I met an old friend.	5. Tony bought a new motorcycle. He had worked and saved his money.

5. Having worked and saved his money, Tony bought a new motorcycle.	6. We left the dance at two o'clock. We decided to go to the Busy Bee for an early breakfast.
6. Leaving the dance at two o'clock, we decided to go to the Busy Bee for an early breakfast.	7. William Faulkner was awarded the Nobel Prize. He is a great American author.
7. William Faulkner, awarded the Nobel Prize, is a great American author.	8. Gordon passed his final examination in accounting. He and his roommate celebrated.
8. Having passed his final examination in accounting, Gordon celebrated with his roommate.	9. Dr. Taylor is a fluent speaker. She holds her audience well.
9. Being a fluent speaker, Dr. Taylor holds her audience well.	10. Sandra tried hard to forget how much was at stake. She concentrated on doing her best.
10. Trying hard to forget how much was at stake, Sandra concentrated on doing her best.	

B. Combine the following pairs of sentences, making one of the sentences an appositive phrase.

EXAMPLE: Betsy was the only girl in the group. She proved to be the best diver.

Betsy, the only girl in the group, proved to be the best diver.

	1. Voltaire was a French philosopher. He said that he would rather be ruled by one lion than by a hundred rats.
1. Voltaire, a French philosopher, said that he would rather be ruled by one lion than by a hundred rats.	2. Emily Dickinson was an American poet. She spent her life in Amherst, Massachusetts.
2. Emily Dickinson, an American poet, spent her life in Amherst, Massachusetts.	3. The University of Texas is located in Austin. Austin is the capital of the state.
3. The University of Texas is located in Austin, the state capital.	4. Mark Twain wrote the book *The Adventures of Tom Sawyer*. In the story Tom maneuvers his friends into doing his work for him.
4. In *The Adventures of Tom Sawyer*, a book by Mark Twain, Tom maneuvers his friends into doing his work for him.	5. Ty Cobb was one of America's most famous athletes. He was born in Georgia.
5. Ty Cobb, one of America's most famous athletes, was born in Georgia.	6. Chaucer was a medieval poet. Readers continue to enjoy his humor.

6. Readers continue to enjoy the humor of Chaucer, a medieval poet.

7. My friend Suzanne is a Girl Scout official. Her office is in San Francisco.

7. My friend Suzanne, a Girl Scout official, has her office in San Francisco.

8. Roger McNeil is my next door neighbor. He is spending the summer in the North Carolina mountains.

8. Roger McNeil, my next door neighbor, is spending the summer in the North Carolina mountains.

9. For dinner we had rare roast beef and baked potatoes. Afterward we played Monopoly for two or three hours.

9. After dinner, rare roast beef and baked potatoes, we played Monopoly for two or three hours.

10. Mary Lou is a senior in high school. She wants to study pharmacy in college.

10. Mary Lou, a senior in high school, wants to study pharmacy in college.

SCORE ______

Exercise 26 PUNCTUATION OF PHRASES

In the following sentences insert all commas required by the rules stated in Chapter 5. Then write the commas with the words which precede them. Write **C** if the sentence is correctly punctuated.

EXAMPLE: Having spent the day sightseeing in Chicago Donna and Phil were too tired to attend the concert.

Having spent the day sightseeing in Chicago, Donna and Phil were too tired to attend the concert.
Chicago,

	1. To finish the float on time we worked all night.
1. time,	2. After eating lunch Bob read the newspaper.
2. lunch,	3. Dorothy Sayers author of numerous mystery novels also translated Dante's *Divine Comedy.*
3. Sayers, novels,	4. The girl wearing the white satin jump suit is an actress.
4. C	5. Beth one of my best friends is a senior at the University of Michigan.
5. Beth, friends,	6. Looking at my watch I hurried to finish painting the chair.

6. watch,	7. Bruce's house built in 1800 has been completely renovated.
7. house, 1800,	8. The young man entering the auditorium is the college's new president.
8. C	9. Mary Ann Noland my employer's wife is a sculptor.
9. Noland, wife,	10. *The Sound and the Fury* a novel by Faulkner is considered by many to be his best.
10. *Fury*, Faulkner,	11. Before shopping for Christmas presents Dad always prepares a list.
11. presents,	12. Being extremely excited Neville couldn't sit still.
12. excited,	13. After playing with the ball of thread the kitten became bored and took a nap.
13. thread,	14. Having put the clothes in the washer Tim settled down to read.

14. washer,	15. Being interested in nature Angie enjoyed living on a farm.
15. nature,	16. To rewrite my report will take a great deal of time.
16. C	17. The convertible a popular type of car in the forties is no longer manufactured.
17. convertible, forties,	18. Before throwing the pass the quarterback was "sacked."
18. pass,	19. The clock having stopped the officials halted the game.
19. stopped,	20. To understand Chapter 5 I had to review Chapter 4.
20. Chapter 5,	SCORE ______

6

Independent Clauses

6a Independent Clauses

A group of words containing a subject and a verb and expressing a complete thought is called a sentence or an **independent clause.** Some groups of words which contain a subject and a verb, however, do not express a complete thought and therefore cannot stand alone as a sentence. Such word groups are dependent on other sentence elements and are called **dependent clauses.**

Sometimes an independent clause stands alone as a sentence. Sometimes two or more independent clauses are combined into one sentence without a connecting word. Then a semicolon is used to connect the independent clauses:

> The day is cold.
> The day is cold; the wind is howling.

Sometimes independent clauses are connected by one of the coordinating conjunctions, *and, but, for, or, nor, so,* and *yet.* As these conjunctions do not subordinate, an independent clause beginning with one of them may stand as a complete sentence. Independent clauses joined by a coordinating conjunction are separated by commas. Therefore, to punctuate correctly, you must distinguish between independent clauses and other kinds of sentence elements joined by coordinating conjunctions. In the following examples note that only independent clauses joined by coordinating conjunctions are separated by commas:

> The day was *dark* and *dreary.* [The conjunction *and* joins two adjectives, *dark* and *dreary.* No comma permitted.]

> The fallen tree *blocked* the highway and *delayed* travel. [The conjunction *and* joins the two verbs. No comma permitted.]

> She ran *up the steps* and *into the house.* [The conjunction *and* joints two phrases. No comma permitted.]

Mrs. Brown caught the fish, and *her husband cooked them.* [The conjunction *and* connects two independent clauses, and these are separted by a comma.]

Sometimes two independent clauses are connected by a **conjunctive,** or **transitional, adverb** such as one of the following:

however	moreover	nevertheless	therefore
then	accordingly	otherwise	thus
hence	besides	consequently	

A semicolon is necessary before any of these words beginning a second clause. After the longer *conjunctive adverbs* a comma is generally used:

We drove all day; *then* at sundown we began to look for a place to camp.

It rained during the afternoon; *consequently,* our trip to the mountains had to be postponed.

NOTE: Conjunctive adverbs can be distinguished from subordinating conjunctions by the fact that the *adverbs* can be shifted to a later position in the sentence, whereas the *conjunctions* cannot:

It rained during the afternoon; our trip to the mountains, *consequently*, had to be postponed.

SUMMARY OF PUNCTUATION: From the foregoing discussion and examples we can establish the following rules for the punctuation of independent clauses:

1. *Two independent clauses connected by a coordinating conjunction are separated by a comma:*

   Our goat chewed up the morning paper, *and* Father is angry.

   You should call Hank tonight, *for* he is all alone.

2. *Two independent clauses which are not connected by a coordinating conjunction are separated by a semicolon.* Remember that this rule also holds true when the second clause begins with a conjunctive adverb:

   Philip is quite strong; he is much stronger than I.

   We both wanted to go to the toboggan race; *however*, Mother had asked us to be home by six.

3. *A semicolon is used to separate independent clauses which are joined by a coordinating conjunction but which are heavily punctuated with commas internally:*

   Harry, George, and Kitty went to Sky Valley for skiing; but Tony and I were too tired to go.

4. *Short independent clauses, when used in a series with a coordinating conjunction preceding the final clause, may be separted by commas:*

   The audience was seated, the lights were dimmed, and the curtain was raised.

NOTE: A series consists of at least three elements.

6b The Comma Splice

Use of a comma between two independent clauses not joined by a coordinating conjunction (Rule 2), is a major error called the **comma splice** (This term comes from the idea of splicing or "patching" together two clauses which should be more strongly separated.):

COMMA SPLICE: I enjoyed his company, I do not know that he enjoyed mine.

CORRECTION: I enjoyed his company, but I do not know that he enjoyed mine. (Using Rule 1)

I enjoyed his company; I do not know that he enjoyed mine. (Using Rule 2)

OR

I enjoyed his company; however, I do not know that he enjoyed mine. (Using Rule 2)

6c The Run-together Sentence

The **run-together sentence** results from omitting punctuation between two independent clauses not joined by a conjunction. Basically the error is the same as that of the comma splice: it shows ignorance of sentence structure:

Twilight had fallen it was dark under the old oak tree near the house.

When you read the sentence just given, you have difficulty in getting the meaning at first because the ideas are run together. Now consider the following sentence:

Twilight had fallen, it was dark under the old oak tree near the house.

The insertion of the comma is not a satisfactory remedy, for the sentence now contains a comma splice. There are, however, four approved devices for correcting the run-together sentence and the comma splice:

1. Connect two independent clauses by a comma and a coordinating conjunction if the two clauses are logically of equal importance:

   Twilight had fallen, and it was dark under the old oak tree near the house.

2. Connect two independent clauses by a semicolon if they are close enough in thought to make one sentence and you want to omit the conjunction:

   Twilight had fallen; it was dark under the old oak tree near the house.

3. Write the two independent clauses as separate sentences if they need separate emphasis:

   Twilight had fallen. It was dark under the old oak tree near the house.

4. Subordinate one of the independent clauses:

   When twilight had fallen, it was dark under the old oak tree near the house.

Exercise 27 THE COMMA SPLICE AND THE RUN-TOGETHER SENTENCE

Mark correct sentences with a **C**, run-together sentences with an **R**, and sentences containing comma splices with **CS**.

EXAMPLE: A quorum was not present therefore, the committee postponed voting.

R

	1. The first professional football game of the season will be broadcast Sunday, we have invited several friends over.
1. CS	2. I spent hours browsing through L. L. Bean's fall catalogue I ordered two pairs of shoes and a coat.
2. R	3. Making a decision is often easy after one has defined the problem.
3. C	4. White-water canoeing is exciting for the experienced sportsman, it can also be dangerous if he becomes over-confident.
4. CS	5. The beach was crowded with college students they were trying to forget the long, cold winter.
5. R	6. When my husband could not get the doctor by telephone, he drove to the doctor's house, the telephone there was out of order.
6. CS	7. The entrance to Mr. Johnson's office is the third door on the left however, I do not think he is in.

7. R	8. The company is planning a major reorganization, I think the staff will applaud it.
8. CS	9. A man who would lie to his friend should never be trusted.
9. C	10. We have seven cats we can't take them to our new apartment.
10. R	11. Although Red is a beautiful animal, he cannot be a pleasure horse, however, he will make an exciting race horse.
11. CS	12. Driving to work on the freeway is boring, I frequently take the back roads for a change of scene.
12. CS	13. I did not ride the roller coaster at Six Flags I wanted to though.
13. R	14. Goats are delightful animals they frequently have a calming effect on nervous horses.
14. R	15. Sweet potatoes are easy to grow and delicious to eat.
15. C	16. The commuter train came to an abrupt halt the commuters were quietly asked to leave the train.
16. R	17. We were terribly embarrassed, we didn't know how to explain our blunder.

17. CS	18. Timmy was used to playing by himself he had quite an adjustment to make when he started school.
18. R	19. I never did understand his attitude I just accepted it.
19. R	20. Roberta looks forward to spending her summers in Maine, nevertheless, she is always glad to head south in the fall.
20. CS	**SCORE** ______

Exercise 28 THE COMMA SPLICE AND THE RUN-TOGETHER SENTENCE

Mark correct sentences with **C**, run-together sentences with **R**, and sentences containing comma splices with **CS**.

EXAMPLE: The main object of this course is to teach the basic principles of mathematics, it is not an advanced course.

CS

	1. Virginia has spent five years working toward a master's degree she still has not completed the requirements.
1. R	2. I never saw a busier person than Fred, however, I don't know what he does.
2. CS	3. On a cold, stormy night the frightened horse broke out of his stall, but he didn't wander away.
3. C	4. *War and Remembrance* is a historical novel its subject is World War II.
4. R	5. Dr. James unlocked the door to his office, he stood there for a moment before entering.
5. CS	6. Francine and Margie will go to a new school in January, and I think that they will miss their old friends.
6. C	7. After Giles had finished breakfast, he went to the office, the sales meeting was scheduled for nine-thirty.

7. CS	8. Celeste was thrilled about being elected to Phi Beta Kappa, she could hardly wait to tell her parents the news.
8. CS	9. The stadium was packed with fans, moreover, many students had been unable to get tickets.
9. CS	10. As I grow older, my necessities are fewer I realize how cumbersome possessions can be.
10. R	11. Byron did not make up the work he had missed, consequently, he failed the course.
11. CS	12. The jury was denied its request, the judge said that the request was unreasonable.
12. CS	13. He always thought that he was right; hence, he was quite a bore.
13. C	14. Determined to win the game, the coach gambled on fourth down the game was lost at that point.
14. R	15. We went first to Florence, and then we went on to Pisa and Venice.
15. C	16. The requirements for the course were time-consuming they were not, however, unreasonable.
16. R	17. The Downtown Rotary Club has elected a new president, he will take office on January 1.

17. CS	18. When Amy and Clyde play bridge, it is serious business, when Bill and Jennifer play, it is for fun and relaxation.
18. CS	19. Jeff has a Seeing Eye dog, and he allows no one to play with it.
19. C	20. Howard took his grandchildren to Disney World, they enjoyed riding the roller coaster most of all.
20. CS	SCORE ______

Exercise 29 PUNCTUATION OF INDEPENDENT CLAUSES

In the following sentences insert all necessary commas and semicolons. Then write the correct punctuation mark with the word that precedes it. Write **C** if the sentence is correct.

EXAMPLE: After much soul-searching Tony decided to try out for the team he did not qualify.

team;

	1. The boys will be home from school next week and we are planning a family reunion.
1. week,	2. The result of the experiment has, strangely enough, not been publicized in years to come its effects will be far reaching.
2. publicized;	3. Harvey was late again however, he did remember to bring the wine.
3. again;	4. Joe and Sarah's new home is modern but it is also cozy.
4. modern,	5. Norma forgot to bring the tickets consequently, we missed the first act.
5. tickets;	6. The students waited thirty minutes for the lab instructor, but he never came.

6. C	7. After Owen and I had climbed the hill, we stopped a few minutes to catch our breath however, we did not rest long.
7. breath;	8. He talks so much that I don't know when he has time to breathe.
8. C	9. There is a vacancy in my apartment building do you want to move in?
9. building;	10. Not everyone shares his optimism about the economy but I do.
10. economy,	11. The boys on the team were determined to win the championship game therefore, they practiced every day.
11. game;	12. I visited some friends in Los Angeles but I was glad to get back to Maine.
12. Los Angeles,	13. Macon's new hospital is being constructed on the outskirts of town it will be dedicated in the fall.

13. town;	14. I have bought *The New Aerobics*, a book about a new concept of exercise however, I have not had time to read it.
14. exercise;	15. The service station attendant said that the car needs new tires and that they will cost over two hundred dollars.
15. C	16. Martin and my brother are studying for their finals so they will not be going with us to the rock concert.
16. finals,	17. Frank never seems interested in helping around the house yet he is always working on that old car of his.
17. house,	18. Minerva will bake a chocolate cake for dessert or she will make chocolate ice cream if you prefer it.
18. dessert,	19. They walked around the lake then they decided to cool off by taking a swim.
19. lake;	20. Patsy is a person who can be trusted and who will not betray your confidence in this matter.
20. C	**SCORE** ______

7
Dependent Clauses

Any clause beginning with a subordinating word like *what, that, who, which, when, since, before, after,* or *if* is a **dependent clause.** Dependent clauses, like phrases, function as grammatical units in a sentence—that is, as nouns, adjectives, and adverbs:

> I went to school.
> Too much time had elapsed. } [Both clauses are independent.]
>
> *When I went to school,* I studied my lessons. [The first clause is subordinate.]
>
> *Since too much time had elapsed,* she remained at home. [The first clause is subordinate.]

In the last two sentences *I studied my lessons* and *she remained at home* are complete statements. But the clauses *When I went to school* and *Since too much time had elapsed* do not express complete thoughts. They depend upon the independent statements to complete their meanings. Both of these dependent clauses function as adverbs.

7a Noun Clauses

A **noun clause** is a dependent clause used as a noun, that is, as a subject, complement, object of a preposition, or appositive. Noun clauses are usually introduced by *that, what, why, whether, who, which,* or *how*. Some of these introductory words can introduce both noun and adjective clauses, since the function of the whole clause in the sentence, and not its introductory word, determines its classification. Most sentences containing noun clauses differ from those containing adjective and adverbial clauses in that with the clause removed they are no longer complete sentences:

> Your *plan* is interesting. [The subject is the noun *plan.*]
>
> *What you intend to do* [your plan] is interesting. [The italicized noun clause is the subject of the verb *is*. Notice that the noun *plan* can be substituted for the clause.]

Tell me *what you intend to do* [your plan]. [The italicized noun clause is the direct object of the verb *tell.*]

That is *what you intend to do* [your plan]. [The italicized noun clause is a predicate nominative.]

I am interested in *what you intend to do* [your plan]. [The italicized noun clause is the object of the preposition *in.*]

The fact *that he had not told the truth soon became apparent.* [The italicized noun clause is in apposition with the noun *fact.*]

PUNCTUATION: Noun clauses used as non-essential appositives are set off by commas.

7b Adjective Clauses

An **adjective clause** is a dependent clause which modifies a noun or pronoun. The common connective words used to introduce adjective clauses are the relative pronouns *who* (and its inflected forms *whom* and *whose*), *which, that*, and relative adverbs like *where, when*, and *why*. (*Where* and *when* can introduce all three kinds of clauses.)

The italicized clauses in the following sentences are all adjective clauses:

She is a woman *who is respected by everyone.*

Mr. Johnson, *whose son attends the University,* is our friend.

He saw the place *where he was born.*

It was a time *when money did not count.*

I know the reason *why I failed the course.*

Adjective clauses are classified as **essential** (restrictive) and **nonessential** (non-restrictive). An *essential* clause, as its name indicates, is necessary in a sentence, for it identifies or points out a certain person or thing; a *nonessential* clause adds information about the word it modifies, but it is not essential in pointing out or identifying a certain person or thing:

Thomas Jefferson, *who was born on the frontier,* became President. [The name *Thomas Jefferson* has identified the person, and the italicized clause is not essential.]

A person *who loves to read* will never be lonely. [The italicized adjective clause is essential in identifying a particular kind of person.]

My father, *who was a country boy,* has lived in the city for years. [Since a person has only one father, an identifying clause is not essential.]

The girl *by whom I sat in class* is an honor student. [The italicized adjective clause is essential to the identification of *girl.*]

To determine whether an adjective clause is essential. you may apply this test: read the sentence leaving out the adjective clause and see whether the removal omits necessary identification. Try this test on the following sentence:

Jet pilots, *who work under a great deal of stress,* must stay in excellent physical condition.

You will see that the removal of the adjective clause does not change the basic meaning of the sentence. The italicized adjective clause is, therefore, nonessential.

Now read the following sentence, leaving out the italicized adjective clause:

Jet pilots *who are not in excellent physical condition* should not be allowed to fly.

If the adjective clause of this sentence is removed, the statement is not at all what the writer meant to say. The adjective clause is, therefore, essential.

PUNCTUATION: Nonessential adjective clauses are set off from the rest of the sentence by commas. (See Chapter 19, Section b.)

7c Adverbial Clauses

An **adverbial clause** is a dependent clause that functions exactly as if it were an adverb. Like an adverb it modifies a verb, an adjective, an adverb, or the whole idea expressed in the sentence's independent clause; e.g., *As luck would have it,* we missed his telephone call.

An adverbial clause is used to show *time, place, cause, purpose, result, condition, concession, manner,* or *comparison.* Its first word is a subordinating conjunction. Common subordinating conjunctions and their uses are listed below:

1. Time (*when, before, since, as, while, until, after, whenever*)

   I will stay *until you come.*

   When the whistle blew, the laborer stopped.

2. Place (*where, wherever, whence, whither*)

   He went *where no one had ever set foot before.*

   Wherever you go, I will go too.

3. Cause (*because, since, as*)

   Since I had no classes on Saturday, I went home.

   Because he was afraid of being late, Bob ran all the way.

4. Purpose (*in order that, so that, that*)

   My family made many sacrifices *so that I could have an education.*

   Men work *that they may eat.*

5. Result (*so . . . that, such . . . that*)

   The weather was *so* cold *that I decided not to walk to school.*

6. Condition (*if, unless*)

   You will hurt your hand *if you are not careful.*

   Unless you apply at once, your name will not be considered.

7. Concession (*though, although*)

   Although she had no money, she was determined to go to college.

8. Manner (*as, as if, as though*)

   She looked *as though she wanted to laugh.*

   Do *as you like,* but take the consequences.

9. Comparison (*as, than*)

   He is older *than his brother.*

   He is as tall *as his brother.*

PUNCTUATION: Introductory adverbial clauses are always set off by commas:

Although he had tests to take and a term paper to write, he went home for the weekend.

While I was eating lunch, I had a phone call from my brother.

7d Kinds of Sentences

For the purpose of varying style and avoiding monotony, you may need to be able to distinguish the four basic types of sentences. According to the number and kind of clauses (phrases do not affect sentence type), sentences may be grouped into four types: **simple**, **compound**, **complex**, and **compound-complex**.

1. A **simple** sentence is a single independent clause; it has one subject and one predicate. But it may have as a subject more than one noun or pronoun and as a predicate more than one verb:

Robert has a new car. [Single subject and single predicate.]

Robert and his *brother* have a new car. [There is one verb, *have*, but the subject consists of two nouns.]

Robert *washed* and *polished* his new car on Sunday. [There is one subject, *Robert*, but two verbs.]

Robert and his *brother washed* and *polished* their new car. [The subject consists of two nouns, *Robert* and *brother*; and the predicate consists of two verbs, *washed* and *polished.*]

2. A **compound** sentence contains at least two independent clauses and no dependent clause:

Mary likes the mountains, but Jackie prefers the seashore.

A lamp was lighted in the house, the happy family was talking together, and supper was waiting.

3. A **complex** sentence contains only one independent clause and one or more dependent clauses (the dependent clauses are in italics):

The toy truck *that you gave Molly for her birthday* is broken.

Why he refused to contribute to the fund we do not know.

4. A **compound-complex** sentence has at least two independent clauses and one or more dependent clauses (the independent clauses are in italics):

My friend was offended by my attitude, and *I was sorry* that she was hurt.

We spent the morning looking for the home of the woman who paints landscapes, but *we were unable to find it.*

Exercise 30 CLAUSES

Underline each dependent clause in the following sentences. Write **Adj** if the clause is an adjective clause, **Adv** if it is an adverbial clause, and **N** if it is a noun clause. If there is no dependent clause in the sentence, leave the space blank.

EXAMPLE: If it doesn't rain soon, our garden will die.

If it doesn't rain soon **Adv**

Answers	Sentences
	1. Nora's door, which is usually open, was closed.
1. which is usually open Adj	2. Lavinia decided that she wanted to go to the Super Bowl game.
2. that she wanted to go to the Super Bowl game N	3. The monotone of the speaker's voice lulled her to sleep.
3.	4. Please call me after you have seen Mr. Booth.
4. after you have seen Mr. Booth Adv	5. While you were gone, this package arrived for you.
5. While you were gone Adv	6. Dick, who had missed a week of classes, was unable to answer the questions.
6. who had missed a week of classes Adj	7. After taking a deep breath, Warren blew out all fifteen candles on his birthday cake.

7.	8. Though Jackie hates driving to Atlanta, she enjoys shopping there.
8. Though Jackie hates driving to Atlanta Adv	9. What you are suggesting is not practical.
9. What you are suggesting N	10. Surely you are not thinking that Bob stole your poetry notes.
10. that Bob stole your poetry notes N	11. If you don't hand in your book report by Friday, you will fail the course.
11. If you don't hand in your book report by Friday Adv	12. The bus which runs from Oglethorpe into town is almost always late.
12. which runs from Oglethorpe into town Adj	13. Please use a ball point pen when you complete this form.
13. when you complete this form Adv	14. The Bermuda grass that I planted last spring seems to grow very slowly.
14. that I planted last spring Adj	15. Walking to school every morning is the only exercise that Tim has.

15. that Tim has Adj	16. I did not know that Virginia had attended Smith College.
16. that Virginia had attended Smith College N	17. The man for whom they named their baby is going to be the baby's godfather.
17. for whom they named their baby Adj	18. Don't forget that we are going to the symphony concert next week.
18. that we are going to the symphony concert next week N	19. Since growing a beard, James looks very distinguished.
19.	20. They soon discovered that Vance was furious.
20. that Vance was furious N	21. That is the child to whom I gave the cookies.
21. to whom I gave the cookies Adj	22. Carl did not recommend the movie because of its violence.
22.	23. Your mother wanted to know where you had been.
23. where you had been N	24. Why he is behaving so peculiarly is hard to understand.

24. Why he is behaving so peculiarly N	25. I respect your opinion though I don't agree with it.
25. though I don't agree with it Adv	SCORE ______

Exercise 31 CLAUSES

Indicate the function of each of the *italicized* clauses by writing

S	for subject of a verb,	**OP**	for object of a preposition,
DO	for direct object,	**Adj**	for adjective modifier,
PN	for predicate nominative,	**Adv**	for adverbial modifier.

EXAMPLE: *That Don was dishonest* was a well-known fact.

S

	1. I never did understand *what the speaker was trying to say*.
1. DO	2. *If you will bake the cookies*, I will make the punch.
2. Adv	3. May's Halloween costume, *which she had made*, won first prize.
3. Adj	4. Have you ever returned to the place *where you were born*?
4. Adj	5. Liz went to several shops before finding the dress *that she wanted.*
5. Adj	6. *When the lecture was over*, Sandra had several questions *that she wanted to ask.*
6. Adv, Adj	7. Do you hold me responsible for *what he does*?
7. OP	8. My family has decided *that we will not buy another van.*

8. DO	9. *What I am worried about* is *where the money is coming from.*
9. S, PN	10. We were fascinated by the man *who was yelling at the umpire.*
10. Adj	11. *Although my aunt believes in witchcraft*, she is no more superstitious *than many other people.*
11. Adv, Adv	12. The novelists *who are most widely read* are not necessarily the best.
12. Adj	13. The chairman told all delegates *that they would be responsible for their own expenses.*
13. DO	14. Mac plays golf *as often as he can.*
14. Adv	15. Please ask Perry *why he wants the car.*
15. DO	16. Lena is a person *whom I can rely on.*
16. Adj	17. I think *that I will write Margie and ask her to visit me.*
17. DO	18. I usually agree with *what Dolores says.*
18. OP	19. *If you can remember Gene Austin's "My Blue Heaven,"* then you're much older *than I.*

19. Adv, Adv	20. I wonder *how she plans to attend two parties in one evening.*
20. DO	21. Ask Ted, *who lives with Jeff*, to tell him the plans.
21. Adj	22. *Before we eat supper*, let's jog around the block.
22. Adv	23. Jack acted *as though he were angry with me.*
23. Adv	24. *What you really mean* is *that you are bored with our company.*
24. S, PN	25. Tell me the reason *why Theo is afraid of my dog.*
25. Adj	SCORE ______

Exercise 32

REVIEW OF CLAUSES

In the following sentences enclose the dependent clauses in parentheses. Be able to tell the function of each dependent clause.

EXAMPLE: We went to the late show because Henry had to work overtime.

We went to the late show (because Henry had to work overtime.)

	1. When Elaine returned to her car, she found that someone had dented her fender.
1. (When Elaine returned to her car,) she found (that someone had dented her fender.)	2. After each matinee performance the audience is invited to participate in open discussions of the play.
2.	3. Nell, who is a student at Georgia Tech, is interested in mechanical engineering.
3. Nell, (who is a student at Georgia Tech,) is interested in mechanical engineering.	4. I will always believe that the car salesman swindled me when he sold me that used car.
4. I will always believe (that the car salesman swindled me) (when he sold me that used car.)	5. How we are going to get across that stream on our horses is a real problem.
5. (How we are going to get across that stream on our horses) is a real problem.	6. As we turned into the drive, we noticed that the kitchen window had been broken.
6. (As we turned into the drive,) we noticed (that the kitchen window had been broken.)	7. The Kansas corn crop was ruined because the rain came too late.

7. The Kansas corn crop was ruined (because the rain came too late.)	8. The committee did not adjourn until four o'clock because some of the members were still arguing.
8. The committee did not adjourn until four o'clock (because some of the members were still arguing.)	9. The game went into extra innings, but our team finally won by one run.
9.	10. Before you plant your seeds, you must prepare the soil.
10. (Before you plant your seeds,) you must prepare the soil.	11. When he was ready to pay his bill, Neal was embarrassed to find that he had left his wallet at home.
11. (When he was ready to pay his bill,) Neal was embarrassed to find (that he had left his wallet at home.)	12. The snapshots that we took on our recent tour of Alaska were beautiful.
12. The snapshots (that we took on our recent tour of Alaska) were beautiful.	13. Our newsboy, who is unaccustomed to his new route, was late in delivering our Sunday paper.
13. Our newsboy, (who is unaccustomed to his new route,) was late in delivering our Sunday paper.	14. I wish that I could guess to whom the first prize will go in the talent show.
14. I wish (that I could guess) (to whom the first prize will go in the talent show.)	15. I tried to finish supper early so that I could get to the basketball game on time.
15. I tried to finish supper early (so that I could get to the basketball game on time.)	16. Mary Lou is visiting her uncle, who is in the hospital with a broken arm.

16. Mary Lou is visiting her uncle, (who is in the hospital with a broken arm.)	17. We did not recognize Emma because she had lost so much weight.
17. We did not recognize Emma (because she had lost so much weight.)	18. Why young people play their stereos so loudly I will never know.
18. (Why young people play their stereos so loudly) I will never know.	19. Bill does not like tea unless it has lemon in it.
19. Bill does not like tea (unless it has lemon in it.)	20. I was so tired that I did not hear the radio when it came on.
20. I was (so) tired (that I did not hear the radio) (when it came on.)	21. Rita does as she pleases about keeping her room cleaned up.
21. Rita does (as she pleases) about keeping her room cleaned up.	22. The woman with whom we shared a table is from Minneapolis.
22. The woman (with whom we shared a table) is from Minneapolis.	23. Dave saved his money so that he could buy the car that he wanted.
23. Dave saved his money (so that he could buy the car) (that he wanted.)	24. The fact that you are five years older than I doesn't make you any wiser than I.
24. The fact (that you are five years older) (than I) doesn't make you any wiser (than I.)	25. Please call to let me know whether you are coming for dinner.
25. Please call to let me know (whether you are coming for dinner.)	SCORE ______

Exercise 33 CLAUSES

Complete each of the sentences below by writing an adjective clause, an adverbial clause, or a noun clause as indicated. (Note that only one correct version of each sentence is given in the answer section.)

EXAMPLE: (adjective clause)
The boy who flew with us to New York will meet us at eight under the clock at the Waldorf.

	(noun clause) 1. My own recommendation is
1. My own recommendation is that we listen to his side of the story.	(adverbial clause) 2. Bill had a terrible headache
2. Bill had a terrible headache because he had lain in the sun too long.	3. Mark and Helen watched the children, (adjective clause)
3. Mark and Helen watched the children, who were building sand castles on the beach.	(adjective clause) 4. This is the list of books
4. This is the list of books which you will be required to read this quarter.	(Adverbial clause) 5. I want to believe her.
5. Although Joy's story sounds peculiar, I want to believe her.	(Noun clause) 6. will be decided tonight.

6. Who will be the class valedictorian will be decided tonight.	(noun clause) 7. He tried to explain
7. He tried to explain how radar works to the class of sixth graders.	8. Raccoons and woodchucks are two little animals (adjective clause)
8. Raccoons and woodchucks are two little animals that are interesting to watch.	(Noun clause) 9. should make you happy and proud.
9. What your son has achieved in college should make you happy and proud.	(adverbial clause) 10. We were delighted
10. We were delighted when Tommy was well enough to return to work.	SCORE ______

Exercise 34 PUNCTUATION OF CLAUSES

In the following sentences supply commas and semicolons where they are needed. Then write the marks of punctuation with the words which precede them. Write **C** if the sentence is correct.

EXAMPLE: The weatherman predicts sunshine but my grandfather's rheumatism calls for rain.

The weatherman predicts sunshine, but my grandfather's rheumatism calls for rain.
sunshine,

	1. The supper dishes were left sitting on the table no one in the family wanted to miss the opening kick-off.
1. table;	2. Have we passed that Mercedes from Texas before or did we see it at the Hammock Shop?
2. before,	3. The newsstand doesn't have a copy of the new issue of *Ebony* but perhaps you can find one at the library.
3. *Ebony,*	4. Her needlework is kept in a basket that sits by her chair.
4. C	5. Weather vanes which once were common sights are now rarely seen in this area.
5. vanes, sights,	6. Harry shined his boots with a vengeance then he sat back to admire them.
6. vengeance;	7. The kites are as different as the boys who fly them.

7. C	8. The stadium was packed the band was playing and the moment had almost arrived for the game to begin.
8. packed, playing,	9. Although the steps were narrow and rough they were the most direct way to the beach.
9. rough,	10. Corn on the cob can be awkward to eat however I know of nothing more delicious.
10. eat; however,	11. The clouds moved across the sun and the sea turned from blue to gray.
11. sun,	12. The watercolors which are on exhibit in the gallery this week are the work of a German painter.
12. C	13. *The Awful Truth* which may be Tom's favorite movie is on television this weekend.
13. *Truth*, movie,	14. Since Genevieve has a weakness for Sherlock Holmes I must send her this T-shirt.
14. Holmes,	15. I knew that it was the first day of fall a crisp, cool breeze blew in from the north.
15. fall;	16. She is going to dye her hair red just as she has vowed to do.
16. red,	17. No one who has ever sampled Pierre's shrimp creole will forget it.

17. C	18. After we caught our first glimpse of the Rockies we rode silently for several miles.
18. Rockies,	19. Juanita seldom misses a garage sale consequently she could have one of her own.
19. sale; consequently,	20. She named her cat for Aubrey Beardsley whose posters she admires.
20. Beardsley,	21. I like to take my lunch to the park when the weather turns warm.
21. C	22. All spring the coach helped the second baseman and the shortstop work on the double play.
22. C	23. Scarab rings one of which I saw at the museum this morning remind me of Poe's story "The Gold Bug."
23. rings, morning,	24. I read the story so long ago however that I cannot remember the details of the plot.
24. ago, however,	25. Mother called from the office and asked me to plan supper.
25. C	**SCORE** ______

Exercise 35 KINDS OF SENTENCES

Identify the type of sentence by writing

S if the sentence is simple,
Cp if the sentence is compound,
Cx if the sentence is complex,
Cp-Cx if the sentence is compound-complex.

EXAMPLE: Before you use the insecticide, read the instructions carefully.

Cx

Answers	Sentences
	1. The recipe called for only a dash of nutmeg, but I didn't have even that much on the shelf.
1. Cp	2. Maggie brought home a handful of red tulips and arranged them in the pitcher.
2. S	3. I don't know whether the last pitch was a knuckle ball or not.
3. Cx	4. Susan enjoyed watching ballet and seldom missed a performance on television.
4. S	5. Late in the afternoon the cat waited expectantly on the front steps; he knew that Henry would be home shortly.
5. Cp-Cx	6. The children were fascinated by the bright pink flamingos that stood near the river bank.
6. Cx	7. Stanley swerved to avoid the broken glass scattered along the street.
7. S	8. Remodeling the old house was a long-term project; the young couple worked on one room at a time.

8. Cp	9. The morning paper is sponsoring a photography contest, but I can't persuade Dennis to submit one of his pictures.
9. Cp	10. Be careful on that skateboard!
10. S	11. One can usually find cattails growing along the edge of the pond.
11. S	12. Do you know where Lucy found the information about the minimum wage?
12. Cx	13. The hardware department, where you can find an extension cord, is at the very back of the store.
13. Cx	14. I cannot remember where I stored my skates; they are certainly not in my closet.
14. Cp-Cx	15. The child walked gingerly across the crushed shells that had been washed up by the waves.
15. Cx	16. You can fly to Toronto, and then you can rent a car for the trip to Newmarket.
16. Cp	17. The three of us slowly made our way through the maze of attractive shops.
17. S	18. Does anyone know when Dad will be home from work?

18. Cx	19. I have no intention of driving until the snowplows clear the streets.
19. Cx	20. The cook popped the potatoes into the microwave oven; they were done before he could mix the cheese sauce.
20. Cp-Cx	21. The travel magazine explains that officials in the People's Republic of China frown upon tipping.
21. Cx	22. The small dog scampered around the corner and disappeared through the doorway of Ida's Wig Shop.
22. S	23. These postage stamps are more attractive than those that I collected when I was a child.
23. Cx	24. Are you going to study, or are you going to watch the election returns on television?
24. Cp	25. I waited ten minutes for the bus; furthermore, I stood up most of the way home.
25. Cp	**SCORE** ______

8
Agreement of Subject and Verb

The verb in every independent or dependent clause must agree with its subject in person and number. (There are **three persons**: the **first person** is the speaker, the **second person** is the person spoken to, and the **third person** is the person or thing spoken about. There are **two numbers**: the **singular**, denoting one person or thing, and the **plural**, denoting more than one person or thing.) A careful study of the conjugation of the verb in Chapter 1 will show you that a verb can change form not only in *tense* but also in *person* and *number*. If you can recognize the subject and the verb, you should have no trouble making the two agree. Although there is ordinarily no problem in doing so, certain difficulties need special attention.

8a Intervening Expressions

The number of the verb in a sentence is not affected by any modifying phrases or clauses standing between the subject and the verb but is determined entirely by the number of the subject:

> The *evidence* which they submitted to the judges *was* [not *were*] convincing. [*Evidence* is the subject of the verb *was*.]

> The new *library* with its many books and its quiet reading rooms *fills* [not *fill*] a long-felt need. [*Library* is the subject of the verb *fills;* the phrase *with its many books. . .* has nothing to do with the verb.]

8b Verb Preceding the Subject

In some sentences the verb precedes the subject. This reversal of common order frequently leads to error in agreement:

> There *is* [not *are*] in many countries much *unrest* today. [*Unrest* is the subject of the verb *is.*]

There *are* [not *is*] a *table,* two *couches,* four *chairs,* and a *desk* in the living room. [*Table, couches, chairs,* and *desk* are the subjects of the verb *are.*]

Where *are* [not *is*] *Bob* and his *friends going*? [*Bob* and *friends* are subjects of the verb *are going.*]

8c Indefinite Pronouns

The indefinite pronouns or adjectives *either, neither,* and *each,* as well as such compounds as *everybody, anybody, everyone, anyone,* are always singular. *None* may be singular or plural. The plural usage is commoner:

Each of the plans *has* [not *have*] its advantages.

Everyone who heard the speech *was* [not *were*] impressed by it.

Every bud, stalk, flower, and seed *reveals* [not *reveal*] a workmanship beyond the power of man.

Is [not *Are*] *either* of you ready for a walk?

None of the men *have* brought their wives.

None of the three *is* [*are*] interested.

None—no, not one—*is* prepared.

8d Compound Subjects

Compound subjects joined by *and* normally require a plural verb:

Correctness and *precision are* required in all good writing.

Where *are* the *bracelets* and *beads*?

NOTE: When nouns joined by *and* are thought of as a unit, the verb is normally singular:

The *sum* and *substance* of the matter *is* [not *are*] hardly worth considering.

My *friend* and *coworker* Mr. Jones *has* [not *have*] gone abroad.

8e Subjects Joined by *Or* and *Nor*

Singular subjects joined by *or* or *nor* take a singular verb. If one subject, however, is singular and one plural, the verb agrees in number and person with the nearer one:

Either the *coach* or the *player was* [not *were*] at fault.

Neither the *cat* nor the *kittens have* been fed. [The plural word *kittens* in the compound subject stands next to the verb *have been fed.*]

Neither the *kittens* nor the *cat has* been fed. [The singular subject *cat* stands next to the verb, which is therefore singular.]

Neither my *brothers* nor *I am* going. [Note that the verb agrees with the nearer subject in person as well as in number.]

8f Nouns Plural in Form

As a general rule use a singular verb with nouns that are plural in form but singular in meaning. The following nouns are usually singular in meaning: *news, economics, ethics, physics, mathematics, gallows, mumps, measles, shambles, whereabouts:*

The *news is* reported at eleven o'clock.

Measles is a contagious disease.

The following nouns are usually plural: *gymnastics, tactics, trousers, scissors, athletics, tidings, acoustics, riches, barracks:*

Athletics attract him.

The *scissors are* sharp.

Riches often *take* wing and fly away.

Plural nouns denoting a mass, a quantity, or a number require a singular verb when the subject is regarded as a unit.

Five *dollars is* too much for her to pay.

Fifty *bushels was* all the bin would hold.

Though usage is mixed, phrases involving addition, multiplication, subtraction, and division of numbers preferably take the singular:

Two and two is [are] four.

Two times three is six.

Twelve divided by six is two.

In expressions like *part of the apple, some of the pie, all of the money,* the number of *part, some,* and *all* is determined by the number of the noun in the prepositional phrase:

Some of the pie *is* missing.

Some of the pies *are* missing.

8g The Subject of Some Form of *To Be*

When one noun precedes and another follows some form of the verb *to be,* the first noun is the subject, and the verb agrees with it and not with the complement even if the complement is different in number:

The only *fruit* on the market now *is* peaches.

Peaches are the only fruit on the market now. [In the first sentence *fruit* is the subject; in the second, *peaches.*]

8h Relative Pronoun as Subject

When a relative pronoun (*who, which,* or *that*) is used as the subject of a clause, the number and person of the verb are determined by the antecedent of the pronoun, the word to which the pronoun refers:

This is the student *who is* to be promoted. [The antecedent of *who* is the singular noun *student;* therefore, *who* is singular.]

These are the students *who are* to be promoted. [The antecedent of *who* is the plural noun *students.*]

Should I, *who am* a stranger, be allowed to enter the contest? [*Who* refers to *I; I* is first person, singular number.]

She is one of those irresponsible persons *who are* always late. [The antecedent of *who* is *persons.*]

If sentences such as the last one give you trouble, try beginning the sentence with the "of" phrase, and you will readily see that the antecedent of *who* is *persons* and not *one*:

Of those irresponsible *persons who are* always late she is one.

8i Collective Nouns

Some nouns are singular in form but plural in meaning. They are called **collective nouns** and include such words as *team, class, committee, crowd,* and *crew.* These nouns may take either a singular or a plural verb: if you are thinking of the group as a unit, use a singular verb; if you are thinking of the individual members of the group, use a plural verb:

The *crew is* striking for higher pay. [The crew is acting as a unit.]

The *crew are* writing reports of the wreck. [The members of the crew are acting as individuals.]

8j Nouns with Foreign Plurals

Some nouns retain the plural forms peculiar to the languages from which they have been borrowed: *alumni, media, crises.* Still other nouns occur with either their original plural forms or plural forms typical of English: *aquaria* or *aquariums, criteria* or *criterions.* If you are in doubt as to the correct or preferred plural form of a noun, consult a good dictionary.

NOTE: Be careful not to use a plural form when you refer to a singular idea. For instance, write *He is an alumnus of Harvard,* not *He is an alumni of Harvard.*

Exercise 36 SUBJECT-VERB AGREEMENT

Write the correct form of the *italicized* verb.

EXAMPLE: Athletics (*are, is*) the principal topic of conversation at the corner drug store.

are

	1. On the sideboard (*are, is*) a bowl of yellow roses and Aunt Annie's tea set.
1. are	2. Pete is one of those persons who (*have, has*) a genius for friendship.
2. have	3. The crew (*have, has*) both good and bad relationships with the ship's cook.
3. have	4. Each member of the Playmakers (*are, is*) responsible for the sale of ten tickets.
4. is	5. Around the corner and up one block (*are, is*) a delicatessen and a coffee shop.
5. are	6. The trousers that I think you should wear with this jacket (*are, is*) navy flannel.
6. are	7. Several members of the squadron (*plan, plans*) to see the show at Cinema I.
7. plan	8. The social committee (*have, has*) promised to present plans for the Christmas party at the next meeting of the chorus.

8. has	9. August was one of those hot, dry months that (*cause, causes*) us to look forward to fall.
9. cause	10. *Robert Andrews and His Wife*, painted by Thomas Gainsborough about the middle of the eighteenth century, (*hang, hangs*) in London's National Gallery.
10. hangs	11. The stranded motorcyclist along with all his gear (*have, has*) squeezed into my small car.
11. has	12. Even I know that neither heavy rains nor severe drought (*contribute, contributes*) to good crops.
12. contributes	13. My grandmother's shortcake, topped with straw-berries and fresh cream, (*were, was*) a masterpiece.
13. was	14. Everybody in the congregation (*are, is*) aware that Mr. Pitts dozes through the sermon.
14. is	15. Economics (*have, has*) been the subject of several articles in recent issues of *Fortune.*
15. has	16. The county agent together with a number of my friends (*are, is*) looking forward to the trip to Chicago.
16. is	17. Four yards (*were, was*) all that Foster could gain on the last play.

17. was	18. My friend and fellow salesman (*have, has*) suggested that I read *Dress for Success.*
18. has	19. (*Are, Is*) the news always followed by such outrageous music?
19. Is	20. Beside the telephone in the kitchen (*are, is*) a pencil and a note pad.
20. are	**SCORE** ______

Exercise 37	SUBJECT-VERB AGREEMENT

Write the correct form of the *italicized* verb.

EXAMPLE: (*Do, Does*) Carol or Julia drive to work tomorrow?

Does

	1. (*Haven't, Hasn't*) everyone seen enough of this soap opera?
1. Hasn't	2. Everyone but you (*want, wants*) to see whether Mary leaves John or John leaves Mary.
2. wants	3. Both the *Journal* and the *Constitution* (*have, has*) endorsed your candidate for governor.
3. have	4. Neither shade of eyeshadow (*are, is*) available at the Dixie Styling Center.
4. is	5. Jenkins as well as two companions (*are, is*) waiting for the bus to Bear Mountain.
5. is	6. Is it I who (*am, is*) to arrange the chrysanthemums for the service?
6. am	7. Charlie's favorite pastime (*are, is*) arguing with his brother or talking to Hortense on the telephone.
7. is	8. The sum and substance of the decision (*are, is*) that Sue Ann will play Sadie Thompson.

8. is	9. I do believe that every man, woman, and child in Bridgeport (*are, is*) Christmas shopping today.
9. is	10. According to my friends who are truckers, fifty-five miles per hour (*are, is*) too slow a speed for their purpose.
10. is	11. You'll find that two quarts of lime sherbet (*are, is*) in the freezer.
11. are	12. My scissors (*are, is*) misplaced again.
12. are	13. Gymnastics (*are, is*) an obsession with my cousin Herbert.
13. are	14. Neither the dogwood trees nor the lilac bush (*were, was*) damaged by the late frost.
14. was	15. Walt Disney Productions (*were, was*) the producer of *Mary Poppins.*
15. was	16. The basis for the outfielder's feud with the front office (*are, is*) obvious.
16. is	17. Either of the Parker twins (*are, is*) an ideal candidate for your beauty contest.
17. is	18. The curriculum of the English Department (*have, has*) always been a good topic for debate.

18. has	19. Billy can never remember whether six times four (*are, is*) twenty-four or thirty-two.
19. is	20. The shambles that resulted from the soccer game (*were, was*) still evident on Monday morning.
20. was	**SCORE** ______

Exercise 38 SUBJECT-VERB AGREEMENT

Write the correct form of the *italicized* verb.

EXAMPLE: Half of the grapes on the lower terrace (*have, has*) been picked.

have

	1. There (*are, is*) a record and a tape of the Gershwin music in the listening lab.
1. are	2. Each of the recipes for trifle (*call, calls*) for rum.
2. calls	3. *Letters from Joseph Conrad* (*have, has*) been published in paperback.
3. has	4. Neither of those governments (*consider, considers*) the individual important.
4. considers	5. Every nook and cranny of Ethel's pantry (*are, is*) filled with jars of pickles and preserves.
5. is	6. Every spring the alumni (*gather, gathers*) in the Quadrangle for a reception.
6. gather	7. The crowd at the rugby match (*have, has*) been standing the entire time.
7. has	8. (*Are, Is*) either of you selling tickets to the film festival?

8. Is	9. Didn't you know that measles (*are, is*) highly contagious?
9. is	10. Neither the striped curtains nor the plaid ones (*seem, seems*) quite right for this bedroom.
10. seem	11. Sad to say, fifty dollars (*were, was*) not enough to pay my October rent.
11. was	12. The long and short of the affair (*are, is*) that Joe's horse came in last.
12. is	13. No one would disagree with Bismarck's observation that "politics (*are, is*) not an exact science."
13. is	14. Readings in American History (*are, is*) a course required for my major.
14. is	15. Mangoes (*are, is*) a rare fruit at my grocery store.
15. are	16. Although it is only February, some of the crocuses (*have, has*) already pushed through the earth.
16. have	17. None of these tennis players (*have, has*) been in a tournament.
17. have/has	18. According to the sign, bacon and eggs (*are, is*) always available here.

18. are	19. (*Are, Is*) one of the news magazines required reading in your current-history class?
19. Is	20. Half of the pound cake (*are, is*) already gone.
20. is	SCORE ______

Exercise 39 **SUBJECT-VERB AGREEMENT**

Write the correct form of the *italicized* verb.

EXAMPLE: Either of you (*are, is*) qualified to be doorkeeper.

is

	1. Lighting the candles (*change, changes*) the atmosphere of the dining room.
1. changes	2. Some of the apples that we picked this morning (*are, is*) on the back porch.
2. are	3. "Liberty, Equality, Fraternity" (*were, was*) the cry of the French Revolution.
3. was	4. There at the back of the chapel (*were, was*) three handsome stained-glass windows.
4. were	5. Most of the yellow paint (*are, is*) too bright even for the breakfast room.
5. is	6. Mathematics (*were, was*) Sally's Waterloo.
6. was	7. (*Do, Does*) the judge or his clerk know about the prosecutor's request?
7. Does	8. As usual, the whereabouts of Uncle Percy (*are, is*) unknown.

8. is	9. Half of the nursing students (*are, is*) on duty in the hospital this morning.
9. are	10. Often it seems that the only criterion for judging a coach (*are, is*) victory.
10. is	11. Much time and effort (*have, has*) gone into planning for the regatta.
11. have	12. Either of these weavers (*are, is*) willing to bring her work to the craft fair.
12. is	13. Two liters of orange juice (*are, is*) more than this pitcher will hold.
13. is	14. Everyone who had seen the slides (*were, was*) ready to sign up for the trip to Alaska.
14. was	15. When (*are, is*) Rosie and her pups to be moved to the barn?
15. are	16. Neither Mark nor his younger brothers (*were, was*) able to squeeze through the picket fence.
16. were	17. A group of his supporters (*were, was*) planning to honor the mayor at a fund-raising dinner.
17. was	18. On the table by his bed (*are, is*) a worn paperback, a handful of change, and some letters.

18. are	19. The Congress (*are, is*) meeting in joint session to hear the President's address.
19. is	20. Either my father or I (*are, am*) to represent the family at this year's reunion.
20. am	SCORE ______

Exercise 40 SUBJECT-VERB AGREEMENT

Complete the following sentences by choosing the correct form of the verb **to be** in the present tense and then writing it in the space provided.

EXAMPLE: How *are* the acoustics in this theater?

	1. My brother agrees with Francis Bacon: "Riches ______ for spending."
1. are	2. Every doctor, lawyer, merchant, and chief ______ interested in lower taxes.
2. is	3. The leaves on the sycamore tree outside my window ______ beginning to turn brown.
3. are	4. Sweet and sour pork ______ always his first choice at the Bamboo Gardens.
4. is	5. The data received from the questionnaires ______ undoubtedly valid.
5. are	6. Kate's favorite breakfast ______ pancakes and sausage.
6. is	7. Buried among the notes at the end of the chapter ______ the answers to the first two questions.
7. are	8. The pecan is one of those trees that ______ able to offer both fruit and shade.

8. are	9. The glad tidings of my promotion ________ to appear in this week's newsletter.
9. are	10. Where ________ Max and the other members of his family going to camp this weekend?
10. are	11. Have you noticed that some of the gulls ________ still following in the wake of the ship?
11. are	12. Neither the members of the orchestra nor the director ________ interested in repeating tonight's program right away.
12. is	13. Marie's friend and attorney ________ to represent her in traffic court.
13. is	14. The Federated States of Europe ________ still a dream, but not an impossibility.
14. is	15. At the far end of the fishing pier ________ the old man and two young children.
15. are	16. The alumnae who graduated in the Class of 1920 ________ invited to sit on the platform.
16. are	17. The great crowd ________ packed in the coliseum, waiting for the heavyweight match to begin.
17. is	18. The media ________ accused of not presenting both sides of the issue.

18. are	19. Twelve hundred miles per hour ______ the *Concorde*'s astonishing rate of speed.
19. is	20. Steve's father and his counselor ______ interested in the possibility of a student loan.
20. are	**SCORE** ______

9

Agreement of Pronoun and Antecedent

Pronouns, as we saw in Chapter 1, are words that are used in the place of nouns when repetition of a noun would be awkward. *The dog hurt the dog's foot* is clearly an unnatural expression. Usually a pronoun has a definite, easily recognized *antecedent* (the noun or pronoun to which it refers), with which it agrees in *person, number,* and *gender.* The *case* of a pronoun, however, is not dependent on the case of its antecedent.

9a Certain Singular Antecedents

Use singular pronouns to refer to singular antecedents. *Each, either, neither, anyone, anybody, everyone, everybody, someone, somebody, no one, nobody* are singular, and pronouns referring to them should be singular:

> *Each* of the girls has *her* own car.
>
> *Neither* of the boys remembered *his* poncho.
>
> Does *everyone* have *his* ticket?

NOTE: In the last of the preceding examples *his* is used even though its antecedent may be either male or female. You should be aware of and sensitive to objections to this traditional practice, but you should also recognize that no completely satisfactory solution exists, inasmuch as our language has no singular form that refers to persons of either sex. Because the expressions *he or she, his or her, his or hers,* and *him and her* are awkward, you are justified in using the masculine pronouns (or possessive adjectives) in a universal sense. It is often possible, however, to avoid the problem by rephrasing the sentence:

> Does *everyone* have *a* ticket?
>
> Do *we* all have *our* tickets?
>
> *Who* doesn't have *a* ticket? etc.

9b Collective Nouns as Antecedents

With *collective nouns* use either a singular or a plural pronoun according to the meaning of the sentence. Since collective nouns may be either singular or plural, their correct usage depends upon (1) a decision as to meaning (See Chapter 8, Section 8i) and (2) consistency:

The *team* has elected Jan as *its* captain. [The team is acting as a unit and therefore requires the singular pronoun *its*.]

The *team* quickly took *their* positions on the field. [Here each member of the team is acting individually.]

Exercise 41 AGREEMENT OF PRONOUN AND ANTECEDENT

After each sentence write the correct form of the *italicized* pronoun.

EXAMPLE: Each of the fencers brought (*their, his*) own foil to the gym.

his

	1. Someone has left (*their, her*) pedometer down by the track.
1. her	2. As an alumna, (*they, she*) will represent the College at the convocation.
2. she	3. Each of the languages has idioms of (*their, its*) own.
3. its	4. I am not certain that every one of the jurors understood (*their, his*) responsibility.
4. his	5. The Gray Panthers is an organization that is recognized for (*their, its*) concern for the elderly.
5. its	6. It is apparent that neither of the joggers has had (*their, her*) warm-up suit very long.
6. her	7. Everyone had (*their, his*) own idea of who should play the young man in *The American Dream.*
7. his	8. Has everybody filed (*their, his*) story about the President's press conference?

8. his	9. Who said that "everyone has at least one sermon in (*them, him*)"?
9. him	10. Unfortunately, Baker is one of those men who are unable to imagine (*themselves, himself*) hanging out the laundry.
10. themselves	11. For a number of years the Organization of American States has expressed (*themselves, itself*) about affairs within our hemisphere.
11. itself	12. The data had lost (*their, its*) significance by the time Eloise presented her report.
12. their	13. His sister and his friend brought (*their, her*) binoculars to the game.
13. their	14. Neither of the airlines wants to raise (*their, its*) fares.
14. its	15. Either Arthur or Leon will have to get out (*their, his*) sleeping bag tonight.
15. his	16. As the questioning began, all the students slipped down in (*their, his*) desks.
16. their	17. After the matinee not one of the actors was really satisfied with (*their, his*) performance.

17. his	18. Although Gatewood says that apples are cheap this year, the news in the *Farm Journal* speaks for (*themselves, itself*).
18. itself	19. Everyone soliciting for the Community Chest must have (*their, her*) report in by Friday.
19. her	20. Each child in the family received (*their, his*) immunization for polio.
20. his	SCORE ______

Exercise 42 AGREEMENT OF PRONOUN AND ANTECEDENT

In the following sentences underline each pronoun that is used incorrectly, and then write the correct form. If necessary, write the correct form of the verb also. Write **C** if the sentence is correct.

EXAMPLE: Each of you will have to order their own ticket to the World Series.

his

	1. Neither the old doctor nor the young intern was ready to offer their diagnosis.
1. their his	2. The dropping temperature sent each of us scurrying to check her antifreeze.
2. C	3. The panel of judges announced their decision just before midnight.
3. their its	4. Probably nobody has ever forgotten the first time they drove an automobile.
4. they he	5. Each of the spelunkers was careful to mark their return route.
5. their his	6. The instructions for assembling the bicycle are so complicated that an engineer is needed to decipher them.

6. C	7. The P.T.A. was more than willing to lend their support to the Halloween carnival.
7. their its	8. Neither the Californian nor the Floridian is willing to concede that their sunshine can be improved upon.
8. their his	9. One thing I know: everyone should spend some of their time reading for pleasure.
9. their his	10. Neither of the radio stations has their own weather forecaster.
10. their its	11. Because my younger brother has mumps, I'm not surprised to learn that I have them, too.
11. them it	12. Every member of the science faculty has their key to the labs.
12. their his	13. Both the United States and Canada recognized the energy problem they had in common.
13. C	14. The alumnus of the University of Iowa whom you met yesterday has recently had their poetry published in *Harper's*.

14. their his	15. Every member of my family, including my grandparents, will spend their Christmas at Olive's house.
15. their his	16. The media concluded that it should inform us of the perils of speeding.
16. it they	17. The audience was unanimous in their approval of the soprano's performance.
17. their its	18. The gallows casts its shadow over every page of *The Ox-Bow Incident.*
18. C	19. Does anybody remember their way to the top of the falls?
19. their his	20. The directions on the bottle state that one should spray themselves with the insect repellent.
20. themselves himself	**SCORE** ______

10
Reference of Pronouns

The word to which a pronoun refers should always be clear to the reader; that is, a **pronoun** and the **antecedent** to which it refers must be instantly identified as belonging together. A pronoun may be used with grammatical correctness and still be confusing or misleading. Therefore, it is sometimes necessary to repeat the antecedent or to reword the whole sentence for the sake of clearness.

10a Ambiguous Reference

Sometimes a sentence contains more than one word to which a pronoun may grammatically refer (the term *ambiguous* means "capable of more than one interpretation"). The sentence should be written in such a way that the reader has no doubt which word is the antecedent:

> Albert told his uncle that his money had been stolen. [The first *his* is clear, but the second *his* could refer to either *Albert* or *uncle*.]
>
> Albert told his uncle that Albert's money money had been stolen. [The meaning is clear, but the sentence is unnatural and awkward.]

To avoid the ambiguous reference of the first sentence and the awkward repetition of the second, reword the sentence:

> Albert said to his uncle, "My money has been stolen."

Another kind of ambiguous reference (sometimes called *divided* or *remote* reference) occurs when a modifying clause is misplaced in a sentence:

> INCORRECT: The colt was almost hit by a car which jumped over the pasture fence.
>
> CORRECT: The colt which jumped over the pasture fence was almost hit by a car.

NOTE: A relative pronoun should always be placed as near as possible to its antecedent. (See Chapter 15.)

10b Broad Reference

Usually a pronoun should not refer broadly to the whole idea of the preceding clause:

> She avoided using slang, which greatly improved her speech. [*Which* has no clearly apparent antecedent but refers broadly to the whole idea in the first clause.]
>
> She talked incessantly about her operation, and this talkativeness was distressing.

A method often used to improve such sentences is to supply a definite antecedent or to substitute a noun for the pronoun:

> She avoid using slang, a practice which greatly improved her speech.
>
> She talked incessantly about her operation, and this talkativeness was distressing.

As you can see, these sentences are awkward, adding unnecessary words. A better method is to get rid of the pronoun and make a concise, informative sentence that says everything in one clause:

> Her avoidance of slang greatly improved her speech.
>
> Her incessant talking about her operation was distressing.

10c Weak Reference

A pronoun should not refer to a word which is merely implied by the context. Nor, as a common practice, should the pronoun refer to a word used as a modifier:

> INCORRECT: My father is a chemist. *This* is a profession I intend to follow. [The antecedent of *This* should be *chemistry,* which is implied in *chemist* but is not actually stated.]
>
> CORRECT: My father is a chemist. Chemistry is the profession I intend to follow.
>
> ALSO CORRECT: My father's profession of chemistry is the one I intend to follow.
>
> INCORRECT: When she thrust a stick into the rat hole, it ran out and bit her. [*Rat* in this sentence is the modifier of *hole.*]
>
> CORRECT: When she thrust a stick into the rat hole, a rat ran out and bit her.

10d Impersonal Use of the Personal Pronoun

Remember that pronouns are frequently used impersonally and when so used do not have antecedents. Notice the correct impersonal use of *it* in statements about *weather, time,* and *distance*:

> *It* looks like rain. [Reference to weather.]
>
> *It* is now twelve o'clock. [Reference to time.]
>
> How far is *it* to the nearest town? [Reference to distance.]

Avoid the use of *you* and *your* unless you are directing your statement specifically to the reader. Instead, use an impersonal word like *one* or *person.* Also note that the pronoun *you* can never refer to an antecedent in the third person:

> INCORRECT: If *you* want to excel in athletics, *you* should watch your diet. [Incorrect when referring to athletes in general.]

CORRECT: If *one* wants to excel in athletics, *he* should watch his diet.

INCORRECT: When a person gets married, *you* take on new responsibilities. [Here *you* refers incorrectly to *person*, an antecedent in the third person.]

CORRECT: When a person gets married, *he* takes on new responsibilities.

INCORRECT: One must always remember to lock *your* doors before leaving home.

CORRECT: One must always remember to lock *his* doors before leaving home.

Exercise 43 REFERENCE OF PRONOUNS

Write **R** after each sentence which contains an error in the reference of a pronoun. Then rewrite the sentence correctly. Write **C** if the sentence is correct.

EXAMPLE: Because her grandparents are Mexicans, she has visited it every summer. **R**

Because her grandparents are Mexicans, she has visited Mexico every summer.

(Note that only one correct version of each sentence is given in the answer section.)

Answers	Sentences
	1. The magnolia leaves have blown all over my neighbor's lawn and driveway, which are now dry and brittle.
1. *R* The magnolia leaves, which are now dry and brittle, have blown all over my neighbor's lawn and driveway.	2. Although Rachel has spent years studying piano, recently she decided not to be a professional one.
2. *R* Although Rachel has spent years studying piano, recently she decided not to play professionally.	3. Someone left the windows open; this caused a minor disaster once the rain began.
3. *R* Because someone left the windows open, a minor disaster occurred once the rain began.	4. It is as far from Kansas to Oz as it has ever been.

4. *C*	5. Cousin Mary Lee knitted Christmas stockings for all twelve of us; this occupied much of her summer.
5. *R* Knitting Christmas stockings for all twelve of us occupied much of Cousin Mary Lee's summer.	6. The corn has burned up in the fields, which is not surprising during a summer so hot and dry as this one.
6. *R* That the corn has burned up in the fields is not surprising during a summer so hot and dry as this one.	7. Since Mitchell's sister is an excellent swimmer, everybody expects him to be one, too.
7. *C*	8. Aunt Elizabeth's diamond brooch was set with three unusually handsome ones.
8. *R* Aunt Elizabeth's brooch was set with three unusually handsome diamonds.	9. We are prohibited by a law from disturbing the sand dunes, which passed at a recent session of the legislature.

9. *R* We are prohibited from disturbing the sand dunes by a law which passed at a recent session of the legislature.	10. I have always been interested in the German people and certainly hope to include it on my tour of Europe.
10. *R* I have always been interested in the German people and certainly hope to include their country on my tour of Europe.	11. Today's weather map indicates that it will probably snow here tomorrow.
11. *C*	12. The lovely hooked rug was admired by her family which she spread before the fireplace.
12. *R* Her family admired the lovely hooked rug which she spread before the fireplace.	13. Before you leave for Campbell's store, we will have to load the bookmobile with some new ones.
13. *R* Before you leave for Campbell's store, we will have to load the bookmobile with some new books.	14. Alice went down the rabbit hole because she had never seen one with a watch and waistcoat.
14. *R* Alice went down the rabbit hole because she had never seen a rabbit with a watch and waistcoat.	**SCORE** ______

Exercise 44 REFERENCE OF PRONOUNS

Write **R** after each sentence which contains an error in the reference of a pronoun. Then rewrite the sentence correctly. Write **C** if the sentence is correct.

EXAMPLE: Peg slept through the alarm, which made her late for work. **R**

Because Peg slept through the alarm, she was late for work.

(Note that only one correct version of each sentence is given in the answer section.)

Answers	Sentences
	1. If you want this brick wall to be four feet high, you will need another truckload of them.
1. *R* If you want this wall to be four feet high, you will need another truckload of bricks.	2. When one is invited to a party at Beth's, you are in for a good time.
2. *R* When one is invited to a party at Beth's, he is in for a good time.	3. Dr. Spencer delivered a speech at the ecology conference, which was at least forty-five minutes long.
3. *R* At the ecology conference Dr. Spencer delivered a speech which was at least forty-five minutes long.	4. The portrait of Dean Bellamy is sitting in the storage room, which was painted by a famous artist.

4. *R* The portrait of Dean Bellamy, which was painted by a famous artist, is sitting in the storage room.	5. Every night he tosses his shoes into the closet, which makes them difficult to find in the morning.
5. *R* Because he tosses his shoes into the closet every night, they are difficult to find in the morning.	6. Mason told his brother that he should hear about his application to business school soon.
6. *R* Mason said to his brother, "You should hear about your application to business school soon."	7. It is more than five hundred miles from my home to New Orleans.
7. *C*	8. The librarian searched for the book about Indian poetry by Mary Austin, who was on duty last night.
8. *R* The librarian who was on duty last night searched for the book about Indian poetry by Mary Austin.	9. The beige sweater I ordered from the catalog has not come; this makes it impossible for me to wear my tweed skirt.

9. *R* Since the beige sweater I ordered from the catalog has not come, I cannot wear my tweed skirt.	10. Jade, which we associate with the Far East, has been called "the stone of heaven."
10. *C*	11. Seashells lined the windowsills of the sun porch, even though Aunt Mae had not been near it for years.
11. *R* Seashells lined the windowsills of the sun porch, even though Aunt Mae had not been near the shore for years.	12. We visited the Hopi village because Don has always been interested in their culture.
12. *R* We visited the Hopi village because Don has always been interested in the culture of that tribe.	SCORE ______

Exercise 45 REFERENCE OF PRONOUNS

Write **R** after each sentence which contains an error in the reference of a pronoun. Then re-write the sentence correctly. Write **C** if the sentence is correct.

EXAMPLE: Mr. Willis is an accountant, and his daughter is interested in it too. **R**

Mr. Willis is an accountant, and his daughter is interested in being one too.

(Note that only one correct version of each sentence is given in the answer section.)

	1. The heat convinced us that we should eat inside the restaurant, which is typical of New Orleans in June.
1. *R* The heat, which is typical of New Orleans in June, convinced us that we should eat inside the restaurant.	2. If one wants to be well informed, you should subscribe to a daily paper as well as a weekly news magazine.
2. *R* If one wants to be well informed, he should subscribe to a daily paper as well as a weekly news magazine.	3. Seeing the orchids was a treat for our garden club, whose cultivation has intrigued Mr. Knapp for years.
3. *R* Seeing the orchids, whose cultivation has intrigued Mr. Knapp for years, was a treat for our garden club.	4. Pumpkins were on sale at the farmer's market; this excited Mrs. Jacobs' second-graders.

4. *R* The pumpkins on sale at the farmer's market excited Mrs. Jacobs' second-graders.	5. It is eight forty-five, and the northbound train is due.
5. *C*	6. We are going to have to buy more shelf paper if we hope to cover every one of them.
6. *R* If we hope to cover every one of the shelves, we're going to have to buy more paper.	7. Although my father was an excellent real estate salesman, I am not very good at it.
7. *R* Although my father was an excellent real estate salesman, I am not very good at selling.	8. Colin told his father that his car needed two new tires.
8. *R* Colin said, "Dad, your car needs two new tires."	9. Obviously, the problem with sundials is that they cannot tell time when it is not out.

9. *R* Obviously, the problem with sundials is that they cannot tell time when the sun is not out.	10. Edith collects stamps; this was also a hobby of Franklin Roosevelt.
10. *R* Edith's hobby, collecting stamps, was also a hobby of Franklin Roosevelt.	11. No reasonable offer was refused, which explains why I got this chemistry text for five dollars.
11. *R* Because no reasonable offer was refused, I got this chemistry text for five dollars.	12. Knife blocks have become popular because they offer an excellent means of protecting their cutting edges.
12. *R* Knife blocks have become popular because they offer an excellent means of protecting cutting edges.	SCORE ______

11
Case of Pronouns

Nouns and pronouns have three case functions: the **nominative**, the **objective**, and the **possessive**. Except in the possessive, nouns do not show case by change of form and consequently do not present any problems of case. The chief difficulties are in the correct use of pronouns.

11a The Nominative Case

The **nominative case** is used (1) as the subject of a verb (*I* shall come); (2) as the complement after *is, are,* and the other forms of the verb *to be* (It is *I*); or (3) as an appositive of the subject or of the complement after forms of the verb *to be* (Two of us–*he* and *I*–called). Ordinarily the case of a pronoun which comes before a verb presents no difficulties, for we naturally write "I am going," not "Me am going." But all constructions requiring the nominative case are not so simple as this one. Study carefully the following more difficult constructions:

1. A clause of comparison introduced by *as* or *than* is often not written out in full. The verb is then understood. The subject of this understood verb is in the nominative case:

   No one can do the work as well as *he* (can).

   He knows more about the subject than *she* (does).

2. After forms of the linking verb *to be*, nouns and pronouns used to identify the subject agree in case with the subject. Nouns and pronouns used in this way are called **predicate nominatives** and are in the nominative case:

   It was *they* [not *them*].

   The persons referred to were her sister and *she* [not *her*].

   He answered, "It could not have been *I* [not *me*]."

3. Pronouns are frequently combined with a noun or used in apposition with a noun. If they are thus used with the subject of the sentence or with a predicate nominative, they are in the nominative case:

> *We* boys will be responsible for the equipment.
>
> Two photographers–*you* and *he*–must attend the convention.

If you read these sentences omitting the nouns, the correct form of the pronoun will at once be clear.

4. The position of the relative pronoun *who* often causes confusion, especially if it follows a verb or a preposition. The role of the relative pronoun within the dependent clause determines its case. Thus if *who* is the subject of the verb in the dependent clause, it is in the nominative case:

> You know *who* sent the money. [Since *who* is the subject of the verb *sent* and not the object of *know*, it must be in the nominative case. The whole clause *who sent the money* is the object of *know*.]
>
> Give the praise to *whoever* deserves it. [*Whoever* is the subject of *deserves.* The whole clause *whoever deserves it* is the object of the preposition *to*.]

5. Parenthetical expressions such as *you think, I believe, I suppose,* and *he says* often stand between a verb and the pronoun which is the subject. The pronoun must still be in the nominative case:

> *Who* do you think called me last night? [The expression *do you think* has nothing to do with the case of *who*. Leave it out, or place it elsewhere in the sentence, and you will see that *who* is the subject of *called*.]
>
> The man *who Jim* says will be our next governor is in the room. [Leave out or place elsewhere *Jim says,* and you will see that *who* is the subject of *will be.*].

11b The Objective Case

The **objective case** of a pronoun is used when the pronoun is the direct or indirect object of a verb, the object of a preposition, or an appositive of an object:

1. Compound subjects present a special difficulty:

> He wrote a letter to Mary and *me*. [Both words *Mary* and *me* are objects of the preposition *to* and therefore in the objective case. Omit *Mary and* or shift *me* to the position of *Mary*, and the correct form is at once apparent.]
>
> She gave George and *him* the address. [*Him* is part of the compound indirect object.]
>
> They invited William and *me* to the barbecue. [*Me* is part of the compound direct object.]

2. You will also have to watch the case of a pronoun combined with a noun in apposition with an object:

She spoke cordially to *us* boys.

They told three of us girls—Mary, Sue, and *me*—to go.

3. *Whom*, the objective case of *who*, deserves special consideration:

Whom were you talking to? [To *whom* were you talking?]

He is the boy *whom* we met on the plane. [*Whom* is the object of the verb *met*. The subject of *met* is *we*. Remember that the case of the relative pronoun is determined by its role within the dependent clause.]

Whom do you think we saw last night? [The parenthetical expression does not change the fact that *whom* is the object of *saw*.]

11c Case of Pronouns Used with Infinitives

An infinitive phrase, as you have learned already, can have both an object and adverbial modifiers. In addition, an **infinitive** may have a subject. There are rules governing the case There are rules governing the case of pronouns when they are subjects or complements of infinitives:

1. When a pronoun is the subject of an infinitive, it will be in the objective case:

We want *him* to be elected.

2. If the infinitive is a form of the verb *to be* and if it has a subject, its complement will also be in the objective case:

She took him to be *me*.

3. If the infinitive *to be* does not have a subject, its complement will be in the nominative case:

The best player was thought to be *he*.

11d The Possessive Case

Personal pronouns and the relative pronoun *who* have **possessive case** forms, which may be used with a noun or a gerund.

1. When the possessive forms *my, our, your, her, his, its,* and *their* modify nouns or gerunds, they are classified as **possessive adjectives**:

My book is on the table. [*My* is a possessive adjective, modifying *book*.]

We appreciate *your* giving to the Community Chest. [Not *you giving*. The object of the verb *appreciate* is the gerund *giving*; therefore, *your* is merely the possessive adjective modifying the gerund.]

2. Personal and relative pronouns form their possessives without the apostrophe:

The boy *whose* car is in the driveway works here.

The dog chewed *its* bone.

NOTE: Notice the difference between *its*, the possessive form, and *it's*, the contraction of *it is*:

It's time for your car to have *its* oil changed.

Exercise 46 CASE OF PRONOUNS

In the following sentences underline each pronoun which is used incorrectly and then write the correct form. Write **C** if the sentence is correct.

EXAMPLE: I know who Humphrey has considered for the job.

whom

	1. Has Mr. Richards decided who to send to meet Burgess's plane?
1. who whom	2. A clear understanding exists between Meredith and I.
2. I me	3. According to the newspaper account, the owner of the filling station is thought to be him.
3. him he	4. Mrs. Coleman explained to Bud and I where to place the movie projector.
4. I me	5. The three of them–Nick, Arthur, and him–plan to attend the craftsmen's fair in Clarksville.
5. him he	6. Between you and I, it will take more than a two-hour hike to reach the top of the mountain.
6. I me	7. My brother Alfred bakes a better lemon meringue pie than I.

7. C	8. The young man by who this stained glass was designed has a studio on Ridge Road.
8. who whom	9. Steve was looking forward to us camping out this weekend.
9. us our	10. Us musicians have played with the same group since we were in high school.
10. Us We	11. Whom did you say is going to scrimmage with us this afternoon?
11. Whom Who	12. Do you think that Dad has tickets to the Patriots' game for she and George?
12. she her	13. Mary Sue has asked her to be the baby's godmother.
13. C	14. This morning Arnold announced whom is to be on the staff at summer camp.
14. whom who	15. My younger sister often walked halfway to school with my friends and I.

15. I me	16. Mr. Frierson considers he and Marcus to be excellent mechanics.
16. he him	17. My mother claims that us children always enjoyed hearing fairy tales.
17. us we	18. Matt can run the mile faster than him.
18. him he	19. I will always remember us driving home on the Blue Ridge Parkway.
19. us our	20. As Ben sped by the house, he waved at us girls.
20. C	**SCORE** ______

Exercise 47 CASE OF PRONOUNS

In the following sentences underline each pronoun which is used incorrectly, and then write the correct form. Write **C** if the sentence is correct.

EXAMPLE: Polly can walk as far as him.

he

	1. Could it have been her who got the job as sports editor?
1. her she	2. Who did Warren buy the opera tickets from?
2. Who Whom	3. The three of us—Terry, Jeff, and me—use the same kind of tennis racket.
3. me I	4. Marvin, who I often play golf with, drives the ball straight down the fairway.
4. who whom	5. Mother is four inches shorter than me.
5. me I	6. The owner of the car with the diesel engine is thought to be him.
6. him he	7. Grandmother gave Tim and I a trip to New York for graduation.

7. I me	8. Whom do you think will win the Davis Cup this year?
8. Whom Who	9. The story opens with him saying, "Call me Ishmael."
9. him his	10. The first thing that Ramsey and I must do is shop for a refrigerator.
10. C	11. The notice of the auction was addressed to she and Reid.
11. she her	12. Father often takes Wilson to be he.
12. he him	13. Sarah does not know whom originated her recipe for oyster stew.
13. whom who	14. Who did they name the new hospital for?
14. Who Whom	15. Every member of the Book Club but her has paid the dues.

15. C	16. Me asking Dad for money to go to Lake Tahoe would be foolhardy.
16. Me My	17. The electrician who you recommended has agreed to rewire my lamp.
17. who whom	18. The card she wrote Aaron and I was mailed from St. Louis.
18. I me	19. Our college has not published it's catalog for next year.
19. it's its	20. Have you seen the film production of *Who's Afraid of Virginia Woolf?*
20. C	**SCORE** ______

Exercise 48 CASE OF PRONOUNS

Write the correct form of the pronoun *who* (*whoever*).

EXAMPLE: By (*who, whom*) was this portrait of Washington painted?

whom

	1. He is the guitarist (*who, whom*) you met at the recording studio.
1. whom	2. (*Who, Whom*) do you think will be selected Woman of the Year?
2. Who	3. (*Who's, Whose*) car are you driving to the rally?
3. Whose	4. You may be surprised to know (*who, whom*) created the character Frankenstein.
4. who	5. I would like to speak to (*whoever, whomever*) is the buyer for the record department.
5. whoever	6. The landscape architect (*who, whom*) I believe planned this garden is Japanese.
6. who	7. (*Whoever, Whomever*) put his money in this stock made a sound investment.
7. Whoever	8. Does she know (*who, whom*) to call about our hotel reservations in Portland?
8. whom	9. (*Who, Whom*) did you ask to bring the sandwiches?

9. Whom	10. I know that (*whoever, whomever*) gave Horace that lime and lavender tie was no friend.
10. whoever	11. Ginny is not certain (*who, whom*) carved her walnut bookends.
11. who	12. The character in the comics with (*who, whom*) I identify is Charlie Brown.
12. whom	13. (*Who's, Whose*) planning to accompany the choir on the spring tour?
13. Who's	14. (*Who, Whom*) did Lily buy the fortune cookies from?
14. Whom	15. (*Whoever, Whomever*) can that be standing on the wharf?
15. Whoever	16. No one (*who, whom*) Jamie saw recognized her in the black wig and stage makeup.
16. whom	17. Aunt Nana discussed the old days when she lived on the farm with (*whoever, whomever*) would listen.
17. whoever	18. The man (*who, whom*) Roger says is the captain of the ship is standing over there by the rail.
18. who	19. Marilyn knows (*who, whom*) sent the jonquils.

19. who	20. The prize was given to the person (*who, whom*) had submitted the most interesting feature story.
20. who	**SCORE** ______

Exercise 49 REVIEW OF AGREEMENT AND CASE

Underline each word that is incorrectly used. Then write the correct word. Write **C** if the sentence is correct.

EXAMPLE: Dave has asked Laura and I to his open house.

me

	1. Have either of your customers tried on the camel-hair coat?
1. Have Has	2. The whereabouts of Gerald's sailboat have just been reported.
2. have has	3. You recall who Mother said painted the admiral's portrait.
3. C	4. Beverly, who I have asked to be our moderator, knows a great deal about recreation programs.
4. who whom	5. No one could be as memorable a cantor as him.
5. him he	6. After completing the last performance of the tour, the chorus separated, each to go their own way.
6. their his	7. Pris is certain that it was me who received the call from South Bend.

7. me I	8. Whitaker's brother looks exactly like him.
8. C	9. This television set needs to go back to the shop; it's picture is faint and fuzzy.
9. it's its	10. Either my roommate or I are going to subscribe to the *Wall Street Journal.*
10. are am	11. The tree with all its brilliant lights attract visitors to the small park.
11. attract attracts	12. The ladle is one of those pieces of silver which is designed at Williamsburg.
12. is are	13. I don't know what Father will think of you driving all night.
13. you your	14. Each of the roses entered in the show appear perfect to me.
14. appear appears	15. Every driver should be taught how to change a tire since you never know when you will have a flat.

15. you, know, you one, knows, one	16. The bond between she and Dick is one of friendship.
16. she her	17. The teller always spoke pleasantly to whoever needed her attention.
17. C	18. I sat in front of he and his brother at the last Penguins' game.
18. he him	19. Who's motorcycle is that parked next to the fire hydrant?
19. Who's Whose	20. Each of the vocalists recognized by the Country Music Association had their own distinctive style.
20. their his	21. Sound asleep on top of the picnic table is our old cat Jabez and the Fuller's new kitten.
21. is are	22. The politician had difficulty remembering exactly who was who.
22. C	23. The consul from Great Britain as well as his wife were invited to the meeting of the Burns Society.
23. were was	24. Is the mailgram for he or his father?

24. he him	25. The sculptor whose work he most admires is to be a guest at Sunday's reception.
25. C	26. Its undoubtedly a fact that Margaret would rather cut class than miss *All My Children.*
26. Its It's	27. Either the president or the treasurer are responsible for issuing the firm's checks.
27. are is	28. Whom does she think will represent the United States in figure skating at the Olympics?
28. Whom Who	29. During the summer a dozen of us children used to play under the street lights after dark.
29. C	30. I could declare that the man wearing the toupee is him.
30. him he	31. My grandfather is accustomed to me being on time for supper.
31. me my	32. I hope that just us four can get together after the play.

32. <u>us</u> we	33. You can play chess every bit as well as him.
33. <u>him</u> he	34. Ethics are the subject of both of those books by Erich Fromm.
34. <u>are</u> is	35. None of the grocery stores have any chutney.
35. have/has	**SCORE** ______

12
Adjectives and Adverbs

Adjectives and adverbs, as you saw in Chapter One, are words which modify, describe, or add to the meaning of other words in a sentence. It is important to remember the special and differing functions of these two kinds of modifier; *adjectives* modify only nouns and other substantives; *adverbs* modify verbs, adjectives, adverbs, and certain phrases and clauses.

12a Adjective and Adverb Forms

An adverb is frequently formed by adding *-ly* to the adjective form of a word: for example, the adjectives *rapid, sure,* and *considerate* are converted into the adverbs *rapidly, surely,* and *considerately* by this method. But there are numerous exceptions to this general rule. Many common adverbs, like *well, then,* and *quite*, do not end in *-ly*; moreover, there are many *adjectives* that do end in *-ly*, like *manly, stately, lonely,* or *unsightly.*

Sometimes the same form is used for both adjective and adverbial forms: *fast, long*, and *much*, for example. (There are no such words as *fastly, longly,* or *muchly.*) Certain adverbs have two forms, one being the same as the adjective and the other ending in *-ly*: *slow, slowly; quick, quickly; loud, loudly;* etc. The first form is often employed in short commands, as in the sentences *Drive slow* and *Speak loud.*

12b Predicate Adjectives

In any sentence which follows a "subject-verb-modifier" pattern, you must be especially careful to determine whether the modifier is describing the subject or the verb:

> John talks *intelligently.*
>
> John is *intelligent.*

In the first sentence the modifier clearly describes how John talks – that is, it modifies the verb *talks*; consequently, the adverb *intelligently* is needed. But in the second sentence the modifier describes the subject *John*; therefore, an adjective is used. In this construction the adjective following the linking verb *is* is called the **predicate adjective.**

The term **linking verb**, as you learned from Chapter One, refers to certain intransitive verbs which make a statement not by expressing action but by expressing a condition or state of being. These verbs "link" the subject of the sentence with some other substantive that renames or identifies it or with an adjective that describes it. Any adjective that appears after a subject-linking verb construction is called the **predicate adjective.** The verbs most commonly used as linking verbs are the following:

appear	become	remain	stay
be	grow	seem	feel (as an emotion)

Along with these are the five "sense" verbs, which are usually linking verbs:

look	feel	smell	taste	sound

The following sentences illustrate the use of predicate adjectives:

The little dog was *glad* to be out of his pen. [*Glad*, a predicate adjective, follows the linking verb *was* and describes *dog.*]

Father appeared *eager* to drive his new car.

Laurie became *angry* at being put to bed.

Jackie seems *happy* in her new job.

Please remain *quiet*, and I will give you your seat assignments. [*Quiet*, the predicate adjective, describes the subject, *you*, understood.]

The day grew *dark* as the clouds gathered.

Peggy looks *sporty* in her new tennis outfit.

I fell *confident* that Ty will win his case.

That cinnamon bread smells *delicious.*

The rain sounds *dismal* beating on the roof.

Almond toffee ice cream tastes *marvelous.*

This warm robe feels *comfortable.*

A practical test to follow in determining whether to use an adjective or an adverb is to try to substitute some form of the verb *to be* for the verb in the sentence. If the substitution does not substantially change the meaning of the sentence, then the verb should be followed by an adjective. For instance, *She is smart in her new uniform* has essentially the same meaning as *She looks smart in her new uniform*; therefore, the adjective *smart* is the correct modifier.

Occasionally, one of the "sense" verbs is followed by an adverb because the verb is being used not as a *linking* verb but as an *action* verb: *He looked nervously for his keys. Nervously* describes the act of looking, so the adverb is used to express how the looking was done. The substitution test would show immediately that an adjective would be incorrect in the sentence.

12c Misuse of Adjectives

Using an adjective to modify a verb is a common error but a serious one. The sentence *The doctor spoke to the sick child very kind* illustrates this error. *Kind* is an adjective and cannot be used to modify the verb *spoke*; the adverb *kindly* must be used.

Four adjectives which are frequently misused as adverbs are *real, good, sure,* and *some.* When the adverbial form of these words is needed, the correct forms are *really, well, surely,* and *somewhat:*

> The mountain laurel is *really* (or *very,* not *real*) colorful.
>
> You did *well* (not *good*) to stop smoking so quickly.
>
> I *surely* (not *sure*) hope to see him before he leaves.
>
> I feel *somewhat* (not *some*) better today.

NOTE: Remember that *well* can also be an adjective, referring to a state of health, as in *I feel well now, after my long illness.*

12d Comparison of Adjectives and Adverbs

When you wish to indicate to what extent one noun has a certain quality in comparison with that of another noun, you change the form of the modifying adjective that describes the quality: My dog is *bigger* than your dog. My dog is the *biggest* dog in town.

Descriptive adverbs, like adjectives, may be compared in the same way:

> We awaited the holidays *more eagerly* than our parents did.
>
> The shrimp and the oysters were the foods *most rapidly* eaten at the party.

Adjectives and adverbs show or imply comparison by the use of three forms, called **degrees**: the **positive, comparative,** and **superlative degrees.**

POSITIVE DEGREE

The **positive degree** of an adjective or adverb is its regular form:

> He is a *fine* man.
>
> John took notes *carefully.*

COMPARATIVE DEGREE

The **comparative degree** of an adjective or adverb compares two things, persons, or actions:

> He is a *finer* man than his brother.
>
> John took notes *more carefully* than Bob did.

SUPERLATIVE DEGREE

The **superlative degree** compares three or more persons, things, or actions:

> He is the *finest* man I know.
>
> John took notes *most carefully* of all the boys in his class.

The comparative degree is regularly formed by adding *-er* to the positive form of an adjective or adverb or by using *more* or *less* before the positive form. The superlative degree is formed either by adding *-est* to the positive or by using *most* or *least* before the positive. The number of syllables in the word determines which of these forms must be used:

	Positive	*Comparative*	*Superlative*
	strong	stronger	strongest
Adj.	pretty	prettier	prettiest
	difficult	more difficult	most difficult
	quietly	more quietly	most quietly
Adv.	easily	more easily	most easily
	fast	faster	fastest

The comparison of some words is irregular, as of *good* (*good, better, best*) and *bad* (*bad, worse, worst*).

Be careful not to use the superlative form when only two persons, groups, objects, or ideas are involved:

Tom is the *healthier* (not *healthiest*) of the two brothers.

Certain adjectives and adverbs such as *perfect* and *unique* cannot logically be used in the comparative or superlative degree; such words represent the superlative in their simple forms, incapable of being added to or detracted from:

ILLOGICAL: Samuel is the *most unique* person I know.

LOGICAL: Samuel is a *unique* person.

Exercise 50 ADJECTIVES AND ADVERBS

For each sentence write the word that is modified by the *italicized* adjective or adverb. Then write **Adj** if the *italicized* word is an adjective, **Adv** if it is an adverb.

EXAMPLE: The temperature is *unusually* low for a May morning.

low **Adv**

Answers	Sentences
	1. As soon as the bugle blew, the campers *quickly* formed a line for breakfast.
1. formed Adv	2. *Not* one of us remembers a surf this high.
2. one Adj	3. Are you *quite* positive that you locked the door to the apartment?
3. positive Adv	4. With the next gust of wind the kite was *free* from the small boy's grasp.
4. kite Adj	5. The Scandinavian pottery may be purchased in *almost* all department stores.
5. all Adv	6. Uncle George *usually* depends on one of us to bring him an evening paper.
6. depends Adv	7. The new highway up the coast is *straight* but certainly not narrow.

7. highway Adj	8. Matt's horse *always* stood patiently in front of the saloon.
8. stood Adv	9. Do *not* decide upon a camper until you have consulted Perry.
9. Do decide Adv	10. Actually Mother feels very *well*, now that her hay fever is better.
10. Mother Adj	11. Hannah and Julius feel *good* about their plans to restore the old house in Ansley Park.
11. Hannah, Julius Adj	12. The gull glided *low* and then dived for the fish.
12. glided Adv	13. The bell rang *sharply*, announcing to student and teacher alike that Biology 106 was over for one more day.
13. rang Adv	14. Each morning at eight o'clock the factory whistle sounded *loud* and *clear.*
14. whistle Adj, Adj	15. Eleanor bought *several* bright scarves to perk up her drab winter clothes.

15. scarves Adj	16. When the sleet began, I became *somewhat* anxious about the children who had gone to the playground.
16. anxious Adv	17. No one can deny that Ike's gift for storytelling is *unique.*
17. gift Adj	18. *Only* a boy like you would want to spend an entire day in a tree house.
18. boy Adj	19. I have *only* seen my new neighbor; I have yet to meet her.
19. have seen Adv	20. Aunt Millicent *obviously* disapproved of not only my beard but also my patched jeans.
20. disapproved Adv	21. The morning sun felt *warm* on her shoulders, as it streamed through the window.
21. sun Adj	22. Evans felt *carefully* along the window ledge; the key was not there.
22. felt Adv	23. I am *really* tired after teaching three classes and then working two hours at the switchboard.

23. tired Adv	24. My *real* problem is time.
24. problem Adj	25. The quilt was *handsome*, a work of art in anyone's judgment.
25. quilt Adj	26. Helen is *sure* that the iris will bloom in time for the flower show.
26. Helen Adj	27. Felix *surely* plans to see St. Mark's while he is in Italy.
27. plans Adv	28. I have *never* ceased to be amazed at the cost of a hot dog at ball games.
28. have ceased Adv	29. The statue seemed *smaller* than I had remembered it.
29. statue Adj	30. The two of us won the sack race *handily*.
30. won Adv	**SCORE** ______

Exercise 51 ADJECTIVES AND ADVERBS

In the following sentences underline each adjective or adverb that is incorrectly used, and then write the correct form. Write **C** if the sentence is correct.

EXAMPLE: Carolyn looks well in sports clothes.

good

Answers	Sentences
	1. Mr. Singer stared thoughtful out the open window.
1. thoughtful thoughtfully	2. Which of these two histories of Russia is the clearest?
2. clearest clearer	3. All weekend the painters worked steady in the candy shop.
3. steady steadily	4. After looking careful at the children, Dr. Shelton decided they had mumps.
4. careful carefully	5. Bailey looked handsomely in his Navy uniform.
5. handsomely handsome	6. These late summer roses are the most perfect ones I have ever raised.
6. most perfect most nearly perfect	7. The team physician is certain that you will feel good enough to play ball Friday night.

7. good well	8. Paul is real anxious to read *Sports Illustrated* when you have finished it.
8. real very, really	9. Very sudden Bernard forgot the name of the guest speaker.
9. sudden suddenly	10. The stars grew dimly as the November dawn broke.
10. dimly dim	11. In order not to wake the baby, Kathleen tiptoed as cautious as possible across the room.
11. cautious cautiously	12. Appearing calmly, Maria waited to hear the outcome of her audition.
12. calmly calm	13. The young reporter had worked hard all week long.
13. C	14. Which of these three maps of Africa is the more up-to-date?
14. more most	15. The child stared intent at Miss Thistleby's hairdo.
15. intent intently	16. When visiting Egypt, Minerva was real apprehensive about the camel ride.

16. real very, really	17. Aunt Catherine sure was pleased with the fruitcake recipe you sent her.
17. sure surely	18. We feel very badly about your missing the first act.
18. badly bad	19. The information you gave me about the Indianapolis 500 is muchly appreciated.
19. muchly greatly	20. Sam's eye is some better since he applied the beef-steak.
20. some somewhat	21. This cough medicine does not go down easy.
21. easy easily	22. Despite the heavy snow, the morning train has been coming as regular as ever.
22. regular regularly	23. Helen's work in chemistry has been completely satisfactory.
23. C	24. She has not, however, done good in psychology.
24. good well	25. I'm afraid that I didn't divide the cake even.

25. even evenly	26. Even with the electric fan, the air felt heavily and close.
26. heavily heavy	27. As long as one of us is out, Mother can not sleep sound.
27. sound soundly	28. Will the Morgan Heights or the Lakewood bus take me downtown most quickly?
28. most more	29. I believe that the clock on the bank is fast.
29. C	30. We both ran fast to escape the torrent of snowballs.
30. C	31. Mr. Levinson has a most unique collection of coins.
31. (omit most) unique	32. My father either speaks kind about a person or says nothing.
32. kind kindly	33. Marvin sure does spend a great deal of time lifting weights.
33. sure surely	34. Because it tastes sharply, I like this brand of Cheddar cheese.

34. sharply sharp	35. Mrs. Freeman smiled broad as I bought a dozen of her cinnamon buns.
35. broad broadly	SCORE ______

Exercise 52	ADJECTIVES AND ADVERBS

For each of the following sentences write the correct form of the *italicized* words.

EXAMPLE: The candidate appears (*confident, confidently*) to me.

confident

	1. The cars moved (*cautious, cautiously*) through the shower of ticker tape.
1. cautiously	2. Occasionally the manager does speak (*curt, curtly*) to Dennis.
2. curtly	3. The host of the talk show usually appears (*warm, warmly*) and gracious to his guests.
3. warm	4. Since turning on the defroster, I can see (*easy, easily*) through the windshield.
4. easily	5. The children in the neighborhood watched (*close, closely*) as the fireman opened the hydrant.
5. closely	6. The wind blew the straw hat (*crazy, crazily*) up the alley.
6. crazily	7. The whole kitchen smells (*spicy, spicily*) when the wassail is simmering.

7. spicy	8. The ring of a telephone sounds especially (*sharp, sharply*) in the middle of the night.
8. sharp	9. Nancy's heart beat (*wild, wildly*) as she listened to the footsteps on the stairs.
9. wildly	10. By walking (*steady, steadily*), we were able to reach the coliseum in time for the concert.
10. steadily	11. During the heavy rain the water ran (*rapid, rapidly*) along the gutters.
11. rapidly	12. The rumor about Molly's engagement proved (*false, falsely*).
12. false	13. Mrs. Breeden speaks Spanish as (*fluent, fluently*) as she speaks English.
13. fluently	14. In spite of the noisy children, the bus driver remained (*patient, patiently*).
14. patient	15. I cannot decide which of these two cats is the (*more, most*) arrogant.

15. more	16. The clerk glared (*cross, crossly*) at the boys running up the escalator.
16. crossly	17. Dave seems (*handy, handily*) with any sort of tool.
17. handy	18. We must think (*positive, positively*) about Dad's decision to buy a wood-burning stove.
18. positively	19. The taxi sped (*straight, straightly*) to the airport.
19. straight	20. Oh, this casserole tastes (*divine, divinely*).
20. divine.	21. The moon appeared (*hazy, hazily*) through the heavy smog.
21. hazy	22. The detective searched (*diligent, diligently*) through the desk drawer.
22. diligently	23. Enjoying the breeze which blew in (*brisk, briskly*) from the lake, Brenda sat on the front steps until midnight.
23. briskly	24. The slight, blonde girl spoke (*serious, seriously*) of running for Congress.

24. seriously	25. Day after day the old woman sat (*quiet, quietly*) on the same bench in the park.
25. quietly	26. My Irish cousins have the (*most, most nearly*) perfect skin I have ever seen.
26. most nearly	27. The sun felt unusually (*warm, warmly*) as I stood on the corner waiting for Wilson.
27. warm	28. I do believe that Lewis is (*some, somewhat*) taller than his father.
28. somewhat	29. A sign reading "No Children Allowed" is posted (*open, openly*) at the apartment house across the street.
29. openly	30. Are you (*real, really*) sure you want to walk to the mall?
30. really	31. My grandmother would not allow us to speak (*rude, rudely*) to anyone.
31. rudely	32. The audience laughed (*hearty, heartily*) at the comedian's jokes.

32. heartily	33. Although Bess has lived in Seattle for several years, she still writes home (*regular, regularly*).
33. regularly	34. The city council is (*sure, surely*) pleased with the plans for the branch library.
34. surely	35. Doesn't Mrs. Winchester wear (*very unique, unique*) hats?
35. unique	SCORE ______

13
Tense, Voice, Mood

In Chapter 1 we found that a single verb may be classified according to **tense**, **voice**, and **mood**; therefore, it is not surprising that choosing the appropriate verb form occasionally presents difficulty.

13a Principal Parts of Verbs

We know that there are three **principal parts** of a verb. These are (1) **the first person singular, present indicative**; (2) **the first person singular, past indicative**; (3) **the past participle**. The first two of these provide the basic forms of the present, past, and future tenses; the third is used as the basis for the three perfect tenses:

PRINCIPAL PARTS: *begin, began, begun*		
Present:	I begin	
Past:	I began	
Future:	I shall (will) begin	(This form based on present tense *begin*)
Present Perfect:	I have begun	(These forms based on past participle *begun*)
Past Perfect:	I had begun	
Future Perfect:	I shall (will) have begun	

If you know the principal parts of a verb and the way to form the various tenses from them, you should never make a mistake such as the one contained in the following sentence: "The play had already began when I arrived." If the speaker had known that the principal parts of *begin* are *begin, began, begun* and that the past perfect tense is formed by using *had* with the past participle, he would have known that the correct form is *had begun.*

Regular verbs—that is, those verbs which form their past tense and past participle by adding *-d* or *-ed* to the present tense—rarely cause difficulty. It is the **irregular verbs** that are most frequently used incorrectly. When necessary, consult a dictionary for their principal parts. The following list contains the principal parts of certain especially troublesome verbs. Learn these forms:

Present	*Past*	*Past Participle*	*Present*	*Past*	*Past Participle*
ask	asked	asked	know	knew	known
bite	bit	bitten	lead	led	led
blow	blew	blown	ride	rode	ridden
break	broke	broken	ring	rang (rung)	rung
burst	burst	burst	run	ran	run
choose	chose	chosen	see	saw	seen
come	came	come	shake	shook	shaken
dive	dived (dove)	dived	sing	sang (sung)	sung
do	did	done	speak	spoke	spoken
drag	dragged	dragged	steal	stole	stolen
draw	drew	drawn	sting	stung	stung
drink	drank	drunk	suppose	supposed	supposed
drown	drowned	drowned	swim	swam	swum
eat	ate	eaten	swing	swung	swung
fall	fell	fallen	take	took	taken
fly	flew	flown	tear	tore	torn
freeze	froze	frozen	throw	threw	thrown
give	gave	given	use	used	used
go	went	gone	wear	wore	worn
grow	grew	grown	write	wrote	written

Note that the past tense and the past participle of the verbs *ask, suppose* and *use* are regularly formed by the addition of *-ed* (or *-d*) to the present tense. Possibly because the *d* is not always clearly sounded in the pronunciation of the past tense and the past participle of these verbs, people frequently make the mistake of writing the present-tense form when one of the other forms is required:

I have *asked* (not *ask*) him to go with me.

I was *supposed* (not *suppose*) to do that job.

He *used* (not *use*) to be my best friend.

13b Two Troublesome Pairs of Verbs

Lie and *lay* and *sit* and *set* are frequent stumbling blocks to correct writing. These verbs need not be confusing, however, if the following points are remembered:

1. Each verb has a distinguishing meaning. *Lay* and *set*, for instance, are clearly distinguished from *lie* and *sit* by their meanings: both *lay* and *set* usually mean *place* and are correctly used when the verb *place* can be substituted for them.

2. *Lay* and *set* are always transitive verbs; that is, they require an object to complete their meaning when they are used in the active voice. *Lie* and *sit* are intransitive verbs and hence do not take an object.
3. Although *lay* and *lie* share the form *lay*, they use it in different tenses. The remaining principal parts are clearly distinguishable.

These three points may be graphically shown:

PRINCIPAL PARTS	
Intransitive (takes no object)	*Transitive (takes an object)*
lie lay lain, *recline, remain in position*	lay laid laid, *place*
sit sat sat, *be in a sitting position*	set set set, *place*

Let us look at a few sentences which illustrate these distinguishing characteristics. Should we say *I set the box on the table* or *I sat the box on the table*? To answer the question, we should try substituting *placed* for *set* and should also see whether there is a direct object following the verb. We can say *I placed the box on the table*; also, *box* is clearly the direct object of the verb. Therefore, the first sentence, employing *set*, is the correct one. But in the sentence *I left the box sitting on the table*, the correct form is *sitting*, not *setting*, since *placing* cannot be substituted for *sitting* and since there is no direct object after *sitting*:

> I *laid* (that is, *placed*) the book by the bed and *lay* (past tense of *lie*) down to rest.

Do not fall into the error of thinking that only animate things can stand as subjects of intransitive verbs. Note the following sentences in which inanimate objects are used as subjects of the intransitive verbs:

> The book *lies* on the table.
>
> The house *sits* near the road.

13c Tense Sequence

Tense sequence demands that a logical time relationship be shown by the verbs in a sentence. Through force of habit we generally indicate accurate time relationships. A few cautions, however, should be stressed:

1. Use the present tense in the statement of a timeless universal truth or a customary happening:

   I wonder who first discovered that the sun *rises* (not *rose*) in the east. [The fact that the sun rises in the east is a universal truth.]

   Joe said that the class *begins* (not *began*) at 10:30. [The clause *that the class begins at 10:30* states a customary happening.]

2. Use the present tense of an infinitive or the present participle if the action it expresses occurs at the same time as that of the governing verb:

Yesterday I really wanted *to go*. [Not *to have gone*. The governing verb *wanted* indicates a past time. At that past time I wanted to do something *then* – that is, yesterday – not at a time prior to yesterday.]

Skipping along, she hummed a merry tune. The skipping and the humming occur at the same time.)

3. When necessary for clarity, indicate time differences by using different tenses:

INCORRECT: I told him that I *finished* the work just an hour before.

CORRECT: I told him that I *had finished* the work just an hour before. [The verb *told* indicates a past time. Since the work was finished before the time indicated by *told*, the past perfect tense *had finished* must be used.]

INCORRECT: *Making* my reservations, I am packing to go to Cape Cod.

CORRECT: *Having made* my reservations, I am packing to go to Cape Cod. [The perfect participle *having made* must be used to denote an action before the time indicated by the governing verb *am packing*.]

13d Voice

Transitive verbs always indicate whether the subject is acting or is being acted upon. When the subject is doing the acting, the verb is said to be in the **active voice**:

I *laid* the book on the table. [*Laid* is in the active voice because the subject *I* is doing the acting.]

When the subject is being acted upon or receiving the action, the verb is in the **passive voice**:

The book *was laid* on the table. [*Was laid* is in the passive voice because the subject *book* is being acted upon.]

NOTE: The passive voice verb always consists of some form of the verb *to be* plus a past participle: *is seen, was laid, have been taken.*

In general, the active voice is more emphatic than the passive and therefore should normally be used in preference to the passive voice:

WEAK: The automobile *was driven* into the garage.

MORE EMPHATIC: She *drove* the automobile into the garage.

When, however, the receiver of the action should be stressed rather than the doer, or when the doer is unknown, the passive voice is appropriate:

Class officers *will be elected* next Thursday. [The receiver of the action should be stressed.]

The dog *was found* last night. [The doer is unknown.]

Generally speaking, one should not shift from one voice to the other in the same sentence:

AWKWARD: John *is* the best athlete on the team, and the most points *are scored* by him.

BETTER: John *is* the best athlete on the team and also *scores* the most points.

AWKWARD: After Dr. Lovett *was conferred* with, I *understood* the assignment.

BETTER: After I *conferred* with Dr. Lovell (OR After *conferring* with Dr. Lovett), I *understood* the assignment.

13e The Subjunctive Mood

The **subjunctive mood** is most frequently used today to express a wish or to state a condition contrary to fact. In both types of statement the subjunctive *were* is used instead of the indicative *was*. Tenses in the subjunctive do not have the same meaning as they do in the indicative mood. For example, the past subjunctive form points toward the present or future, as seen in the sentence *If I WERE you, I would give his suggestion strong consideration.* The present subjunctive form usually points toward the future with a stronger suggestion of hopefulness than does the past subjunctive. (*I move that John Marshall BE named chairman of our committee.*) The present subjunctive form of the verb *to be* is invariably *be* for all persons, and the past subjunctive form of the verb *to be* is invariably *were.* In all other verbs the subjunctive form varies from the indicative only in that in the present tense the third person singular ending is lost, as in *I suggest that he TAKE the subway to his friend's house.* Note the following examples of verbs in the subjunctive mood:

I wish that I *were* (not *was*) going with you to Hawaii this summer.

If I *were* (not *was*) king, I couldn't be happier.

The subjunctive mood may also be used in the following instances:

If the report *be* true, we will have to modify our plans. [To express a doubt or uncertainty.]

She commanded that the rule *be* enforced. [To express a command.]

Even though he *disagree* with me, I will still admire him. [To express a concession.]

It is necessary that he *see* his parents at once. [To express a necessity.]

I move that the proposal *be* adopted. [To express a parliamentary motion.]

Exercise 53 TWO TROUBLESOME PAIRS OF VERBS

Choose the correct form from each pair of *italicized* verbs and write it in the space provided.

EXAMPLE: (*Lay, Lie*) your packages on the counter.

Lay

	1. Just beneath the surface of the water (*lies, lays*) a coral reef.
1. lies	2. The wind blew away the papers (*lying, laying*) on the steps.
2. lying	3. In the laundromat the young woman carefully folded the towels and (*lay, laid*) them in a basket.
3. laid	4. We always find our morning paper (*lying, laying*) at our door.
4. lying	5. All week a blanket of smoke has (*lain, laid*) over the canyon.
5. lain	6. In the bakery window (*lay, laid*) my heart's desire, a freshly baked pound cake.
6. lay	7. Our cat really prefers to (*lie, lay*) in Father's chair.

7. lie	8. Bring some water to the player (*lying, laying*) on the field!
8. lying	9. Mervin (*lay, laid*) the map on the table and began searching for Burbank.
9. laid	10. Only one subdivision (*lies, lays*) beyond Cedar Glen.
10. lies	11. Mother is in the habit of (*lying, laying*) her car keys on the piano.
11. laying	12. Have you already (*lain, laid*) the pattern on the material?
12. laid	13. The bridge (*lay, lain*) across a great stretch of swampland.
13. lay	14. The board of directors has authorized us to (*lie, lay*) several miles of new track.
14. lay	15. In the opening scene of the opera the heroine is (*lying, laying*) on a couch.

15. lying	16. Please (*sit, set*) the chair in front of the window.
16. set	17. An eagle (*sitting, setting*) on a bare branch was the subject of the prize-winning photograph.
17. sitting	18. In the warehouse (*sits, sets*) row after row of metal desks.
18. sits	19. Through the window we could see the violets which Mr. Parkman had (*sat, set*) on narrow glass shelves.
19. set	20. The clock (*sitting, setting*) on the mantel is almost correct.
20. sitting	21. The small boy (*sat, set*) stiffly in the barber's chair, waiting for Mr. Ludwig to begin.
21. sat	22. I should have (*sat, set*) the casserole in the oven fifteen minutes ago.
22. set	23. Roger, ask the guests to come in and (*sit, set*) down.

23. sit	24. By all means (*sit, set*) the picnic table in the shade of the sycamore tree.
24. set	25. I could have (*sat, set*) half the night listening to Uncle Dan's tales.
25. sat	26. After standing in line at the box office, we were delighted to (*sit, set*) down.
26. sit	27. Kate (*sat, set*) her mortarboard squarely on her head.
27. set	28. In the shadow of the skyscraper (*sat, set*) the old cotton exchange.
28. sat	29. The pilot (*sat, set*) the helicopter down on the roof of the office building.
29. set	30. Mr. Jacobs often (*sits, sets*) at the door of his hardware store.
30. sits	**SCORE** ______

Exercise 54 TWO TROUBLESOME PAIRS OF VERBS

Write the correct form of **lie, lay** or **sit, set** wherever an incorrect form is used. Write **C** if a sentence is correct.

EXAMPLE: Behind us laid a long stream of traffic.

lay

	1. I had lain the letter opener beside the morning mail.
1. laid	2. Laying crumpled on the subway platform was a dollar bill.
2. Lying	3. October arrived, and the usual blanket of leaves was laying over the campus.
3. lying	4. The grave of the famous poet lays in the heart of the city.
4. lies	5. First, lie all the pieces of the jigsaw puzzle on a table.
5. lay	6. The old tires continue to lay in a great heap on the vacant lot.
6. lie	7. Can you believe that the contractor has already lain the foundation for our new church?

7. laid	8. Hugo left the tattered paperback laying on the seat of the bus.
8. lying	9. The huge ocean liner had laid at anchor for several days.
9. lain	10. I was foolish to leave my bicycle lying in the driveway.
10. C	11. Lying my sunglasses on the edge of the dock was equally careless.
11. Laying	12. Winnie lain her golden chain in the jewelry box.
12. laid	13. The snow laid in huge drifts along the freeway.
13. lay	14. Jack always lies his briefcase on the back seat of his car.
14. lays	15. I can tell that the streets of this city were not lain out according to a plan.
15. laid	16. The nurse sat the pitcher of water on the bedside table.

16. set	17. Across from the park where we have lunch sets the tallest building in the city.
17. sits	18. We set on the edge of the pool while Horace completed his laps.
18. sat	19. The stack of newspapers had been set on the steps, waiting for the delivery boy to arrive.
19. C	20. Setting at the entrance to the museum was a pair of imposing lions.
20. Sitting	21. Sit the tomatoes in the window if you want them to ripen.
21. Set	22. The diesel locomotive was setting on a siding.
22. sitting	23. Johnson hurriedly sat the ball on the kicking tee.
23. set	24. Monday through Friday she sets in the information booth at the department store.
24. sits	25. Anticipating the parade, the children have been setting on the curb since early morning.

25. sitting	26. Aunt Sally spent the afternoon sitting out tulip bulbs.
26. setting	27. The hitchhiker sat his pack beside the highway.
27. set	28. Skillfully the pilot sat the plane down on the narrow runway.
28. set	29. Have you noticed that the house that sets on the corner of Second and Green Streets is empty?
29. sits	30. The transportation department has set stop signs at Bradford Crossing.
30. C	**SCORE** ______

Exercise 55 TENSE AND MOOD

A. Write the correct form of each *italicized* verb.

EXAMPLE: The bitter wind (*sting*) my face yesterday.

stung

	1. We (*fly*) to Boston and then on to Montreal last summer.
1. flew	2. How many pairs of basketball shoes has Lou (*wear*) out?
2. worn	3. *Masterpiece Theatre* is (*suppose*) to be on television tonight.
3. supposed	4. His roommate (*shake*) him and reminded him of his eight-o'clock class.
4. shook	5. By noon the tourists had already (*ride*) around the entire island.
5. ridden	6. Marilyn has already (*sing*) at two or three weddings this summer.
6. sung	7. Every morning last week the boys (*swim*) at the Y.M.C.A.

7. swam	8. Have you heard that Sara Sessions has been (*ask*) to work in summer stock?
8. asked	9. By the time I joined Marsha, she had (*drink*) her cup of tea and eaten her sandwich.
9. drunk	10. Nick declares that he has (*see*) a flying saucer.
10. seen	11. Have you (*come*) to a conclusion about your plans for the spring holidays?
11. come	12. Last Saturday Bert (*drag*) me along to still another football game.
12. dragged	13. For its cover the magazine has (*choose*) an illustration by Norman Rockwell.
13. chosen	14. Although Grandfather's apartment is uptown, he has recently (*lead*) a quiet life.
14. led	15. We (*use*) to enjoy window-shopping on summer nights.
15. used	

B. Write the past tense of each verb in the following sentences.

EXAMPLE: The stagehand *draws* the curtain at eight-thirty.

drew

	1. He *thinks* the moon especially beautiful as it *rises* over the dark hills.
1. thought rose	2. Aunt Jane *goes* to the mall every Wednesday where she *eats* lunch with friends.
2. went ate	3. The fly *buzzes* around my head and *keeps* me from concentrating on my accounting problem.
3. buzzed kept	4. Naturally, when the temperature *falls* below zero degrees Celsius, the water in the birdbath *freezes.*
4. fell froze	5. When my mother *buys* tangerines at the super-market, I *know* the holidays *are* not far off.
5. bought knew were	

C. Write the correct form of each *italicized* verb.

EXAMPLE: It is necessary that the salesman (*mail, mails*) his report at once.
mail

Answers	Exercises
	1. (*Having walked, Walking*) five or six blocks, Pam finally reached the White House.
1. Having walked	2. When I was a small boy, I hoped (*to join, to have joined*) a circus.
2. to join	3. The reporter stated that the Shannon River (*is, was*) over two hundred miles long.
3. is	4. After much discussion the commissioner moved that the meeting (*was, be*) adjourned.
4. be	5. If I (*was, were*) your cat Sheba, I would consider life to be perfect.
5. were	**SCORE** ______

Exercise 56 TENSE AND MOOD

Underline each verb that is incorrectly used; then write the correct form. Write **C** if a sentence is correct.

EXAMPLE: The temperature has fell in the last two hours.

fallen

	1. Miss Sheffield lead the first graders up the steps and into the museum.
1. lead led	2. Aunt Harriet's ceiling fan once hanged in Norman's Pharmacy.
2. hanged hung	3. The brochure stated that the ferry left daily for Prince Edward Island.
3. left leaves	4. Margie has ran to catch many a bus.
4. ran run	5. Playing kickball last night, Shirley had difficulty getting up this morning.
5. Playing Having played	6. The coach has gave Baker one last chance to lose weight.
6. gave given or has	7. I rode by the drive-in but saw none of my friends.

7. C	8. Your reminder that examinations begin next week has shooken my confidence.
8. shooken shaken	9. As soon as the referee blown the whistle, the crowd stood to watch the kick-off.
9. blown had blown	10. If that was my locker, I would consider its condition alarming.
10. was were	11. The marshal drawed his gun and shot the wretched villain.
11. drawed drew	12. Where have the Pratts chose to go on their vacation?
12. chose chosen	13. Dizzy Dean should have said that the player slid, not "slud," into home.
13. C	14. Our English teacher has fell time and again for Nora's excuses.
14. fell fallen or has	15. Why do you suppose no one has came up with a cure for the common cold?

15. came come	16. Mortimer is suppose to put away the screen and projector.
16. suppose supposed	17. The master of ceremonies drew three tickets from the bowl before he called the winning number.
17. drew had drawn	18. Are you sure that John Paul Jones said, "I have not yet began to fight"?
18. began begun	19. I must have showed you a dozen times how to put gas in the car.
19. showed shown	20. This very minute I wish that I was at the beach watching the sun go down.
20. was were	21. When the comedian imitated the politician, the audience busted out laughing.
21. busted burst	22. Sheila has already broke the eggs for the omelet.
22. broke broken	23. The quarterback overthrowed his receiver down field.

Answer	Sentence
23. overthrowed overthrew	24. Clara is accustom to leaving for work at seven-thirty.
24. accustom accustomed	25. Have you already went to see the movie *Superman*?
25. went gone	26. I held my breath as the small girl dived from the high board.
26. C (or dove)	27. Grandmother always use to serve cranberry relish at Thanksgiving.
27. use used	28. It is necessary that all of us are on the bus by eight o'clock.
28. are be	29. My brothers and I have often swam at the Boys Club.
29. swam swum	30. The cook done the best she could with what she had.
30. done did; or *has done*	31. We ask to see the baby, but her father said that she was asleep.

31. ask asked	32. I'm afraid that I have tore my jacket getting out of the car.
32. tore torn	33. If I was you, I would give Aunt Lillian the box of toffee.
33. was were	34. Introducing the speaker, Dean Kibler returned to his chair on the platform.
34. Introducing Having introduced	35. Albert flown for the first time when he went to Hawaii.
35. flown flew	36. When Josh was a young man, he wanted to have been a violinist.
36. have been be	37. My cousin has chose not to go to school this quarter.
37. chose chosen or has	38. If that puppy has bit me once, he has bit me a dozen times.
38. bit, bit bitten, bitten	39. One can find poetry wrote by Robert Frost in numerous anthologies.

39. wrote written	40. My father is accustom to reading the Sunday *Times.*
40. accustom accustomed	41. If the truth is known, Aunt Mae has enjoyed too much of her own cooking.
41. is be	42. The pine trees growed at a surprising rate.
42. growed grew	43. Celia has certainly never rode a motorcycle.
43. rode ridden	44. Listening to her new tapes, Eloise painted the desk as well as a bookcase.
44. C	45. Because his hands and feet were all but freezing, Mr. Bolton wished the game was over.
45. was were	46. I am afraid that Edison has wore out his favorite jeans.
46. wore worn	47. Both of us wish that we had took a course in music appreciation.
47. took taken	48. Tony moved that the committee's report was accepted.

48. was be	49. How long has the portrait of Dr. Wilkes hung in the conference room?
49. C	50. It was four o'clock Christmas morning when the children stolen down the steps to see their gifts.
50. stolen stole	**SCORE** ______

Exercise 57 VOICE

Revise the following sentences, changing all verbs which are in the passive voice to the active voice.

EXAMPLE: Every morning the mail was delivered by Mr. Benchley.

Every morning Mr. Benchley delivered the mail.

	1. The Egyptian pyramids were built by slave labor and were designed to be tombs for members of the royal family.
1. Slave labor built the Egyptian pyramids as tombs for members of the royal family.	2. The game was played by the Boston Red Sox and the New York Yankees before thousands of fans, whose tickets had been bought weeks in advance.
2. The Boston Red Sox and the New York Yankees played the game before thousands of fans, who had bought tickets weeks in advance.	3. The class schedule for next year has been approved by Dean Reynolds, and it will be made available to students on Monday.
3. Dean Reynolds has approved next year's class schedule and will make it available to students on Monday.	4. Last December *The Nutcracker*, which was composed by Tchaikovsky, was presented by our local ballet company.

4. Last December our local ballet company presented Tchaikovsky's *The Nutcracker.*

5. In the *Atlantic Monthly* was published an article which had been written by Theodore H. White about his early life in Dorchester.

5. Theodore H. White's account of his early life in Dorchester appeared in the *Atlantic Monthly.*

6. By afternoon the snow, which was waded through by all of us on our way to class, had been melted by the sun.

6. By afternoon the sun had melted the snow, which all of us had waded through on our way to class.

7. Although the picnic had been planned by Aunt Isabel, tasks were assigned by her to all the other members of the family.

7. Although Aunt Isabel had planned the picnic, she assigned tasks to all the other members of the family.

8. The top two stories of the old brownstone were used as a parsonage by the minister and his wife, but the first floor was reserved for the church offices.

8. The minister and his wife used the top two stories of the old brownstone as a parsonage, but the church offices occupied the first floor.

9. Every morning, after my father had been driven to the station by my mother, the train was boarded by him for the ride into the city.

9. Every morning, after my mother had driven my father to the station, he boarded the train for the ride into the city.

10. After my hair had been cut by my favorite barber, it was blown dry.

10. After my favorite barber cut my hair, he blew it dry.

11. On the wall of the building was a mural which had been painted by two art students; it was enjoyed by the whole community.

11. The whole community enjoyed the mural which two art students had painted on the wall of the building.

12. Although the telephone was answered by each of us living on the hall, more often than not Felicia was asked for by the caller.

12. Although each of us living on the hall answered the telephone, more often than not the call was for Felicia.

13. As children we were taken by my father to the corner bakery, where apple turnovers could be bought for a few cents apiece.

13. My father took us as children to the corner bakery, where we could buy apple turnovers for a few cents apiece.

14. The boat, which had recently been purchased by Dan, was taken by him in early September down the Inland Waterway.

14. In early September Dan took his new boat down the Inland Waterway.	15. A trip to Mecca, which had been made by a Muslim family, was described in the *National Geographic.*
15. An account of a Muslim family's trip to Mecca appeared in the *National Geographic.*	SCORE ______

14
Dangling Modifiers

A **modifier** must always have a word to modify. This fact seems almost too obvious to warrant discussion. And yet we frequently see sentences similar in construction to this one: "Hearing a number of entertaining stories, our visit was thoroughly enjoyable." *Hearing a number of entertaining stories* is a modifying phrase. But where in the sentence is there a word for it to modify? Certainly the phrase cannot logically modify *visit*: it was not our visit that heard a number of entertaining stories. Who did hear the stories? *We* did. Since, however, the word *we* does not appear in the sentence for the phrase to modify, the phrase is said to "dangle." Any modifier dangles, or hangs unattached, when there is no obvious word to which it is clearly and logically related. (Note the similarity of this problem of modifiers and the problem of pronouns and their antecedents.)

14a Recognizing Dangling Modifiers

It is important that you recognize dangling modifiers when you see them. Such modifiers usually appear as two types of constructions–as *verbal phrases* and as *elliptical clauses.* (An elliptical clause, as applicable to this lesson, is a dependent clause in which the subject and/or verb are omitted.)

> *Hearing a number of entertaining stories,* our visit was thoroughly enjoyable. [Dangling participial phrase.]
>
> *On entering the room,* refreshments were being served. [Dangling gerund phrase.]
>
> *To play tennis well,* the racket must be held properly. [Dangling infinitive phrase.]
>
> *When only three years old,* my father took me to a circus. [Dangling elliptical clause.]

In each of the examples given above, the dangling modifier stands at the beginning of the sentence. If the modifier were *not* dangling–that is, if it were correctly used–it would be related to the subject of the sentence. In none of these sentences, however, can the introductory modifier logically refer to the subject. If the error is not immediately apparent, try placing the modifier just after the subject. The dangling nature of the modifier becomes easily recognizable because of the illogical meaning which results when you say, "Our visit, *hearing a number of entertaining stories, . .* " or "Refreshments, *on entering the room, . . .*"

Dangling modifiers frequently appear at the end as well as at the beginning of sentences. The participial phrase dangles in the sentence "The dog had only one eye, *caused by an accident.*"

At this point an exception to the rules governing the recognition of dangling modifiers should be noted: some introductory verbal phrases are general or summarizing expressions and therefore need not refer to the subject which follows:

CORRECT: *Generally speaking,* the boys' themes were more interesting than the girls'.

CORRECT: *To sum up,* our vacation was a disaster from start to finish.

14b Correcting Dangling Modifiers

Sentences containing dangling modifiers are usually corrected in one of two ways. One way is to leave the modifier as it is and to recast the remainder of the sentence so that the word to which the modifier should refer becomes the subject of the sentence. Remember that when modifiers such as those discussed in this lesson stand at the beginning of the sentence, they must always clearly and logically modify or be related to the subject of the sentence:

Hearing a number of entertaining stories, *we* thoroughly enjoyed our visit.

On entering the room, *I* found that refreshments were being served.

To play tennis well, *one* must hold the racket properly.

When only three years old, *I* was taken to a circus by my father.

You may test the correctness of these sentences, as you tested the incorrectness of the others, by placing the modifier just after the subject. Then see whether the sentence reads logically; if it does, the modifier has been correctly used. The following sentence, though awkward, is clear and logical: "We, hearing a number of entertaining stories, thoroughly enjoyed our visit."

The other way to correct sentences containing dangling modifiers is to expand the modifiers into dependent clauses:

Since we heard a number of entertaining stories, our visit was thoroughly enjoyable.

When I entered the room, refreshments were being served.

If one wishes to play tennis well, he must hold the racket properly.

When I was only three years old, my father took me to a circus.

Exercise 58 DANGLING MODIFIERS

Rewrite in correct form all sentences which contain dangling modifiers. Write **C** if a sentence is correct.

EXAMPLE: To rake all these leaves, a sturdy rake is needed.

To rake all these leaves, one must have a sturdy rake.

(Only one correct version of each sentence is given in the answer section.)

	1. Having watched television all afternoon, her head ached dreadfully.
1. Having watched television all afternoon, she had a dreadful headache.	2. When growing up, my parents often took my sisters and me on outings in the park.
2. When my sisters and I were growing up, my parents often took us on outings in the park.	3. After talking with the counselor, Mona's problems seemed smaller.
3. After Mona had talked with the counselor, her problems seemed smaller.	4. To build a log cabin these days, a book of instructions is needed.
4. To build a log cabin these days, one needs a book of instructions.	5. Having been out of town all summer, there was much news I had missed.

5. Having been out of town all summer, I had missed much news.

6. Sitting on the wooden stool, it was easy for Mrs. Mills to plant the pansies.

---

6. Sitting on the wooden stool, Mrs. Mills easily planted the pansies.

7. Generally speaking, she prefers biography to fiction.

---

7. C

8. The afternoon seemed unusually hot walking home from the grocery store.

---

8. The afternoon seemed unusually hot when I was walking home from the grocery store.

9. Having brought the tree into the house, the next task was finding the ornaments.

---

9. Once Phil had brought the tree into the house, the next task was finding the ornaments.

10. After locking the door, the lights were turned out.

---

10. After locking the door, Emma turned out the lights.

11. While riding the bus to town, it began to rain.

---

11. While Phyllis was riding the bus to town, it began to rain.

12. To find one's way through the hospital corridors, the directional signs must be read.

12. To find one's way through the hospital corridors, one must read the directional signs.	13. The stage seemed far away when sitting in the second balcony.
13. The stage seemed far away when we were sitting in the second balcony.	14. Having completed the corner cupboard, the cabinet shop was closed for the day.
14. Having completed the corner cupboard, the cabinetmaker closed the shop for the day.	15. To think clearly, at least eight hours of sleep were needed by Gilbert.
15. To think clearly, Gilbert needed at least eight hours of sleep.	16. Swinging on the trapeze high up in the circus tent, Violet's eyes caught sight of her fiancé.
16. Swinging on the trapeze high up in the circus tent, Violet caught sight of her fiancé.	17. Having thanked his hostess for a delicious dinner, a taxi was waiting for Winston at the curb.
17. Having thanked his hostess for a delicious dinner, Winston found a taxi waiting at the curb.	18. While speeding along the freeway, the rain forced the motorcyclist to stop under a bridge.

18. While the motorcyclist was speeding along the freeway, the rain forced him to stop under a bridge.	19. After arranging to videotape the soap opera, attending the garden club did not seem a burden.
19. After Agatha had arranged to videotape the soap opera, attending the garden club did not seem a burden.	20. Flapping in the breeze, I could scarcely read the motto on the state flag.
20. I could scarcely read the motto on the state flag, which was flapping in the breeze.	SCORE ______

Exercise 59 DANGLING MODIFIERS

Using the following phrases and elliptical clauses as introductory modifiers, write complete sentences.

EXAMPLE: When studying for an examination,

When studying for an examination, *I make a pot of coffee.*

(Note that only one illustrative version of each sentence is given.)

	1. Having hung our coats in the closet,
1. Having hung our coats in the closet, we joined Grandfather's other guests in the living room.	2. To spend the night in the wilderness camp,
2. To spend the night in the wilderness camp, one must carry his own equipment.	3. Although always interested in soccer,
3. Although always interested in soccer, I never find time to play.	4. Once completed,
4. Once completed, the manuscript was mailed to the publisher.	5. Standing in the mud puddle,
5. Standing in the mud puddle, the child enjoyed his squishy shoes.	6. While in the midst of writing a letter home,

6. While in the midst of writing a letter home, I received a call from my parents.	7. Having missed the five-thirty train,
7. Having missed the five-thirty train, I joined the crowd in the waiting room.	8. Flying low over the lake,
8. Flying low over the lake, we could see the swimmers from the summer camp.	9. To find an exciting book to read,
9. To find an exciting book to read, Janet usually consults the librarian.	10. When working at a department store during the holidays,
10. When working at a department store during the holidays, I need a great deal of patience.	11. Having once again powdered her nose,
11. Having once again powdered her nose, Miriam was ready for the interview.	12. To play bridge well,
12. To play bridge well, one must be able to concentrate and must have a good memory.	13. Making a final appearance as a three-year-old,
13. Making a final appearance as a three-year-old, the Derby winner ran at Aqueduct.	14. Once fumbled,

14. Once fumbled, the ball could not be recovered.	15. To sum up,
15. To sum up, it is clear that Columbus was not the first European to come to the Americas.	16. After dialing Betsy's number a dozen times,
16. After dialing Betsy's number a dozen times, Andy called Louise.	17. Disturbed by the great claps of thunder,
17. Disturbed by the great claps of thunder, the collie crawled under the steps.	18. Having seen the film for the second time,
18. Having seen the film for the second time, Chris appreciated the complicated plot.	19. To find the most direct route to Independence,
19. To find the most direct route to Independence, we consulted the map of Missouri.	20. Not taking time to open my umbrella,
20. Not taking time to open my umbrella, I made a dash for the car.	21. Never having appeared on television,
21. Never having appeared on television, the trumpet player was extremely nervous.	22. After getting on the elevator,

22. After getting on the elevator, I remembered that the key to my room was at the hotel desk.	23. Having made his eighth goal of the season,
23. Having made his eighth goal of the season, the hockey player was jubilant.	24. After switching on the hall light,
24. After switching on the hall light, I saw the small mouse scurry across the floor.	25. Instead of ordering tickets to the musical,
25. Instead of ordering tickets to the musical, Mrs. Fowler decided to buy them at the box office.	SCORE ______

15
Misplaced Modifiers

Modifiers must always be so placed that there will be no uncertainty about the words they modify. A modifier should, in general, stand as close as possible to the word that it modifies. This does not mean, however, that in every sentence there is only one correct position for a modifier. The following sentence, in which the adverb *today* is shifted from one position to another, is equally clear in any one of these three versions:

Today she arrived in Chicago.

She arrived *today* in Chicago.

She arrived in Chicago *today*.

The position of the modifier *today* can be shifted because, no matter where it is placed, it clearly modifies the verb *arrived*.

15a Misplaced Phrases and Clauses

When, however, a modifier can attach itself to two different words in the sentence, the writer must be careful to place it in a position which will indicate the meaning intended:

They argued the subject while I tried to study *at fever pitch*.

This sentence is illogical as long as the phrase *at fever pitch* seems to modify *to study*. The phrase must be placed where it will unmistakably modify *argued*:

CORRECT: They argued the subject *at fever pitch* while I tried to study.

ALSO CORRECT: *At fever pitch* they argued the subject while I tried to study.

A relative clause—that is, a clause introduced by a relative pronoun—should normally follow the word which it modifies:

ILLOGICAL: A piece was played at the dance *which was composed of dissonant chords.*

CORRECT: A piece *which was composed of dissonant chords* was played at the dance.

15b Ambiguous Modifiers

When a modifier is placed between two elements so that it may be taken to modify either element, it is **ambiguous.** These ambiguous modifiers are sometimes called **squinting modifiers**:

The girl who had been dancing *gracefully* entered the room.

Does the speaker mean that the girl had been dancing gracefully or that she entered the room gracefully? Either of these meanings may be expressed with clarity if the adverb *gracefully* is properly placed:

The girl who had been *gracefully* dancing entered the room. [*Gracefully* modifies *had been dancing.*]

The girl who had been dancing entered the room *gracefully.* [Here *gracefully* modifies *entered.*]

15c Misplaced Words Like *Only, Nearly,* and *Almost*

Words such as *only, nearly,* and *almost* are frequently misplaced. Normally these modifying words should immediately precede the word they modify. To understand the importance of properly placing these modifiers, consider in the following sentences the different meanings which result when *only* is shifted:

Only I heard John shouting at the boys. [*Only* modifies *I.* Meaning: I was the only one who heard John shouting.]

I *only* heard John shouting at the boys. [*Only* modifies *heard.* Implied meaning: I heard but didn't see John shouting.]

I heard *only* John shouting at the boys. [*Only* modifies *John.* Meaning: John was the only one whom I heard shouting.]

I heard John *only* shouting at the boys. [*Only* modified *shouting.* Possible implied meaning: I didn't hear John hitting the boys–I heard him only shouting at them.]

I heard John shouting at the boys *only.* [*Only* modifies *boys.* Possible implied meaning: The boys were the ones I heard John shouting at–not the girls.]

Misplacing *only, nearly,* or *almost* will frequently result in an illogical statement:

ILLOGICAL: The baby *only* cried until he was six months old.

CORRECT: The baby cried *only* until he was six months old.

ILLOGICAL: Since his earnings amounted to $97.15, he *nearly* made a hundred dollars.

CORRECT: Since his earnings amounted to $97.15, he made *nearly* a hundred dollars.

ILLOGICAL: At the recent track meet Ralph *almost* jumped six feet.

CORRECT: At the recent track meet Ralph jumped *almost* six feet.

15d Split Infinitives

A **split infinitive** is a construction in which the sign of the infinitive *to* has been separated from the verb with which it is associated. *To vigorously deny* and *to instantly be killed* are split infinitives. Unless emphasis or clarity demands its use, such a construction should be avoided:

AWKWARD: He always tries *to efficiently and promptly do* his work.

CORRECT: He always tries *to do* his work *efficiently and promptly.*

CORRECT: We expect *to more than double* our sales in April. [Placing the modifiers *more than* anywhere else in this sentence would result in ambiguity or changed meaning.]

Exercise 60	MISPLACED MODIFIERS

Rewrite all sentences containing misplaced modifers. If a misplaced modifier can be placed in more than one position, indicate each correct position with a separate sentence. Write **C** if a sentence is correct.

EXAMPLE: Bernard has almost painted the entire hallway.

Bernard has painted almost the entire hallway.

	1. Recently I read about a unique wedding that took place in the newspaper.
1. Recently I read in the newspaper about a unique wedding. In the newspaper I recently read about a unique wedding.	2. I read the billboard quickly passing on the train.
2. Passing quickly on the train, I read the billboard. Passing on the train, I quickly read the billboard.	3. Because Gloria is dieting, she has hardly eaten a bite of cheesecake.
3. Because Gloria is dieting, she has eaten hardly a bite of cheesecake.	4. The studio produced a film about the Middle Ages in 1977.
4. In 1977 the studio produced a film about the Middle Ages. The studio in 1977 produced a film about the Middle Ages.	5. The gray pigeon stared at the gray accountant sitting on the ledge.

5. Sitting on the ledge, the gray pigeon stared at the gray accountant.
The gray pigeon sitting on the ledge stared at the gray accountant.

6. Little Red Riding Hood went to visit her grandmother wearing a cape.

---

6. Wearing a cape, Little Red Riding Hood went to visit her grandmother.
Little Red Riding Hood, wearing a cape, went to visit her grandmother.

7. The judge presided at the trial of the embezzler who had recently been appointed by the governor.

---

7. The judge who had recently been appointed by the governor presided at the trial of the embezzler.

8. Margaret often spent the afternoon with her three-year-old reading Mother Goose rhymes.

---

8. Margaret often spent the afternoon reading Mother Goose rhymes with her three-year-old.

9. Claudia's fingers were covered with rings which were short and plump.

---

9. Claudia's fingers, which were short and plump, were covered with rings.
Claudia's short, plump fingers were covered with rings.

10. The garage repaired my car which has recently opened on Barton Way.

---

10. The garage which has recently opened on Barton Way repaired my car.

11. The door which swung open at once revealed a room decorated in bright greens and yellows.

11. The door which at once swung open revealed a room decorated in bright greens and yellows.
The door which swung open revealed at once a room decorated in bright greens and yellows.

12. Myra's pearls reached her waist, which she had inherited in June.

---

12. Myra's pearls, which she had inherited in June, reached her waist.

13. The fudge which I was cooking slowly thickened.

---

13. The fudge which I was slowly cooking thickened.
The fudge which I was cooking thickened slowly.

14. Will you put the butter in the refrigerator sitting on the counter?

---

14. Will you put the butter sitting on the counter in the refrigerator?

15. Uncle Seth has nearly lost all his hair.

---

15. Uncle Seth has lost nearly all his hair.

16. We ate at the Chinese restaurant on the north side of town which had recently been opened.

---

16. We ate at the Chinese restaurant which had recently been opened on the north side of town.

17. Alicia is wearing a flower in her hair made of pink silk.

17. In her hair Alicia is wearing a flower made of pink silk. Alicia is wearing a pink silk flower in her hair.	18. If you intend to securely hang the wreath, you will need some strong cord.
18. If you intend to hang the wreath securely, you will need some strong cord.	19. Barry almost ate all the doughnuts you left in the pantry.
19. Barry ate almost all the doughnuts you left in the pantry.	20. The fans greeted the team in spite of its defeat with enthusiasm.
20. The fans greeted the team with enthusiasm in spite of its defeat. In spite of its defeat the fans greeted the team with enthusiasm.	SCORE ______

Exercise 61 MISPLACED MODIFIERS

Rewrite all sentences containing misplaced modifiers. If a misplaced modifier can be placed in more than one position, indicate each correct position with a separate sentence. Write **C** if a sentence is correct.

EXAMPLE: I nearly have all his albums.

I have nearly all his albums.

Answers	Exercises
	1. The cherry trees were covered with ice in the back yard.
1. In the back yard the cherry trees were covered with ice. The cherry trees in the back yard were covered with ice.	2. My roommate wrote a research paper about Cook's voyage around the world during his freshman year.
2. During his freshman year my roommate wrote a research paper about Cook's voyage around the world.	3. As far as oil is concerned, the United States cannot even supply its own needs.
3. As far as oil is concerned, the United States cannot supply even its own needs.	4. The stalled car was pulled to the side of the street which was tying up traffic.

4. The stalled car which was tying up traffic was pulled to the side of the street.	5. The congressman explained his position on tax revision to the voters appearing on television.
5. Appearing on television, the congressman explained his position on tax revision to the voters. The congressman, appearing on television, explained his position on tax revision to the voters.	6. His dream is to eventually see Greece.
6. His dream is to see Greece eventually.	7. We put the air conditioner in the bedroom window which we had bought at the warehouse sale.
7. We put the air conditioner which we had bought at the warehouse sale in the bedroom window.	8. The two combs secured her black curls which Hugh had given her.
8. The two combs which Hugh had given her secured her black curls.	9. On our trip to Phoenix my father almost drove the whole way.
9. On our trip to Phoenix my father drove almost the whole way.	10. Professor Gildersleeve wrote a book about corruption in high places with a young assistant.

10. With a young assistant, Professor Gildersleeve wrote a book about corruption in high places.
Professor Gildersleeve with a young assistant wrote a book about corruption in high places.

11. The actor playing the lead now lives in our apartment complex.

---

11. The actor now playing the lead lives in our apartment complex.
The actor playing the lead lives now in our apartment complex.

12. This winter I have had hardly a chance to go skiing.

---

12. C

13. Mother only wants two or three onions from the grocery store.

---

13. Mother wants only two or three onions from the grocery store.

14. The young saleswoman helped me find the book about Joe Namath with horn-rimmed glasses.

---

14. The young saleswoman with horn-rimmed glasses helped me find the book about Joe Namath.

15. The ball was a gift to the coach autographed by the whole team.

---

15. The ball, autographed by the whole team, was a gift to the coach.
Autographed by the whole team, the ball was a gift to the coach.

16. The patrol car barely missed the detour sign speeding down the narrow road.

16. Speeding down the narrow road, the patrol car barely missed the detour sign. The patrol car, speeding down the narrow road, barely missed the detour sign.	17. Behind the counter the young girl demonstrated skillfully tying scarves.
17. Behind the counter the young girl skillfully demonstrated tying scarves. Behind the counter the young girl demonstrated tying scarves skillfully.	18. The rays of the flashlight revealed a small black kitten piercing the darkness.
18. Piercing the darkness, the rays of the flashlight revealed a small black kitten. The rays of the flashlight, piercing the darkness, revealed a small black kitten.	19. My father seldom hesitated to immediately respond to a request for help.
19. My father seldom hesitated to respond immediately to a request for help.	20. The dancer who tripped had suddenly regained her composure.
20. The dancer who had suddenly tripped regained her composure. The dancer who had tripped regained her composure suddenly. Suddenly the dancer who had tripped regained her composure.	SCORE _______

16
Parallelism

Frequently in our writing and speaking we need to indicate equality of ideas. To show this equality, we should employ **parallel** grammatical constructions. In other words, we should convey parallel thought in parallel language; and conversely, we should use parallel language only when we are conveying parallel thoughts.

16a Coordinate Elements

In employing parallelism, we should balance nouns against nouns, infinitives against infinitives, prepositional phrases against prepositional phrases, adjective clauses against adjective clauses, etc. We should never make the mistake of saying, "I have always liked *swimming* and *to fish*." Since the object of *have liked* is two parallel ideas, we should say:

> I have always liked *swimming* and *fishing*. (*And* joins two gerunds.)
>
> OR
>
> I have always liked *to swim* and *to fish*. (*And* joins two infinitives.)

Parallel prepositional phrases are illustrated in the following sentence. The parallel elements appear immediately after the double bar:

> Government ‖ of the people,
> ‖ by the people,
> and ‖ for the people shall not perish from the earth.

Next we see an illustration of parallel noun clauses:

> He said ‖ that he would remain in the East,
> ‖ that his wife would travel through the Northwest,
> and ‖ that his son would attend summer school in the South.

The following sentence contains parallel independent clauses:

> I came;
> I saw;
> I conquered.

Parallel elements are usually joined either by simple coordinating conjunctions or by correlative conjunctions. The most common coordinating conjunctions used with parallel constructions are *and, but, or.* Whenever one of these connectives is used, you must be careful to see that the elements which are being joined are coordinate or parallel in construction:

FAULTY: Ann is a girl with executive ability and who therefore should be elected class president.

This sentence contains faulty parallelism, since *and* is used to join a phrase (*with executive ability*) and a dependent clause (*who therefore should be elected class president*). To correct the sentence, (1) expand the phrase into a *who* clause, or (2) make an independent clause of the *who* clause:

CORRECT: Ann is a girl || who has executive ability
and || who therefore should be elected class president.

NOTE: A safe rule to follow is this: *And who* or *and which* should never be used unless preceded by another *who-* or *which-*clause.

ALSO CORRECT: || Ann is a girl with executive ability;
|| she therefore should be elected class president.

A common error results from making a construction appear to be parallel when actually it is not:

Mr. Lee is honest, intelligent, and works hard.

The structure of the sentence suggests an *a, b,* and *c* series; yet what we have is not three parallel elements but two adjectives (*honest, intelligent*) and a verb (*works*). The sentence can be corrected in two ways: we can use three adjectives in a series or two independent clauses in parallel construction, thus:

CORRECT: Mr. Lee is || honest,
|| intelligent,
and || industrious.

ALSO CORRECT: || Mr. Lee is honest and intelligent,
and || he works hard.

16b Use of Correlative Conjunctions

Correlative conjunctions are used in pairs: *either . . . or . . . ; neither . . . nor . . . ; both . . . and . . . ; not only . . . but also . . . .* When these conjunctions are employed in a sentence, they must be followed by parallel constructions:

INCORRECT: I hope *either* to spend my vacation in Mexico *or* Cuba. [In this sentence *either* is followed by an infinitive, *or* by a noun.]

CORRECT: I hope to spend my vacation either ‖ in Mexico
or ‖ in Cuba.

ALSO CORRECT: I hope to spend my vacation in either ‖ Mexico
or ‖ Cuba.

INCORRECT: She knew *not only* what to say, *but also* she knew when to say it.

CORRECT: She knew not only ‖ what to say
but also ‖ when to say it.

16c Repetition of Certain Words

In order to make parallel constructions clear, you must sometimes repeat an article, a preposition, an auxiliary verb, the sign of the infinitive (*to*), or the introductory word of a dependent clause. Three of these types of necessary repetition are illustrated in the sentences which follow:

OBSCURE: He must counsel all employees who participate in sports and also go on recruiting trips throughout the Southwest.

CLEAR: He must counsel all employees who participate in sports and *must* also go on recruiting trips throughout the Southwest.

OBSCURE: The instructor wants to meet those students who enjoy barber-shop harmony and organize several quartets.

CLEAR: The instructor wants to meet those students who enjoy barber-shop harmony and *to* organize several quartets.

OBSCURE: He thought that economic conditions were improving and the company was planning to increase its dividend rate.

CLEAR: He thought that economic conditions were improving and *that* the company was planning to increase its dividend rate.

16d *Than* and *As* in Parallel Constructions

Than and *as* are frequently used to join parallel constructions. When these two connectives introduce comparisons, you must be sure that the things compared are similar. Don't compare, for instance, a janitor's salary with a teacher. Compare a janitor's salary with a teacher's salary:

INCORRECT: A janitor's salary is frequently larger than a teacher.

CORRECT: ‖ A janitor's salary is frequently larger
than ‖ a teacher's (salary).

16e Incorrect Omission of Necessary Words

A very common kind of faulty parallelism is seen in the following sentence:

I always have and always will *remember* to send my first-grade teacher a Christmas card.

In this sentence *remember* is correctly used after *will*, but after *have* the form needed is *remembered.* Consequently, *remember* cannot serve as the understood participle after *have*:

CORRECT: I ‖ always have *remembered*
and ‖ always will remember to send my first-grade teacher a Christmas card.

Other sentences containing similar errors are given below:

INCORRECT: I *was* mildly surprised, but all of my friends gravely shocked. [After *all of my friends* the incorrect verb form *was* seems to be understood.]

CORRECT: I was mildly surprised, but all of my friends *were* gravely shocked.

INCORRECT: He gave me an apple and pear. [Before *pear* the incorrect form *an* seems to be understood.]

CORRECT: He gave me an apple and *a* pear.

INCORRECT: I was interested and astounded *by* the story of his latest adventure.

CORRECT: I was ‖ interested *in*
and ‖ astounded by the story of his latest adventure

INCORRECT: She is as tall if not taller *than* her sister.

CORRECT: She is as tall *as* her sister, if not taller. [The reader understands *than her sister.*]

ALSO CORRECT: She is as tall *as*, if not taller than, her sister.

16f Correct Use of "Unparallel" Constructions

A caution should be added to this lesson. Parallelism of phraseology is not always possible. When it is not, do not hesitate to use natural, "unparallel" constructions:

CORRECT THOUGH "UNPARALLEL": He spoke *slowly* and *with dignity.*

Here *slowly* and *with dignity* are parallel in a sense: they are both adverbial modifiers.

Exercise 62 PARALLELISM

Rewrite in a correct form all sentences containing faulty parallelism. Write **C** if the sentence is correct.

EXAMPLE: The cafe is small, inviting, and serves splendid pizza.

The small, inviting cafe serves splendid pizza.

(Only one correct version of each sentence is given in the answer section.)

Answers	Exercises
	1. The boy wore a pair of jeans, a shirt with "Aspen" printed on it, and he had on his favorite tennis shoes.
1. The boy wore a pair of jeans, a shirt with "Aspen" printed on it, and his favorite tennis shoes.	2. Jenny was a young woman with a sparkle in her eye and who also had a quick smile.
2. Jenny, a young woman with a sparkle in her eye, also had a quick smile.	3. Our entire family is delighted and interested in the new television series.
3. Our entire family is delighted with and interested in the new television series.	4. My compact car is smaller than Aunt Martha.
4. My compact car is smaller than Aunt Martha's.	5. In her desk drawer she found several odds and ends: a collection of ticket stubs, empty checkbook, and a lone glove.

5. In her desk drawer she found several odds and ends: a collection of ticket stubs, an empty checkbook, and a lone glove.

6. The children are neither too old nor are they too young to enjoy the story of Aladdin.

---

6. The children are neither too old nor too young to enjoy the story of Aladdin.

7. Frances climbed on the bus, gave the driver her transfer slip, and then she looked for a seat.

---

7. Frances climbed on the bus, gave the driver her transfer slip, and then looked for a seat.

8. The models in the fashion show were tall, slender, and wore evening clothes designed in Paris.

---

8. Tall and slender, the models in the fashion show wore evening clothes designed in Paris.

9. The Coopers had a marvelous week in the mountains: swimming, hiking, and visiting old friends.

---

9. C

10. My father always has and always will watch the bowl games on New Year's Day.

---

10. My father always has watched and always will watch the bowl games on New Year's Day.

11. I must put the pot roast on either before leaving for classes, or I must run back home between second and third periods.

11. I must either put the pot roast on before leaving for classes or run back home between second and third periods.	12. The tourists were Japanese and who enjoyed taking pictures.
12. The Japanese tourists enjoyed taking pictures.	13. Ralph decided that he would work this winter in Colorado and to go back to college for the spring quarter.
13. Ralph decided to work this winter in Colorado and to go back to college for the spring quarter.	14. The novel by Scott Fitzgerald is as good if not better than any other American novel.
14. The novel by Scott Fitzgerald is as good as if not better than any other American novel.	15. The longshoreman had broad shoulders, thick arms, and his hands were large and powerful.
15. The longshoreman had broad shoulders, thick arms, and large, powerful hands.	16. We stopped at Aunt Celia's to hear about her trip to New Mexico and for a visit with our cousins.
16. We stopped at Aunt Celia's to hear about her trip to New Mexico and to visit with our cousins.	17. On Tuesday Coach Lombard hopes to meet with those girls who play field hockey and discuss the tournament schedule.

17. On Tuesday Coach Lombard hopes to meet with those girls who play field hockey and to discuss the tournament schedule.	18. It is not unusual for a man's salary to be greater than a woman.
18. It is not unusual for a man's salary to be greater than a woman's.	**SCORE** ______

Exercise 63 PARALLELISM

Complete each of the following sentences by adding a construction which is parallel to the *italicized* construction.

EXAMPLE: Joseph found her to be *lively, intelligent,* and

Joseph found her to be *lively, intelligent,* and *appealing.*

(Only one correct version of each sentence is given in the answer section.)

	1. I am thinking of *cutting my hair* or
1. I am thinking of *cutting my hair* or wearing it in a bun.	2. Every morning the broker first *read the financial page* and
2. Every morning the broker first *read the financial page* and then turned to the comics.	3. *Either we will have to open the window*, or
3. *Either we will have to open the window*, or we will have to turn on the air conditioner.	4. This map of Los Angeles is *clear* and
4. This map of Los Angeles is *clear* and accurate.	5. Ray wants *to drive his motorcycle for the rest of the summer* and
5. Ray wants *to drive his motorcycle for the rest of the summer* and to trade it for a car in the fall.	6. Next week the supermarket not only *will open at seven in the morning* but also

6. Next week the supermarket not only *will open at seven in the morning* but also will not close until midnight.	7. Grandfather left everything on the dock: *his fishing pole,*
7. Grandfather left everything on the dock: *his fishing pole*, his straw cap, and his sunglasses.	8. The sports editor reported that the pitcher could either *accept the contract* or
8. The sports editor reported that the pitcher could either *accept the contract* or become a free agent.	9. I need to discuss the plans for our trip to the Southwest *with my parents* and
9. I need to discuss the plans for our trip to the Southwest *with my parents* and with a travel agent.	10. The meals at the Penguin Grill are neither *nourishing* nor
10. The meals at the Penguin Grill are neither *nourishing* nor appetizing.	**SCORE** ______

17 Subordination

Parallelism enables you to indicate equality of ideas. More often, however, your writing will include sentences in which some ideas are more important than others. The main device for showing the difference between major and minor emphasis is **subordination**: we reserve the independent clause for the main idea and use dependent clauses, phrases, and single words to convey subordinate ideas:

> In our garden there is a birdbath *which is carved from marble.* [Subordinate idea placed in a dependent clause.]
>
> In our garden there is a birdbath *carved from marble.* [Subordinate idea reduced to a participial phrase.]
>
> In our garden there is a *marble* birdbath. [Subordinate idea reduced to a one-word modifier.]

17a Primer Style

It is necessary to understand the principle of subordination, for without subordination you would be unable to indicate the relative importance of ideas or their various shades of meaning in your thinking. The following group of sentences is both childish and monotonous because six dissimilar ideas have been presented in six simple sentences and thus appear to be of equal importance:

> A pep meeting was held last Friday night. Memorial Stadium was the scene of the meeting. The meeting was attended by thousands of students. Over a hundred faculty members were there too. It rained Friday night. There was also some sleet.

As you know, coordinating conjunctions are used to join ideas of equal importance. Consequently, the six sentences given above would not be improved if they were joined by such conjunctions. As a matter of fact, a type of sentence which you should avoid is the long, stringy one which is tied together by *and, but, so,* or *and so*. Instead of using this kind of sentence, weigh the relative importance of your several ideas, and show their importance by the use of main and subordinate sentence elements. Notice how the six ideas can be merged into one clear sentence:

> Despite rain and some sleet the pep meeting held last Friday night at Memorial Stadium was attended by thousands of students and over a hundred faculty members.

In combining the six sentences, the writer has chosen to use the fact about student and faculty attendance as the main idea. Another writer might have chosen otherwise, for there will not always be complete agreement as to which idea can be singled out and considered the most important. You may be sure, however, that if your sentence reads with emphasis and effectiveness you have chosen a correct idea as the main one.

17b Upside-down Subordination

When there are only two ideas of unequal rank to be considered, you should have no difficulty in selecting the more important one:

1. He showed some signs of fatigue.
2. He easily won the National Open Golf Tournament.

Of these two sentences the second is undoubtedly the more important. Hence, when the two sentences are combined, the second should stand as the independent clause, and the first should be reduced to a dependent clause or even a phrase. If you made an independent clause of the first sentence and a subordinate element of the second, your sentence would contain upside-down subordination:

> FAULTY (upside-down subordination): Though he easily won the National Open Golf Tournament, he showed some signs of fatigue.
>
> CORRECT: Though he showed some signs of fatigue, he easily won the National Open Golf Tournament.

17c Choice of Subordinating Conjunctions

In introducing a subordinate element, be sure that you choose the right subordinating conjunction. The following sentences illustrate the correct use of certain conjunctions:

> I don't know *whether* (or *that*; not *as* nor *if*) I can see you tomorrow.
>
> *Although* (not *while*) she isn't a genius, she has undeniable talent.
>
> I saw in the autobiography of the actor *that* (not *where*) there is a question about the exact date of his birth.

(See Chapter 22, Glossary of Faulty Diction, for further discussion of accurate word choice.)

Exercise 64 SUBORDINATION

Combine the ideas in each of the following groups of sentences into one effective simple or complex sentence.

EXAMPLE: Mathew Brady was a photographer.
He is most often remembered for his photographs of the Civil War.
He also photographed many Presidents of the United States.

Mathew Brady, a photographer most often remembered for his photographs of the Civil War, also took pictures of many Presidents of the United States.

(Only one correct version of each sentence is given in the answer section.)

	1. Daniel Defoe wrote the novel *Robinson Crusoe.* He relates the story of a man shipwrecked on a remote island. The story is based upon actual events in the life of Alexander Selkirk.
1. *Robinson Crusoe*, a novel written by Daniel Defoe about a man shipwrecked on a remote island, is based upon actual events in the life of Alexander Selkirk.	2. Henry Ford was the father of the "Model T." He conceived the idea of producing it on an assembly line. The car remains a symbol of American ingenuity.
2. Henry Ford—the father of the "Model T," that symbol of American ingenuity—conceived the idea of producing it on an assembly line.	3. The Greek alphabet was derived from that of the Phoenicians. According to a myth, it was taken to Greece by Cadmus. Cadmus was the son of the King of Phoenicia.

3. A myth relates that the Greek alphabet, derived from that of the Phoenicians, was taken to Greece by Cadmus, son of the King of Phoenicia.	4. The White Nile and the Blue Nile are joined at Khartoum. Here they become the Nile. The Nile is the longest river in the world.
4. At Khartoum, the White Nile and the Blue Nile are joined and become the Nile, the longest river in the world.	5. Robert Burns was a Scottish poet. He wrote a poem entitled "Auld Lang Syne." He explained that it was based upon an old folk song.
5. The Scottish poet Robert Burns wrote a poem entitled "Auld Lang Syne," which, he explained, was based upon an old folk song.	6. Daniel O'Connell was born in County Kerry, Ireland, in 1775. He was often referred to as the "Liberator." He represented the interests of Ireland as a member of the House of Commons and as lord mayor of Dublin.
6. Born in County Kerry, Ireland, in 1775, Daniel O'Connell, the "Liberator," represented the interests of his country as a member of the House of Commons and as lord mayor of Dublin.	7. Langston Hughes was a black poet. He was a moving spirit in the Harlem Renaissance. The Harlem Renaissance is a name used to identify the creative movement among black artists during the 1920's.

7. The black poet Langston Hughes was a moving spirit in the Harlem Renaissance, a creative movement among black artists during the 1920's.	8. Benjamin Franklin invented a stove. It was called the "Pennsylvania fireplace." Subsequently, stoves of various designs have been associated with his name.
8. Although Benjamin Franklin invented a stove called the "Pennsylvania fireplace," stoves of various designs have subsequently been associated with his name.	9. William Clark and Meriwether Lewis led an expedition across the western United States. Sacagawea served as their guide. She was a Shoshoni Indian. Her name may be translated "Bird Woman."
9. Sacagawea, a Shoshoni Indian whose name may be translated "Bird Woman," served as a guide for William Clark and Meriwether Lewis in their expedition across the western United States.	SCORE ______

Exercise 65 SUBORDINATION

Combine the ideas in each of the following groups of sentences into one effective simple or complex sentence.

EXAMPLE: Mincemeat pie is my favorite dessert.
It contains minced or chopped fruits and spices.
It is frequently served with a slice of sharp Cheddar cheese.

Mincemeat pie, my favorite dessert, contains minced or chopped fruits and spices and is frequently served with a slice of sharp Cheddar cheese.

(Only one correct version of each sentence is given in the answer section.)

1. Anders Celsius was born in Sweden in 1701.
He was an astronomer.
He developed the centigrade temperature scale.
On this scale, water freezes at zero degrees and reaches its boiling point at one hundred.

1. Anders Celsius, a Swedish astronomer born in 1701, developed the centigrade temperature scale, on which water freezes at zero degrees and reaches its boiling point at one hundred.

2. The Cabot Trail overlooks the sea.
It offers the traveler magnificent views.
It is located on Cape Breton Island.
Cape Breton is a part of Nova Scotia.

2. The Cabot Trail, located on Cape Breton Island, Nova Scotia, overlooks the sea and offers the traveler magnificent views.	3. Paul Bunyan is the hero of a series of tall tales. Their setting is the American Northwest. He has a great blue ox named Babe. The ox's strength is as memorable as Paul's.
3. Paul Bunyan, the hero of a series of tall tales set in the American Northwest, has a great blue ox named Babe, whose strength is as memorable as Paul's.	4. Adam Smith was an eighteenth-century economist. He wrote a book entitled *The Wealth of Nations.* In this book he advocated *laissez-faire.* *Laissez-faire* is a concept that opposes the government's excessive intervention in economic affairs.
4. Adam Smith, an eighteenth-century economist, wrote a book entitled *The Wealth of Nations*, in which he advocated *laissez-faire*, a concept that opposes the government's excessive intervention in economic affairs.	5. Many species of butterflies migrate. One of these is the monarch butterfly. It travels great distances in regular patterns. Scientists do not understand this phenomenon.

5. The monarch butterfly, one of the many species of migrating butterflies, travels great distances in regular patterns, a phenomenon that scientists do not understand.	6. Thomas à Becket was Archbishop of Canterbury. He was a friend of Henry II, King of England. He questioned Henry's authority. While at a service in the Cathedral, he was murdered by four of the King's followers.
6. Thomas à Becket, Archbishop of Canterbury, questioned the authority of his friend King Henry II of England and, while at a service in the Cathedral, was murdered by four of the King's followers.	7. Margaret Mead was an outstanding anthropologist. She was born in Philadelphia in 1901. She died in New York in 1978. At the time of her death she had become interested in the feminist movement.
7. Margaret Mead, an outstanding anthropologist who was born in Philadelphia in 1901, had become interested in the feminist movement at the time of her death in New York in 1978.	8. The entrance to the harbor at San Francisco is called the Golden Gate. It is spanned by a suspension bridge. The bridge is more than a mile long. It is the second-longest suspension bridge in the world.

8. The entrance to San Francisco's harbor, the Golden Gate, is spanned by a suspension bridge more than a mile long, the second-longest such bridge in the world.

SCORE ______

Exercise 66 SUBORDINATION

The following sentences contain upside-down subordination or too much coordination. Rewrite each sentence to make it an effective simple or complex sentence.

EXAMPLE: Dorothy has several of Joan Baez's recordings, and she lent them to me, and I enjoyed listening to them.

Dorothy lent me several of Joan Baez's recordings, which I enjoyed listening to.

(Only one correct version of each sentence is given in the answer section.)

	1. Hitting a grand slam home run, Pete made contact with a fast ball.
1. Making contact with a fast ball, Pete hit a grand slam home run.	2. Sue, who won a trip to Puerto Rico, works at Blume's Music Store.
2. Sue, who works at Blume's Music Store, won a trip to Puerto Rico.	3. We asked Jane and Charles to be our guests for dinner, and we made reservations at the Chesapeake Inn, and they agreed to meet us at seven o'clock.
3. Having asked Jane and Charles to be our guests for dinner, we made reservations at the Chesapeake Inn, where they agreed to meet us at seven o'clock.	4. At last finding the courage to propose to Mary Sue, Horace took her hand in his.

4. Taking her hand in his, Horace at last found the courage to propose to Mary Sue.	5. Bradley, who easily climbed to the summit of Mt. Mitchell, was in excellent physical condition.
5. Bradley, who was in excellent physical condition, easily climbed to the summit of Mt. Mitchell.	6. Although we had the best pecan crop in years, the squirrels ate many of the nuts.
6. Although the squirrels ate many of the nuts, we had the best pecan crop in years.	7. The streets were torn up, and the traffic was heavy, and I missed my train to Beverly.
7. Because the streets were torn up and the traffic was heavy, I missed my train to Beverly.	8. The *Double Eagle II*, which is the first balloon to have crossed the Atlantic, flew from the east coast of the United States to France.
8. The *Double Eagle II*, which flew from the east coast of the United States to France, is the first balloon to have crossed the Atlantic.	9. Though the children could manage the subway ride by themselves, they were very young.

9. Though the children were very young, they could manage the subway ride by themselves.	10. We were walking along Madison Avenue, and we saw a crowd gathered at a corner, and they were watching a crew of window washers high up on a building.
10. As we were walking along Madison Avenue, we saw a crowd gathered at a corner, watching a crew of window washers high up on a building.	SCORE ______

18
Illogical Comparisons and Mixed Constructions

Correctness and clarity are essential to good writing. To reach these goals, you must know the rules of grammar and punctuation. But further, you must think logically and find the exact words in which to express your thoughts. Nothing is more bothersome to a reader than inexact, illogical, or confusing sentences. Some of the lessons which we have already studied have stressed means of avoiding certain errors which produce vagueness or confusion in writing; among these errors are faulty reference of pronouns, dangling or misplaced modifiers, and upside-down subordination. This lesson will consider certain other errors which obstruct clarity of expression.

18a Illogical Comparisons

When you make comparisons, you must be sure not only that the things compared are similar (a matter considered in the lesson on parallelism) but that all necessary elements of the comparison are included.

Note the following sentence:

> Harold is taller than any boy in his class.

Since *Harold*, the first term of the comparison, is included in the classification *any boy in his class*, the comparison is obviously illogical: the sentence might be interpreted to mean *Harold is taller than Harold.* Therefore, the first term of the comparison must be compared with a second term or classification which excludes the first term, thus:

> CORRECT: Harold is taller than any *other* boy in his class.
>
> ALSO CORRECT: Harold is taller than any *girl* in his class.

It should also be pointed out that when the superlative is followed by *of,* the object of *of* must be plural:

ILLOGICAL: Harold is the tallest of any other boy in his class.

CORRECT: Harold is the tallest of *all the boys* in his class.

ALSO CORRECT: Harold is the *tallest boy* in his class.

Ambiguity results from a comparison like this one:

I helped you more than Jim.

Does the sentence mean *I helped you more than I helped Jim* or *I helped you more than Jim did*? The writer should use one sentence or the other, according to whichever meaning is intended.

The type of incomplete comparison illustrated by the following vague sentences is particularly popular with writers of advertising copy and with careless speakers:

VAGUE: Eastern Rubber Company makes a tire which gives twenty percent more mileage.

CLEAR: Eastern Rubber Company makes a tire which gives twenty percent more mileage *than any tire it made ten years ago.*

ALSO CLEAR: Eastern Rubber Company makes a tire which gives twenty percent more mileage *than any other tire made in the United States.*

VAGUE: Litter is more of a problem in cities.

CLEAR: Litter is more of a problem in cities *than in small towns.*

ALSO CLEAR: Litter is more of a problem in cities *than it used to be.*

18b Mixed on Confused Constructions

Mixed constructions are frequently the result of some sort of shift in a sentence. Through ignorance or forgetfulness the writer starts a sentence with one type of construction and then switches to another. Notice the shift of construction in the following sentence:

She bought an old, dilapidated house which by having it extensively repaired converted it into a comfortable home.

The sentence reads correctly through the relative pronoun *which*. The reader expects *which* to introduce an adjective clause; however, he is unable to find a verb for *which.* Instead, he finds that the sentence is completed by a construction in which a gerund phrase stands as the subject of the verb *converted.* The sentence may be corrected in various ways. Two correct versions are:

She bought an old, dilapidated house which after extensive repairs was converted into a comfortable home.

By means of extensive repairs she converted into a comfortable home an old, dilapidated house which she had bought.

Other examples of mixed constructions are given below:

MIXED: Bob realized that during the conference how inattentive he had been. [This sentence is confusing because *that* as used here is a subordinating conjunction and should introduce a noun clause. However, the *that*-construction is left incomplete. Futher on, *how* introduces a noun clause. What we find then is only one noun clause but two words, *that* and *how*, used to introduce noun clauses. Obviously, only one such word should introduce the one dependent clause.]

CORRECT: Bob realized that during the conference he had been inattentive.

ALSO CORRECT: Bob realized how inattentive he had been during the conference.

MIXED: Because she had to work in the library kept her from attending the party. [A dependent clause introduced by *because* is always adverbial; hence such a clause can never be used as the subject of a sentence.]

CORRECT: Having to work in the library kept her from attending the party.

ALSO CORRECT: Because she had to work in the library, she could not attend the party.

MIXED: He pulled a leg muscle was why he failed to place in the broad jump. [*He pulled a leg muscle* is an independent clause standing as the subject of *was*. An independent clause, unless it is a quotation, can never be used as the subject of a sentence.]

CORRECT: Because he pulled a leg muscle, he failed to place in the broad jump.

MIXED: By attending the reception as a guest rather than as a butler was a new experience for him. [The preposition *by* introduces a modifying phrase, and a modifying phrase can never be used as the subject of a sentence.]

CORRECT: Attending the reception as a guest rather than as a butler was a new experience for him.

ALSO CORRECT: By attending the reception as a guest rather than as a butler, he enjoyed a new experience.

MIXED: A pronoun is when a word is used in the place of a noun. [Never use *is when* or *is where* in defining a word. Remember that a *when-* or *where-*clause which is clearly adverbial cannot be used as a predicate nominative.]

CORRECT: A pronoun is a word used in the place of a noun.

MIXED: I was the one about whom she was whispering to my father about. [To correct this sentence, omit either *about*.]

MIXED: We know that if he were interested in our offer that he would come to see us. [To correct this sentence, omit the second *that*. The first *that* introduces the noun clause *that . . . he would come to see us. If he were interested in our offer* is an adverbial clause within the noun clause.]

Exercise 67

ILLOGICAL COMPARISONS AND MIXED CONSTRUCTIONS

The following sentences contain illogical comparisons and mixed constructions. Rewrite each sentence in a correct form. Write **C** if a sentence is correct.

EXAMPLE: Why I never see him any more is because he has moved to Texas.

I never see him any more because he has moved to Texas.

	1. Lamar likes Sam less than Lucile.
1. Lamar likes Sam less than he does Lucile. Lamar likes Sam less than Lucile does.	2. I understand that Mr. Griffin is the richest of any man in Colorado.
2. I understand that Mr. Griffin is the richest man in Colorado.	3. Starlite Electric Company will repair your lamps better and more cheaply.
3. Starlite Electric Company will repair your lamps better and more cheaply than any other electric company.	4. In football a hand-off is where one player gives the ball to another player nearby.
4. In football a hand-off occurs when one player gives the ball to another player nearby.	5. I never doubted that if I were given a chance, that I could win the yodeling contest.

5. I never doubted that if I were given the chance, I could win the yodeling contest.	6. In trying to find a rain scarf was Molly's excuse for keeping us waiting.
6. Molly's excuse for keeping us waiting was that she was trying to find a rain scarf.	7. Because he was new in town made Phil shy and uncomfortable.
7. Phil was shy and uncomfortable because he was new in town.	8. I have always thought that with a colonial house what a pretty shrub boxwood is.
8. I have always thought that with a colonial house boxwood is a pretty shrub.	9. My bicycle, which after I had it painted and repaired, I think it looked like new.
9. My bicycle, after I had it painted and repaired, looked like new.	10. The new elementary school has a much larger enrollment.
10. The new elementary school has a much larger enrollment than the old one had.	11. Pete likes girls more than his brothers.
11. Pete likes girls more than his brothers do.	12. Chuck is a better hitter than any other player on the team.

12. C

13. Isabel said she remembered that how good Jackie used to be at diving.

13. Isabel said she remembered how good Jackie used to be at diving.

14. This spaghetti is tasteless; my father makes the best spaghetti.

14. This spaghetti is tasteless; my father makes the best spaghetti I have ever had.

15. The commercial says that Bubbly Yeast will help me make better bread.

15. The commercial says that Bubbly Yeast will help me make better bread than I can make with any other yeast.

16. Janice, after she had tried several roommates, she finally found a congenial one.

16. Janice, after she had tried several roommates, finally found a congenial one.

17. A sonnet is when you have a poem of fourteen lines.

17. A sonnet is a poem of fourteen lines.

18. Eating his lunch too fast was the cause of his indigestion.

18. C

19. Blue is her favorite of any other color.

19. Blue is her favorite color.	20. By framing the picture in gold is why it is so attractive.
20. Framing the picture in gold has made it attractive.	21. Fresh vegetables are harder to find.
21. Fresh vegetables are harder to find now than they were in June and July.	22. When I need money, I count on Father more than Aunt Amanda.
22. When I need money, I count on Father more than on Aunt Amanda.	23. Jerry explained that marinating is when you soak food in a flavored sauce.
23. Jerry explained that marinating is soaking food in a flavored sauce.	24. Isn't it wonderful that the crime rate is less?
24. Isn't it wonderful that this year's crime rate is less than last year's?	25. This has been the worst day; everything has gone wrong.
25. This has been the worst day of the week; everything has gone wrong. This has been a terrible day; everything has gone wrong.	SCORE ______

19
Punctuation

Punctuation depends largely upon the grammatical structure of a sentence. In order to punctuate correctly, you must therefore have an understanding of grammatical elements. For this reason, rules of punctuation in this text have been correlated, whenever applicable, with your study of grammar and sentence structure. You learned, for instance, how to punctuate certain phrases when you studied the phrase as a sentence unit.

In order that this chapter may present a reasonably complete treatment of punctuation, you will find here, along with additional rules, a summary of the rules already studied and reference to the chapters in which they are discussed. The rules given below have become to a large extent standardized; hence they should be clearly understood and practiced. Following the principle of punctuating "by ear" or of using a comma wherever there is a vocal pause results in an arbitrary and frequently misleading use of punctuation.

19a Terminal Marks

The terminal marks of punctuation—that is, those marks used to end a sentence—are the period, the question mark, and the exclamation mark.

Use a period after a declarative sentence, an imperative sentence, or an indirect question:

DECLARATIVE: John answered the telephone.

IMPERATIVE: Answer the telephone.

INDIRECT QUESTION: She asked whether John had answered the telephone.

NOTE: A request which is stated as a polite question should be followed by a period. Such a request frequently occurs in business correspondence:

Will you please send me your special summer catalogue.

Use a period also after most abbreviations:

Mr., Ms., Dr., B.S., Jr., *i.e.*, viz., etc., A.D., B.C., A.M., P.M.

Use three periods to indicate an omission of a word or words within a quoted sentence, three periods plus a terminal mark to indicate an omission at the end of a quoted sentence:

"Fourscore and seven years ago our fathers brought forth . . . a new nation . . . ."

Use a question mark after a direct question:

Did John answer the telephone?

"Have you finished your work?" she asked.

Use an exclamation mark after an expression of strong feeling. This mark of punctuation should be used sparingly:

"Halt!" he shouted.

How disgusting!

There goes the fox!

19b The Comma

1. Use a comma to separate independent clauses when they are joined by *and, but, or, nor, for, so,* and *yet*. (See Chapter 6.) If the clauses are long or are complicated by internal punctuation, a semicolon may be used instead of a comma:

The game was over, but the crowd refused to leave the park.

2. Use a comma to separate words, phrases, and clauses written as a series of three or more coordinate elements. This includes short independent clauses when used in a series, as shown in the third example sentence below:

A trio composed of Marie, Ellen, and Frances sang at the entertainment.

Jack walked into my office, took off his hat, and sat down.

I washed the dishes, I dried them, and I put them away.

3. Use a comma to separate two or more coordinate adjectives that modify the same noun:

The noisy, enthusiastic freshman class assembled in Section F of the stadium. [*Noisy* and *enthusiastic* are coordinate adjectives; therefore they are separated by a comma. But *freshman*, though an adjective, is not coordinate with *noisy* and *enthusiastic*; actually *noisy* and *enthusiastic* modify not just *class* but the word group *freshman class*. Hence no comma precedes *freshman*.]

To determine whether adjectives are coordinate, you may make two tests: if they are coordinate, you will be able (1) to join them with *and* or (2) to interchange their positions in the sentence. You can certainly say *the noisy and enthusiastic freshman class* or *the enthusiastic, noisy freshman class*; thus *noisy* and *enthusiastic* are clearly coordinate. However, to say *the noisy and freshman class* or *the freshman noisy class* would be absurd; thus *freshman* is not structurally parallel with *noisy*:

a blue wool suit [Adjectives not coordinate.]

an expensive, well-tailored suit [Adjectives coordinate.]

a new tennis court [Adjectives not coordinate.]

a muddy, rough court [Adjectives coordinate.]

4. Use a comma to separate sharply contrasted coordinate elements:

He was merely ignorant, not stupid.

5. Use commas to set off all nonessential modifiers. Do not set off essential modifiers. (See Chapter 7 for a discussion of essential and nonessential clauses.)

NONESSENTIAL CLAUSE: Sara Sessions, *who is wearing red shorts today,* was voted the most versatile girl in her class.

NONESSENTIAL PHRASE: Sara Sessions, *wearing red shorts today,* was voted the most versatile girl in her class.

ESSENTIAL CLAUSE: The girl *who is wearing red shorts today* is Sara Sessions.

6. Use a comma after an introductory adverbial clause, verbal phrase, or absolute phrase. (See Chapter 7 for a discussion of dependent clauses, Chapter 5 for a discussion of phrases).

INTRODUCTORY ADVERBIAL CLAUSE: *When he arose to give his speech,* he was greeted with thunderous applause.

INTRODUCTORY PARTICIPIAL PHRASE: *Being in a hurry,* I was able to see him only briefly.

INTRODUCTORY GERUND PHRASE: *On turning the corner,* Tom ran squarely into a a police officer.

INTRODUCTORY INFINITIVE PHRASE: *To get a seat*, we have to arrive by 7:30 P.M.

INTRODUCTORY ABSOLUTE PHRASE: *My schedule having been arranged,* I felt like a full-fledged college freshman.

7. Use commas to set off nonesssential appositives. (See Chapter 5.)

Tom, *the captain of the team,* was injured in the first game of the season.

Sometimes an appositive is so closely "fused" with the word which it follows that it constitutes an essential element in the sentence and thus is not set off by commas:

William *the Conqueror* died in 1087.

The poet *Keats* spent his last days in Italy.

The word *bonfire* has an interesting history.

8. Use commas to set off items in dates, geographical names, and addresses and to set off titles after names:

July 22, 1977, was a momentous day in his life.

Birmingham, Alabama, gets its name from Birmingham, England.

Do you know who lives at 1600 Pennsylvania Avenue, Washington, D.C.?

Alfred E. Timberlake, Ph.D., will be the principal speaker.

9. Use commas to set off words used in direct address:

It is up to you, *Dot*, to push the campaign.

I think, *sir,* that I am correct.

You, *my fellow Americans,* must aid in the fight against inflation.

10. Use a comma after a mild interjection and after *yes* and *no*:

Oh, I suppose you're right.

Yes, I will be glad to go.

11. Use a comma to separate an independent clause from a question dependent on the clause:

You will try to do the work, won't you?

12. Use commas to set off expressions like *he said* or *she replied* when they interrupt a sentence of direct quotation. (But see rule 1 under The Semicolon, below.)

"I was able," *she replied,* "to build the bookcase in less than an hour."

13. Use commas to set off certain parenthetic elements:

I was, *however*, too tired to make the trip.

My hopes, *to tell the truth,* had fallen to a low ebb.

14. Use a comma to prevent the misreading of a sentence:

Above, the mountains rose like purple shadows.

To John, Harrison had been a sort of idol.

19c The Semicolon

1. Use a semicolon to separate independent clauses when they are not joined by *and, but, or, nor, for, so,* or *yet*. (See Chapter 6.)

Wade held the ball for an instant; then he passed it to West.

"He is sick," she said; "therefore, he will not come."

2. Use a semicolon to separate coordinate elements which are joined by a coordinating conjunction but which are internally punctuated:

His tour included concert appearances in Austin, Texas; Little Rock, Arkansas; Tulsa, Oklahoma; and Kansas City, Kansas.

3. Use a semicolon to punctuate independent clauses which are joined by a coordinating conjunction in sentences which are heavily punctuated with commas internally:

I invited Sara, Susan, Leon, and John to the party; but Joe, Robert, and Charles also dropped in.

19d The Colon

1. Use a colon after a clause which introduces a formal list. Do not use a colon unless the words preceding the list form a complete statement:

INCORRECT: The poets I like best are: Housman, Yeats, and Eliot.

CORRECT: The poets I like best are these: Housman, Yeats, and Eliot.

ALSO CORRECT: The poets I like best are Housman, Yeats, and Eliot.

INCORRECT: The basket was filled with: apples, oranges, and bananas.

CORRECT: The basket was filled with the following fruits: apples, oranges, and bananas.

ALSO CORRECT: The basket was filled with apples, oranges, and bananas.

2. Use a colon after a statement which introduces an explanation or amplification of that statement:

One characteristic accounted for his success: complete honesty. [A dash, which is less formal than the colon, may be substituted for the colon in this sentence.]

There was only one way to solve the mystery: we had to find the missing letter.

3. Use a colon after expressions like *he said* when they introduce a long and formal quotation:

The speaker rose to his feet and said: "Students and teachers, I wish to call your attention to . . . ."

4. Use a colon after the formal salutation of a letter, between the hour and minute figures in time designations, between a chapter and verse reference from the Bible, and between a title and subtitle:

Dear Sir:

8:40 P.M.

John 3:16

Victorian England: Portrait of an Age

19e The Dash

1. Use a dash to indicate an abrupt shift or break in the thought of a sentence or to set off an informal or emphatic parenthesis:

Harvey decided to go to—but you wouldn't be interested in that story.

Mary told me—would you believe it?—that she preferred a quiet vacation at home.

At the age of three—such is the power of youth—Mary could stand on her head.

2. Use dashes to set off an appositive or a parenthetic element which is internally punctuated:

Her roommates—Jane, Laura, and Ruth—are spending the weekend with her.

19f Quotation Marks

1. Use quotation marks to enclose direct quotations, but do not use them to enclose indirect quotations:

INCORRECT: He said that "I was old enough to know better."

CORRECT: He said, "You are old enough to know better."

ALSO CORRECT: He said that I was old enough to know better.

If a direct quotation is interrupted by an expression like *he said*, use quotation marks to enclose only the quoted material. This necessitates the use of two sets of quotation marks:

INCORRECT: "It's just possible, Mary responded, that I'll get up before six in the morning."

CORRECT: "It's just possible," Mary responded, "that I'll get up before six in the morning."

If there are two or more consecutive sentences of quoted material, use only one set of quotations marks to enclose all the sentences, not one set for each sentence:

INCORRECT: Ruby shouted, "Wait for me." "I'll be ready in two minutes."

CORRECT: Ruby shouted, "Wait for me. I'll be ready in two minutes."

Use single marks to enclose a quotation with a quotation:

The instructor asked, "Who said, 'Change the name of Arkansas? Never!'?"

Place the comma and the period inside the quotation marks, the semicolon outside. Place the question mark and exclamation mark inside the quotation marks when they apply to the quoted material, outside when they apply to the entire sentence:

"Of course," he replied, "I remember you." [Comma and period inside the quotation marks.]

Her favorite poem was Kipling's "If."

Several times the witness said, "I swear to the truth of my statement"; yet the jury remained unconvinced. [Semicolon outside the quotation marks.]

He asked, "Where are you going?" [The question mark comes within the quotation marks because only the quoted material is a question.]

Did she definitely say, "I accept your invitation"? [The question mark comes outside the quotation marks because the entire sentence is a question.]

2. Use quotation marks to enclose the titles of short works (short stories, short poems, articles, one-act plays, songs, and speeches) and of smaller units of books. (See Rule 3 under Italics, Chapter 20, Section b.)

Benét's story "The Devil and Daniel Webster" was first published in the *Saturday Evening Post.*

The kindergarten children sang "America" for us.

"Who Will Be the New Bishop?" is the title of the first chapter of *Barchester Towers.*

3. Use quotation marks to enclose words taken from special vocabularies or used in a special sense:

All the money he had won on the quiz program was invested in "blue chips."

In certain sections of the United States a man who is both honest and good-natured is known as a "clever man."

19g Parentheses

Use parentheses to enclose certain parenthetic elements. From a study of the preceding marks of punctuation you will remember that commas and dashes are also used to set off parenthetic material. There are no clearly defined rules by which you can always determine which marks to use. In general, however, commas are used to set off a parenthetic element which is fairly closely connected with the thought of the sentence. Dashes are used to set off a loosely connected element such as an abrupt break in the thought of the sentence; they tend to emphasize the element set off. Parentheses are used to enclose (1) material that is supplementary or explanatory and (2) figures repeated to insure accuracy or used to designate an enumeration. An element enclosed by parentheses is usually even more loosely connected with the sentence than one set off by dashes; and parentheses, unlike dashes, tend to minimize the element set off:

> The *Ville de Nantes* (see Plate 5) is a large, semidouble, red and white camellia.
>
> I am enclosing a check for thirty-five dollars ($35.00).
>
> Please write on the card (1) your full name, (2) your home address, and (3) a parent's or guardian's full name.

19h Brackets

Use brackets to enclose any interpolation, or insertion, which you add to material that is being quoted. (You will note that in this text brackets are used to enclose explanations which follow illustrative sentences.)

> In September, 1793, Robert Burns wrote a letter which included this sentence: "So may God ever defend the cause of truth and liberty as he did that day [the day of Bruce's victory over Edward II at Bannockburn]."

Exercise 68	THE COMMA

In the following sentences insert commas wherever they are needed. If a sentence is correctly punctuated, mark it **C**.

	1. Katherine I am surprised at your laziness.
1. Katherine, I am surprised at your laziness.	2. Though he hates to say so Jack is a little nervous about flying.
2. Though he hates to say so, Jack is a little nervous about flying.	3. Richard the Lionhearted won fame fighting in the Crusades but failed to win Jerusalem.
3. C	4. When playing tennis one should wear cool loose clothing.
4. When playing tennis, one should wear cool, loose clothing.	5. Terry is really just thoughtless not deliberately unkind.
5. Terry is really just thoughtless, not deliberately unkind.	6. My duty having been done by waxing the kitchen floor I lay down to read the newspaper.
6. My duty having been done by waxing the kitchen floor, I lay down to read the newspaper.	7. Mr. Hanson our church sexton rings the bells faithfully every Sunday.
7. Mr. Hanson, our church sexton, rings the bells faithfully every Sunday.	8. For Mary Margaret would do almost anything.
8. For Mary, Margaret would do almost anything.	9. The puppy that is alone in the corner is my favorite one of the litter.

9. C	10. The long dark road up the mountain seemed endless to the lost hikers.
10. The long, dark road up the mountain seemed endless to the lost hikers.	11. While cooking the steaks Mimi got grease on her new wraparound skirt.
11. While cooking the steaks, Mimi got grease on her new wraparound skirt.	12. I still say that Golden Colorado is a prettier town than Tuscaloosa Alabama.
12. I still say that Golden, Colorado, is a prettier town than Tuscaloosa, Alabama.	13. Being late to class is a good way to antagonize one's teacher.
13. C	14. Being late to class Brad was afraid he would antagonize the teacher.
14. Being late to class, Brad was afraid he would antagonize the teacher.	15. Millie Jeannette and Florence were all on hand for the big bake sale.
15. Millie, Jeannette, and Florence were all on hand for the big bake sale.	16. After the show they walked all the way home I hear.
16. After the show they walked all the way home, I hear.	17. I know that you want to learn to drive Kitty but you are too young.
17. I know that you want to learn to drive, Kitty, but you are too young.	18. His sporty expensive new car costs too much to maintain.
18. His sporty, expensive new car costs too much to maintain.	19. To be ready for the big moment Harry rehearsed his one line in the play over and over.

19. To be ready for the big moment, Harry rehearsed his one line in the play over and over.	20. Dinner was ready the table was set and our guest was late.
20. Dinner was ready, the table was set, and our guest was late.	21. I am happy to know that by January 1 1983 my car will be paid for.
21. I am happy to know that by January 1, 1983, my car will be paid for.	22. The author Ernest Hemingway wrote a gripping novel about the Spanish Civil War.
22. C	23. The happy smiling faces of the children were reward enough for our work in preparing the party.
23. The happy, smiling faces of the children were reward enough for our work in preparing the party.	24. Frances made sandwiches poured tea and sliced chocolate cake for dessert.
24. Frances made sandwiches, poured tea, and sliced chocolate cake for dessert.	25. The name *Eugene* comes from a Greek word that means "well born."
25. C	26. Toni and Bill who are there on the first tee play golf almost every day.
26. Toni and Bill, who are there on the first tee, play golf almost every day.	27. On learning that Benjy was safe I burst into tears.
27. On learning the Benjy was safe, I burst into tears.	28. My great-uncle a colonel in the Army was stationed in Germany for several years.
28. My great-uncle, a colonel in the Army, was stationed in Germany for several years.	29. You must remember my warning Eloise and you must also abide by it.

29. You must remember my warning, Eloise, and you must also abide by it.	30. Flying was great fun; below the buildings of New York looked like toys.
30. Flying was great fun; below, the buildings of New York looked like toys.	31. Oh I suppose I must get dressed and go to the lecture.
31. Oh, I suppose I must get dressed and go to the lecture.	32. Billy was as a matter of fact much later than I had expected.
32. Billy was, as a matter of fact, much later than I had expected.	33. "You know" Mother said "that it is past your bedtime."
33. "You know," Mother said, "that it is past your bedtime."	34. To Marian Ellis had always seemed a pleasant person.
34. To Marian, Ellis had always seemed a pleasant person.	SCORE ______

Exercise 69 THE COMMA

In the following sentences insert commas wherever they are needed. If a sentence is correctly punctuated, mark it **C**.

	1. After I had written my letter of resignation I relaxed and began to enjoy the situation.
1. After I had written my letter of resignation, I relaxed and began to enjoy the situation.	2. Joyce Kilmer's poem "Trees" has been familiar to generations of school children.
2. C	3. I'm afraid my dear that you may be disappointed in the taste of caviar.
3. I'm afraid, my dear, that you may be disappointed in the taste of caviar.	4. Hoping to find the Erwins at home we drove over to see them yesterday.
4. Hoping to find the Erwins at home, we drove over to see them yesterday.	5. The two children hammering busily when we found them were building a tree house.
5. The two children, hammering busily when we found them, were building a tree house.	6. Jim was ashamed of his rudeness; he refused however to apologize.
6. Jim was ashamed of his rudeness; he refused, however, to apologize.	7. Ruth's swim suit—a splashy red yellow and white model—was quite becoming.
7. Ruth's swim suit—a splashy red, yellow, and white model—was quite becoming.	8. Rob tried over and over to get the kite from the tree but never succeeded in dislodging it.
8. C	9. Margaret who goes swimming every day has just bought herself a hair dryer.

9. Margaret, who goes swimming every day, has just bought herself a hair dryer.	10. A person who swims often certainly needs a hair dryer.
10. C	11. Flannery O'Connor a Georgia author wrote powerful tales of the rural South.
11. Flannery O'Connor, a Georgia author, wrote powerful tales of the rural South.	12. For a beautiful complexion color it sparingly.
12. For a beautiful complexion, color it sparingly.	13. Being almost ready for bed we turned down the thermostat and went upstairs.
13. Being almost ready for bed, we turned down the thermostat and went upstairs.	14. Well I hope you're satisfied with the fine mess you've got us in.
14. Well, I hope you're satisfied with the fine mess you've got us in.	15. Mark took a taxi to the hotel from Buckingham Palace because he was tired of walking.
15. C	16. For Frances Martin's appearance on the scene was a godsend.
16. For Frances, Martin's appearance on the scene was a godsend.	17. It's time to start our Christmas shopping isn't it?
17. It's time to start our Christmas shopping, isn't it?	18. The man's footsteps slowed as his own slowed and Jason felt certain that he was being followed.

18. The man's footsteps slowed as his own slowed, and Jason felt certain that he was being followed.	19. Last fall I went to all the Los Angeles Rams' home games.
19. C	20. Halifax located in the province of Nova Scotia has a very large harbor.
20. Halifax, located in the province of Nova Scotia, has a very large harbor.	21. Barbara looked in the bread box in the pantry and in the refrigerator but never found the missing cake.
21. Barbara looked in the bread box, in the pantry, and in the refrigerator but never found the missing cake.	22. Luckily for us all Liz we could depend on you for directions to the lake.
22. Luckily for us all, Liz, we could depend on you for directions to the lake.	23. A person who never has time for his friends will probably never have many friends.
23. C	24. Having intended to stop after two sets of tennis Tom and Midge played on until dark.
24. Having intended to stop after two sets of tennis, Tom and Midge played on until dark.	25. While Sue fed the baby I was packing the car for our trip.
25. While Sue fed the baby, I was packing the car for our trip.	26. Why Alice are you trying to make excuses for your lateness?
26. Why, Alice, are you trying to make excuses for your lateness?	27. I will try to get to a telephone and let you know how the roads are up ahead.

27. C	28. Without batting an eye Horace said that he would pay the check for our delicious New England dinner.
28. Without batting an eye, Horace said that he would pay the check for our delicious New England dinner.	29. Three of my friends–Marcia Mimi and Mabel–have signed up for trampoline classes this year.
29. Three of my friends–Marcia, Mimi, and Mabel–have signed up for trampoline classes this year.	30. I tried to call Mattie Lou for I needed to tell her about Helen's illness.
30. I tried to call Mattie Lou, for I needed to tell her about Helen's illness.	31. On July 4 1979 there was a big celebration in Piedmont Park.
31. On July 4, 1979, there was a big celebration in Piedmont Park.	32. Trying to stop smoking in just one week was probably expecting too much.
32. C	SCORE ______

Exercise 70	THE COLON AND THE DASH

In the following sentences insert colons and dashes wherever they are needed. If a sentence is correctly punctuated, mark it **C**.

	1. John had a good explanation for his lateness he had gotten lost in Ansley Park.
1. John had a good explanation for his lateness: he had gotten lost in Ansley Park.	2. His schedule this semester includes courses in French, mathematics, and philosophy.
2. C	3. We took a bus to Milwaukee and then why are you yawning, Melissa? caught a plane to Salem, Oregon.
3. We took a bus to Milwaukee and then—why are you yawning, Melissa?—caught a plane to Salem, Oregon.	4. The following members will serve on the nominating committee Robert Jones, Margaret Allen, Terence Matthews, and Phyllis Hartford.
4. The following members will serve on the nominating committee: Robert Jones, Margaret Allen, Terence Matthews, and Phyllis Hartford.	5. I can't get this seat belt oh, now it is buckled.
5. I can't get this seat belt—oh, now it is buckled.	6. Anyone who likes long historical novels Michener's *Hawaii*, for example will probably enjoy reading *The Thorn Birds.*
6. Anyone who likes long historical novels—Michener's *Hawaii*, for example—will probably enjoy reading *The Thorn Birds.*	7. In the big cooler Mother had packed sandwiches, fruit, coconut cake, and lemonade.

7. C	8. Jim found the missing ten-dollar bill in an incriminating spot Danny's shoe.
8. Jim found the missing ten-dollar bill in an incriminating spot: Danny's shoe.	9. Our friends Dave and Adelaide I'm sure you have met them will be going with us on a trip to Rome.
9. Our friends Dave and Adelaide–I'm sure you have met them–will be going with us on a trip to Rome.	10. I've been trying to remember the road w took last summer when oh, I believe it was Highway 53.
10. I've been trying to remember the road we took last summer when–oh, I believe it was Highway 53.	11. Janet's letter to her supervisor began, "Dear Mr. Allen I hope you will understand my recent absence."
11. Janet's letter to her supervisor began, "Dear Mr. Allen: I hope you will understand my recent absence."	12. Joe, try to remember what I told you about changing a tire first, be sure to get the car well off the road.
12. Joe, try to remember what I told you about changing a tire: first, be sure to get the car well off the road.	13. When Sarah told me about Rudy's accident, she said he oh, were you there when it happened?
13. When Sarah told me about Rudy's accident, she said he–oh, were you there when it happened?	14. Two novels Hardy's *Tess of the d'Urbervilles* and Dickens's *Hard Times* are noted for their ability to produce drowsiness.
14. Two novels–Hardy's *Tess of the d'Urbervilles* and Dickens's *Hard Times*–are noted for their ability to produce drowsiness.	15. Here is a list for U. S. Customs of my European purchases one linen tablecloth, one hand-knit man's sweater, two silk neckties, and one antique silver bowl.

15. Here is a list for U. S. Customs of my European purchases: one linen tablecloth, one hand-knit man's sweater, two silk neckties, and one antique silver bowl.	16. When you leave for the lake, Cissy, be sure to take your why, you already have your tennis shoes on.
16. When you leave for the lake, Cissy, be sure to take your–why, you already have your tennis shoes on.	17. With all his faults, Godfrey has one trait that always wins me over his sense of humor.
17. With all his faults, Godfrey has one trait that always wins me over: his sense of humor.	18. It looks as though heaven help us another ninety-degree day is in store.
18. It looks as though–heaven help us–another ninety-degree day is in store.	19. Three kinds of dessert apple pie, peach ice cream, and strawberry tart were placed on the table.
19. Three kinds of dessert–apple pie, peach ice cream, and strawberry tart–were placed on the table.	20. This quotation from Shakespeare is an example of his use of figurative language "Macbeth does murder sleep."
20. This quotation from Shakespeare is an example of his use of figurative language: "Macbeth does murder sleep."	SCORE ______

Exercise 71 QUOTATION MARKS

In the following sentences insert quotation marks wherever they are needed. If a sentence is correctly punctuated, mark it **C**.

	1. Good gracious! Aunt Virginia cried. Surely you're not serious about this hang-gliding plan.
1. "Good gracious!" Aunt Virginia cried. "Surely you're not serious about this hang-gliding plan."	2. Have you ever heard an automobile mechanic referred to as a grease monkey?
2. Have you ever heard an automobile mechanic referred to as a "grease monkey"?	3. Randolph said to me, Bill Anderson, the country music star, wrote his song City Lights in a hotel room in Commerce, Georgia.
3. Randolph said to me, "Bill Anderson, the country music star, wrote his song 'City Lights' in a hotel room in Commerce, Georgia."	4. James Michener must have done a great deal of research before writing his novel *Chesapeake.*
4. C	5. After working hard all day yesterday, Jim says he has the blahs this morning.
5. After working hard all day yesterday, Jim says he has "the blahs" this morning.	6. After the cricket match the bank played God Save the Queen.
6. After the cricket match the band played "God Save the Queen."	7. We noticed that the motel near the airport is called a skytel.
7. We noticed that the motel near the airport is called a "skytel."	8. Frank began his letter to me with Hi, Kiddo! This is a great place.

8. Frank began his letter to me with "Hi, Kiddo! This is a great place."	9. On the last night of camp we ended the songfest with I've Been Working on the Railroad and Someone's in the Kitchen with Dinah.
9. On the last night of camp we ended the songfest with "I've Been Working on the Railroad" and "Someone's in the Kitchen with Dinah."	10. The unpopulated back country of Australia is known to natives as The Outback.
10. The unpopulated back country of Australia is known to natives as "The Outback."	11. My grandfather is fond of saying that he is a gentleman of the old school.
11. My grandfather is fond of saying that he is a "gentleman of the old school."	12. In *A Child's Garden of Verses* there is a wonderful poem entitled The Lamplighter.
12. In *A Child's Garden of Verses* there is a wonderful poem entitled "The Lamplighter."	13. In his latest phone call home Irby reported that he is happy as a clam.
13. In his latest phone call home Irby reported that he is "happy as a clam."	14. Mrs. Kent asked the class, Does everyone know what a gerund is?
14. Mrs. Kent asked the class, "Does everyone know what a gerund is?"	15. Larry wanted to know Why does Tom always forget the words to the second stanza of America?
15. Larry wanted to know, "Why does Tom always forget the words to the second stanza of 'America'?"	16. When asked what bedtime story he wanted, the little boy always requested Little Red Riding Hood.
16. When asked what bedtime story he wanted, the little boy always requested "Little Red Riding Hood."	17. Bess announced last Tuesday that she is going to marry Mr. Scarborough.

17. C	18. Ron referred to his sociology teacher as that old biddy.
18. Ron referred to his sociology teacher as "that old biddy."	19. You should go to Nova Scotia someday Helen said Joanna; however, you should not plan to go in winter.
19. "You should go to Nova Scotia someday, Helen," said Joanna; "however, you should not plan to go in winter."	20. Alice, I wish you would stop saying every thing is meaningful; it is a trite expression
20. Alice, I wish you would stop saying everything is "meaningful"; it is a trite expression.	SCORE ______

Exercise 72	REVIEW OF PUNCTUATION

In the following sentences insert all necessary marks of punctuation. If a sentence is correctly punctuated, mark it **C**.

	1. The new member of the basketball team although he is almost seven feet tall is too clumsy to make a good player.
1. The new member of the basketball team, although he is almost seven feet tall, is too clumsy to make a good player.	2. Carol couldn't start the car after leaving the football game fortunately however Roger came along and spotted the trouble quickly.
2. Carol couldn't start the car after leaving the football game; fortunately, however, Roger came along and spotted the trouble quickly.	3. Swimming in the heated water of an indoor pool was a new experience for Beth.
3. C	4. Although all things considered we were lucky to have won at all I wish that we had won by more than two points and I imagine you feel the same way.
4. Although, all things considered, we were lucky to have won at all, I wish that we had won by more than two points; and I imagine you feel the same way.	5. Yes I think that those big gas guzzlers are a threat to the ecology don't you?
5. Yes, I think that those big "gas guzzlers" are a threat to the ecology, don't you?	6. Here are the things you should always remember about driving keep your mind on your driving and your eyes on the road.

6. Here are the things you should always remember about driving: keep your mind on your driving and your eyes on the road.	7. Throughout the Elton John concert was a success in the eyes of the enthusiastic audience.
7. Throughout, the Elton John concert was a success in the eyes of the enthusiastic audience.	8. Marge asked her psychiatrist friend whether she ever gets tired of being called a shrink.
8. Marge asked her psychiatrist friend whether she ever gets tired of being called a "shrink."	9. Frank we agreed not to argue any more about the Yankees and the Red Sox didn't we?
9. Frank, we agreed not to argue any more about the Yankees and the Red Sox, didn't we?	10. The dinner table is no place for a discussion of your pet snake Ellen said Mother.
10. "The dinner table is no place for a discussion of your pet snake, Ellen," said Mother.	11. The man who is preparing the report on fuel conservation is a graduate of this university.
11. C	12. Jones knew that there was only one play that might give the Wildcats their first down a pass to McIntosh.
12. Jones knew that there was only one play that might give the Wildcats their first down: a pass to McIntosh.	13. Jackie please see whether the postman has oh there he is now.
13. Jackie, please see whether the postman has–oh, there he is now.	14. The first chapter of the science-fiction novel that I was talking about is Exodus of the Satellites.

<table>
<tr><td>14. The first chapter of the science-fiction novel that I was talking about is "Exodus of the Satellites."</td><td>15. She closed her letter by saying Enclosed is my check for one thousand dollars $1,000 which I hope you will find useful in your charitable work.</td></tr>
<tr><td>15. She closed her letter by saying, "Enclosed is my check for one thousand dollars ($1,000), which I hope you will find useful in your charitable work."</td><td>16. Naturally Howell said I will expect you to return the book as soon as you have finished reading it.</td></tr>
<tr><td>16. "Naturally," Howell said, "I will expect you to return the book as soon as you have finished reading it."</td><td>17. Remember these three rules about driving a golf ball 1 Keep your head down 2 Keep your eye on the ball and 3 Follow through in your swing.</td></tr>
<tr><td>17. Remember these three rules about driving a golf ball: (1) Keep your head down, (2) Keep your eye on the ball, and (3) Follow through in your swing.</td><td>18. When replacing the bolts on the wheel see Figure 4 be sure to tighten them with a wrench.</td></tr>
<tr><td>18. When replacing the bolts on the wheel (see Figure 4), be sure to tighten them with a wrench.</td><td>19. Did Lucy really say I refuse to ride with George?</td></tr>
<tr><td>19. Did Lucy really say, "I refuse to ride with George"?</td><td>20. Her remark was I know you won't believe this abrupt to the point of rudeness.</td></tr>
<tr><td>20. Her remark was—I know you won't believe this—abrupt to the point of rudeness.</td><td>21. She wants pink and green curtains in her bedroom I believe that blue and white would be prettier.</td></tr>
<tr><td>21. She wants pink and green curtains in her bedroom; I believe that blue and white would be prettier.</td><td>22. While I was waiting patiently for Jim to meet me he was watching a football game on television.</td></tr>
</table>

22. While I was waiting patiently for Jim to meet me, he was watching a football game on television.	23. It is time my fellow sufferers for us to protest the terrible food we are getting in the cafeteria.
23. It is time, my fellow sufferers, for us to protest the terrible food we are getting in the cafeteria.	24. She was hot she was tired and she was getting a headache.
24. She was hot, she was tired, and she was getting a headache.	25. Our revised itinerary includes Copenhagen Denmark Stockholm Sweden Bergen Norway and Helsinki Finland.
25. Our revised itinerary includes Copenhagen, Denmark; Stockholm, Sweden; Bergen, Norway; and Helsinki, Finland.	SCORE ______

Exercise 73 REVIEW OF PUNCTUATION

In the following sentences insert all necessary marks of punctuation. If a sentence is correctly punctuated, mark it **C**.

	1. Every club member Tom Walter Gene and the rest believes that Charlie will be a fine president.
1. Every club member–Tom, Walter, Gene, and the rest–believes that Charlie will be a fine president.	2. There is a problem that most large universities seem to have in common the confusion of registration day.
2. There is a problem that most large universities seem to have in common: the confusion of registration day.	3. While looking for the lost quarter I found a four-leaf clover.
3. While looking for the lost quarter, I found a four-leaf clover.	4. It was Franklin D. Roosevelt I believe who said The only thing we have to fear is fear itself.
4. It was Franklin D. Roosevelt, I believe, who said, "The only thing we have to fear is fear itself."	5. At half time Fred excitedly called his family to report that the Tigers were ahead seven to zilch.
5. At half time Fred excitedly called his family to report that the Tigers were ahead, seven to "zilch."	6. My teacher Mrs. Flanagan said that she would help us girls learn to twirl a baton.
6. C	7. She is a friendly warm-hearted person I know that she will be popular with everyone.

7. She is a friendly, warm-hearted person; I know that she will be popular with everyone.	8. Washington Irving's famous tale The Legend of Sleepy Hollow makes a good ghost story for Halloween.
8. Washington Irving's famous tale "The Legend of Sleepy Hollow" makes a good ghost story for Halloween.	9. Steve is a wonderful person but he has one little flaw his tendency to gossip.
9. Steve is a wonderful person, but he has one little flaw: his tendency to gossip.	10. In his address the senator made the following statement George Washington the first President of the United States could have been king if he had wished.
10. In his address the senator made the following statement: "George Washington, the first President of the United States, could have been king if he had wished."	11. A sports cartoonist named Dorgan was the man who first called wieners hot dogs they were first sold under this name at the New York Polo Grounds.
11. A sports cartoonist named Dorgan was the man who first called wieners "hot dogs"; they were first sold under this name at the New York Polo Grounds.	12. As he went back up the chimney Saint Nicholas said Happy Christmas to all and to all a good night.
12. As he went back up the chimney, Saint Nicholas said, "Happy Christmas to all and to all a good night."	13. Jim Jackson Martha Scott and Sarah Hawkins made *A*'s on their essays but the rest of us barely passed.
13. Jim Jackson, Martha Scott, and Sarah Hawkins made *A*'s on their essays; but the rest of us barely passed.	14. I have decided can you blame me not to try out a fourth time for the gymnastics team.
14. I have decided–can you blame me?–not to try out a fourth time for the gymnastics team.	15. The book reviewer wrote Actually he Sherlock Holmes never said Elementary my dear Watson.

15. The book reviewer wrote, "Actually he [Sherlock Holmes] never said, 'Elementary, my dear Watson.' "	16. Alfred the Great was an English king in the ninth century.
16. C	17. The author Hans Christian Andersen born in Odense Denmark was a much-loved writer of children's stories.
17. The author Hans Christian Andersen, born in Odense, Denmark, was a much-loved writer of children's stories.	18. On September 1 1984 he will be twenty years old.
18. On September 1, 1984, he will be twenty years old.	19. The runner who crosses the finish line first will win a red T-shirt.
19. C	20. Mary Martin who appeared on television years ago as Peter Pan was the star of many a Broadway musical.
20. Mary Martin, who appeared on television years ago as Peter Pan, was the star of many a Broadway musical.	21. Duluth Minnesota must be a cold place to spend the winter.
21. Duluth, Minnesota, must be a cold place to spend the winter.	22. I'm counting on you Jane to influence the children to get to bed on time.
22. I'm counting on you, Jane, to influence the children to get to bed on time.	23. Sally Mobley she's the girl over there in the blue shorts will probably be our tennis champion this year.
23. Sally Mobley–she's the girl over there in the blue shorts–will probably be our tennis champion this year.	24. Wearing a pretty green chiffon dress Miriam shook hands cordially with each of her guests.

24. Wearing a pretty green chiffon dress, Miriam shook hands cordially with each of her guests.	25. Laurie I asked you for a piece of chocolate cake not all of it.
25. Laurie, I asked you for a piece of chocolate cake, not all of it.	SCORE ______

20 Mechanics: Capital Letters, Italics, the Apostrophe, the Hyphen

20a Capital Letters

1. Capitalize the first word of a sentence, of a line of traditional poetry, and of a direct quotation:

> All the students attended the meeting.
>
> Under a spreading chestnut-tree
> The village smithy stands.
>
> He said, "She does not wish to see you."

2. Capitalize proper nouns, words used as proper nouns, and adjectives derived from proper nouns:

> Great Britain, William, the Bible
>
> President, Senator, Captain, University (when these are used with or substituted for the name of a particular president, senator, captain, or university), and similarly
>
> Mother, Grandfather, Uncle (as in *We told Mother to go to bed, We bought Grandfather a bicycle,* and *We buried Uncle in Arlington Cemetery,* but not in *My mother is ill, His grandfather is eighty-two,* and *Our uncle was wounded at Gettysburg*)
>
> British, Shakespearean, Biblical, Scandinavian

3. Capitalize the names of days, months, and holidays:

> Monday, February, Fourth of July, Ash Wednesday, Veterans Day

4. Capitalize the names of historical periods and events:

> The Middle Ages, the French Revolution, the Battle of the Bulge, the Reformation

5. Capitalize the first word in the titles of books, chapters, essays, short stories, short

poems, songs, and works of art. Capitalize also all other words in these titles except articles. prepositions, and conjunctions:

> *The Last of the Mohicans,* "Without Benefit of Clergy," "Ode to the West Wind," "Only a Bird in a Gilded Cage," El Greco's *View of Toledo*

6. Capitalize names of the Deity, religions, and religious organizations:

> Jehovah, God, the Redeemer, Buddhism, Church of England, Society of Jesus, Order of St. Francis

7. Capitalize the names of governing bodies, political parties, governmental agencies, and civic and social organizations:

> The House of Commons, the Senate, the Democratic Party, the Internal Revenue Department, the Chamber of Commerce, Daughters of the American Revolution

8. Capitalize the points of the compass when they refer to a specific region but not when they indicate direction:

> He lived in the East all his life.
>
> They traveled west for about a hundred miles and then turned south.

9. Capitalize the names of studies only if they are derived from proper nouns or are the names of specific courses of instruction:

> He was studying physics, chemistry, and German.
>
> He failed in Mathematics 101 and in Human Biology 1.

10. Capitalize personfications:

> O wild West Wind, thou breath of Autumn's being.
>
> Daughters of Time, the hypocritic Days.
>
> Be with me, Beauty, for the fire is dying.

20b Italics

1. Italicize words that you wish to emphasize. (In manuscript indicate italics by underlining.)

> Do you mean to say that she ate them *all*?
>
> It could hardly have been *the* Robert Frost.

NOTE: Use this device sparingly. Frequent use of italics for emphasis is a sign of an immature style.

2. Italicize numbers, letters, and words referred to as such:

> He made his *7* and his *9* very much alike.
>
> She has never yet learned to pronounce *statistics.*
>
> In his handwriting he employs the old-fashioned *s.*

3. Italicize the names of books, magazines, and newspapers. (Smaller units of books, such as chapters, stories, essays, and poems, are usually set in quotation marks.)

A Tale of Two Cities, the *Atlantic Monthly*, the Atlanta *Journal*

NOTE: In the names of newspapers or magazines it is not always necessary to italicize the definite article or the name of a city.

4. Italicize the names of ships, trains, and airplanes:

The *Queen Elizabeth*, the *Twentieth-Century Limited*, the *Spirit of St. Louis*

5. Italicize foreign words and phrases in an English context:

The *coup d'état* led to his becoming emperor.

6. Italicize the titles of paintings, statues, and other works of art:

Gainesborough's *Blue Boy*, Rodin's *The Thinker*

20c The Apostrophe

1. Use the apostrophe and *s* to form the possessive case of singular nouns:

The boar's head, Mary's lamb, the boss's orders

NOTE: Proper names ending in *s* may form the possessive by adding *'s* if the resulting word is not unpleasant or difficult to sound:

Keats's poems, Charles's work, *but* Ulysses' return

2. Use an apostrophe without *s* to form the possessive of plural nouns ending in *s*:

Soldiers' quarters, boys' clothes

3. Use an apostrophe and *s* to form the possessive of plural nouns not ending in *s*:

Men's coats, children's shoes, the alumni's contributions

4. The possessive of words indicating time is formed like the possessive of other nouns:

A week's delay, a day's journey, *but* a two days' visit

5. The apostrophe is frequently omitted in the names of organizations and institutions:

The Farmers Hardware Company, Boys High School, State Teachers College

6. In forming the possessives of compounds, use the apostrophe according to the meaning and the logic of the construction:

Beaumont and Fletcher's plays [Plays written by Beaumont and Fletcher jointly.]
Smith's and Jones's children [The children of Smith and the children of Jones.]
John and Mary's house [The house belonging to John and Mary.]
Somebody else's business [The business of somebody else.]

7. Use an apostrophe to indicate the omission of letters in contractions and of digits in numerals:

Isn't, don't, 'tis
The cat's had kittens.
The Class of '23

NOTE: Be sure that the apostrophe is placed at the exact point where the letter or digit is omitted. Do not write *is'nt, do'nt.*

8. Use an apostrophe and *s* to indicate the plural of letters, numerals, signs, and words used as such:

> Dot your *i*'s and cross your *t*'s.
>
> His telephone number contains four *8*'s.
>
> In your next theme omit the *&* 's.
>
> He uses too many *so*'s.

20d The Hyphen

In English, compounds are made in three ways:

(1) by writing the words solid (*bedroom, watchmaker, starlight*),

(2) by writing them separately (*ice cream, motion picture, mountain lion*), or

(3) by separating the words with a hyphen (*name-caller, ne'er-do-well, finger-paint*).

The resulting confusion, like so much confusion in English, lies in the fact that the language is constantly changing. A compound may begin its career as two words; then it may move on to the form with a hyphen; and finally it may end as a solid formation—its destiny accomplished, as it were. So we have *bedroom* (written solid) but *dining room* (two words). We have the noun *bluepoint* to refer to an oyster, but we use the two words *blue point* to describe a Siamese cat. A decision may be *far-reaching*, but a forecaster is *farseeing*. The only solution to this confusing problem is to consult a dictionary. But this authority is not always satisfactory because many compounds are made for the occasion and are not in the dictionary—and dictionaries may disagree. Furthermore, a compound with a hyphen may be correct in one part of a sentence and incorrect in another, or it may be correct as a noun and incorrect as a verb. The stylebook of one publisher says, "If you take hyphens seriously, you will surely go mad." Nevertheless, there is a sort of logic in the use of the hyphen, as well as a kind of common sense; furthermore, one can learn some of the pitfalls to avoid.

Consider the following sentences:

> He is a great admirer of Henry Kissinger, the ex-Republican Secretary of State. [Is Mr. Kissinger no longer a Republican? The phrase should read *the former Republican Secretary of State.*]
>
> The parents enjoyed their children's recreation of the first Thanksgiving. [In this sentence *re-creation* is the appropriate word, and the hyphen distinguishes it from *recreation.*]
>
> I would think that your sixteen year old brother could scramble an egg. [In this sentence *sixteen, year,* and *old* form a compound modifier and should be hyphenated. The phrase should read *your sixteen-year-old brother.*]
>
> He introduced me to his uncle, an old car enthusiast. [Is his uncle old? Or is his uncle interested in old cars? The phrase is clarified with a hyphen: *an old-car enthusiast.*]
>
> Did you hear the reporter's interview with the singing whale authority? [Did the reporter interview a whale authority who sings or an authority on singing whales? Appropriate hyphenation clears up the confusion; the phrase should read *with the singing-whale authority.*]

The following rules indicate common practice and are fairly reliable:

1. Compound numerals (*twenty-one* through *ninety-nine*) are always written with a hyphen:

Twenty-six, forty-eight, fifty-two

2. Fractions are written with a hyphen if they are adjectival:

His speech was one-third fact and two-thirds demagoguery.

But Three fourths of the apples are rotten.

3. Compounds with *self* are written with a hyphen:

Self-styled, self-taught, self-centered

Note the exceptions *selfsame, selfhood, selfless.*

4. The hyphen is used in certain expressions of family relationship:

Great-grandfather, great-aunt

5. Most compounds beginning with *ex, pre,* and *pro* are written with a hyphen:

Ex-president, pre-Christian, pro-British

6. The hyphen is commonly used with compounds with prepositional phrases:

Mother-in-law, stick-in-the-mud, heart-to-heart

7. One of the commonest uses of hyphens is to form compound modifiers for nouns and pronouns:

An eight-year-old child, a well-done steak, a blue-green sea

NOTE: Such compounds are hyphenated when they immediately precede the word they modify, but frequently they are not hyphenated when they are used predicatively:

His well-spoken words pleased the audience [*but* His words were well spoken].

She made a number of off-the-record comments [*but* Her comments were made off the record].

8. Hyphens are used in coined or occasional compounds:

She gave him a kind of you-ought-to-know-better look.

Her bird-on-the-nest hat was sensational.

9. The hyphen is used in compound nouns that name the same person in two different capacities:

Author-publisher, musician-statesman, tycoon-playboy

10. The hyphen is frequently used to avoid confusion between words:

Re-claim [to distinguish from *reclaim*]

Re-cover [to distinguish from *recover*]

11. Hyphens are used to avoid clumsy spellings:

Bull-like, semi-independent, ante-election, pre-empt

NOTE: *Cooperate* and *coordinate* are common enough to be accepted.

12. The hyphen is used at the end of a line of writing to indicate the division of a word continued on the next line. The division must always come at the end of a syllable. Do not divide words of one syllable:

PROPER DIVISIONS: con-tin-ued, in-di-cate, au-di-ence

IMPROPER DIVISIONS: wo-rd, laugh-ed, comp-ound

NOTE: If you are uncertain about the division of a word, consult your dictionary.

Exercise 74	CAPITALS

In the following sentences change small letters to capital letters wherever necessary and vice versa. If a sentence needs no change, mark it **C**.

EXAMPLE: when harry tried to reach meg on the telephone, he found that she had already left for chicago.

W H M
when harry tried to reach meg on the telephone, he found that she had already
C
left for chicago.

	1. My friend dr. gillespie is my grandfather's age.
D G 1. My friend dr. gillespie is my grandfather's age.	2. I believe that columbus day was on saturday last year, wasn't it?
C D 2. I believe that columbus day was on S saturday last year, wasn't it?	3. That wind from the east means that we will have rain soon.
3. C	4. Dorothy, are the anglican church and the church of england one and the same?
A C 4. Dorothy, are the anglican church and C E the church of england one and the same?	5. Frost's "stopping by woods on a snowy evening" is a poem concerned with making choices.
S W 5. Frost's "stopping by woods on a S E snowy evening" is a poem concerned with making choices.	6. On our first trip to the west we were awed by the grandeur of the rocky mountains.

6. On our first trip to the ~~w~~West we were awed by the grandeur of the ~~r~~Rocky ~~m~~Mountains.	7. May, I believe that history 304 is a good choice for you as an elective.
7. May, I believe that ~~h~~History 304 is a good choice for you as an elective.	8. My sociology professor says that *the mind of the south* is an excellent book.
8. My sociology professor says that *~~t~~The ~~m~~Mind of the ~~s~~South* is an excellent book.	9. When last heard from, uncle fred was on the the isle of capri.
9. When last heard from, ~~u~~Uncle ~~f~~Fred was on the ~~i~~Isle of ~~c~~Capri.	10. Janice replied, "you shouldn't say that, mother."
10. Janice replied, "~~y~~You shouldn't say that, ~~m~~Mother."	11. My sister and my brother are leaving for toronto on july 20.
11. My sister and my brother are leaving for ~~t~~Toronto on ~~j~~July 20.	12. Facing south, we could see the gulf of mexico far in the distance.
12. Facing south, we could see the ~~g~~Gulf of ~~m~~Mexico far in the distance.	13. Harvey had always hoped to be a shakespearean actor someday.
13. Harvey had always hoped to be a ~~s~~Shakespearean actor someday.	14. Last summer he realized his ambition when he played in *the merchant of venice* at stratford-on-avon.

14. Last summer he realized his ambition
T M
when he played in *the merchant of*
V S A
venice at stratford-on-avon.

15. Dad predicted that I would have trouble with accounting 101 if I didn't study regularly.

15. Dad predicted that I would have
A
trouble with accounting 101 if I
didn't study regularly.

SCORE ______

Exercise 75 ITALICS

In the following sentences underline all words that should be *italicized.* If a sentence needs no change, mark it **C**.

EXAMPLE: After reading Shakespeare's drama Romeo and Juliet, Frances decided to see the movie version.

After reading Shakespeare's drama <u>Romeo and Juliet,</u> Frances decided to see the movie version.

	1. Didn't you realize that there is only one b in Sandy Robins's last name?
1. Didn't you realize that there is only one <u>b</u> in Sandy Robins's last name?	2. Father says that it is good to see Life magazine back on the newsstands after all these years.
2. Father says that it is good to see <u>Life</u> magazine back on the newsstands after all these years.	3. It is Ellie's habit to work the crossword puzzle in the Sunday New York Times before reading the comics.
3. It is Ellie's habit to work the crossword puzzle in the Sunday New York <u>Times</u> before reading the comics.	4. I'll never forget Negley Farson's description of salmon migration in his book The Way of a Transgressor.
4. I'll never forget Negley Farson's description of salmon migration in his book <u>The Way of a Transgressor</u>.	5. Handwriting experts agree that there is significance in the way a person writes the capital letter I.
5. Handwriting experts agree that there is significance in the way a person writes the capital letter <u>I</u>.	6. Jake, can you tell me what expediency means?

6. Jake, can you tell me what *expediency* means?

7. Eight Cousins, a wonderful book by Louisa May Alcott, is a sequel to her popular Little Women.

7. *Eight Cousins*, a wonderful book by Louisa May Alcott, is a sequel to her popular *Little Women*.

8. Jamie uses two m's instead of one when he writes the word coming.

8. Jamie uses two *m*'s instead of one when he writes the word *coming*.

9. Shirley Jackson, author of "After You, My Dear Alphonse," wrote many other short stories.

9. C

10. Henry's family gave him a subscription to Bon Appétit for Christmas.

10. Henry's family gave him a subscription to *Bon Appétit* for Christmas.

11. Jeanne wanted to lend me her copy of Grimm's Fairy Tales, but she couldn't find it.

11. Jeanne wanted to lend me her copy of *Grimm's Fairy Tales*, but she couldn't find it.

12. Susie and Jim were having a tête-à-tête when we saw them at the restaurant.

12. Susie and Jim were having a *tête-à-tete* when we saw them at the restaurant.

13. When you see the abbreviation op. cit., George, you know that it means "the work quoted from."

13. When you see the abbreviation *op. cit.*, George, you know that it means "the work quoted from."

14. It was interesting to learn that the French luxury liner Liberté had once been a German ship, the Europa.

14. It was interesting to learn that the French luxury liner <u>Liberté</u> had once been a German ship, the <u>Europa</u>.	15. There's an intriguing article in the January Reader's Digest about the U. S. Supreme Court.
15. There's an intriguing article in the January <u>Reader's Digest</u> about the U. S. Supreme Court.	16. At the Smithsonian Institution the children were fascinated by Lindbergh's little plane, The Spirit of Saint Louis.
16. At the Smithsonian Institution the children were fascinated by Lindbergh's little plane, <u>The Spirit of Saint Louis</u>.	17. Almost everyone I know seems to mispronounce the word liaison.
17. Almost everyone I know seems to mispronounce the word <u>liaison</u>.	18. Everybody wanted Joe to play "When the Saints Go Marching In" on his trumpet.
18. C	19. There are four 6's in our new telephone number.
19. There are four <u>6</u>'s in our new telephone number.	20. No crêpes suzette are as delicious as those at Antoine's in New Orleans.
20. No <u>crêpes suzette</u> are as delicious as those at Antoine's in New Orleans.	SCORE ______

Exercise 76 THE APOSTROPHE

In the following sentences underline all words that should have apostrophes, and then write the words with the apostrophes correctly placed. If a sentence is correct, mark it **C**.

EXAMPLE: Pollys news is exciting: she is getting married in April.

Polly's

Answers	Exercises
	1. Havent I already told you to unload the dishwasher, Martha?
1. Havent I already told you to unload the dishwasher, Martha? *Haven't*	2. Whats going to happen to your goldfish when you move to Seattle?
2. Whats going to happen to your goldfish when you move to Seattle? *What's*	3. Many in the Class of 80 will be taking postgraduate work.
3. Many in the Class of 80 will be taking postgraduate work. *'80*	4. Morris and Pattys two-year-old son is a real handful.
4. Morris and Pattys two-year-old son is a real handful. *Patty's*	5. Europeans have a distinctive way of making 7s.
5. Europeans have a distinctive way of making 7s. *7's*	6. The Franklins are going to New Jersey to visit their daughters family.
6. The Franklins are going to New Jersey to visit their daughters family. *daughter's*	7. She asked the bank teller to give her two dollars worth of nickels for parking-meter money.

7. She asked the bank teller to give her two dollars worth of nickels for parking-meter money. *dollars'*	8. Nows the time for you to speak up about your problems, Nancy.
8. Nows the time for you to speak up about your problems, Nancy. *Now's*	9. The Joneses and the Walkers houses are next door to each other.
9. The Joneses and the Walkers houses are next door to each other. *Joneses' Walkers'*	10. Las Vegas famous luxury hotels feature big-name entertainers.
10. Las Vegas famous luxury hotels feature big-name entertainers. *Las Vegas's*	11. One of baseballs all-time great players was Ty Cobb.
11. One of baseballs all-time great players was Ty Cobb. *baseball's*	12. The bear stood on its hind legs and pawed the air.
12. *C*	13. Henry James novel *The Golden Bowl* is on the reading list for Dr. Lintons class this quarter.
13. Henry James novel *The Golden Bowl* is on the reading list for Dr. Lintons class this quarter. *Henry James' or Henry James's Dr. Linton's*	14. Hank always has to ask, "Whats in it for me?"
14. Hank always has to ask, "Whats in it for me?" *What's*	15. I heard only recently that youre going to major in psychology in college.

15. I heard only recently that youre going to major in psychology in college. *you're*	16. After his two years leave of absence Ted returned to his job with renewed interest and energy.
16. After his two years leave of absence Ted returned to his job with renewed interest and energy. *years'*	17. Its going to be cold tonight, Scotty; you had better take your red flannels.
17. Its going to be cold tonight, Scotty; you had better take your red flannels. *It's*	18. My eyes, nose, and mouth are like my sisters; but my hair is much straighter than hers.
18. My eyes, nose, and mouth are like my sisters; but my hair is much straighter than hers. *sister's*	19. Rogers and Hammersteins collaborations have added a great deal to the world of popular music.
19. Rogers and Hammersteins collaborations have added a great deal to the world of popular music. *Hammerstein's*	20. His bachelors degree from Northwestern proved valuable to him from the day of graduation.
20. His bachelors degree from Northwestern proved valuable to him from the day of graduation. *bachelor's*	SCORE ______

Exercise 77 **THE HYPHEN**

In the sentences below underline the compounds that are wrong, and then write the correct forms. If a sentence is correctly punctuated, mark it **C**.

EXAMPLE: I am sorry to say that Tom's tongue in cheek attitude has got him into trouble.

tongue-in-cheek

	1. Mr. Lee, the Chinese porcelain authority, will lecture at the Carnegie Library tomorrow morning at ten o'clock.
1. Mr. Lee, the Chinese porcelain authority, will lecture at the Carnegie Library tomorrow morning at ten o'clock. *Chinese-porcelain*	2. This is a well written, unbiased report on conditions in Central America.
2. This is a well written, unbiased report on conditions in Central America. *well-written*	3. Hetty's stage fright made her tongue tied.
3. Hetty's stage fright made her tongue tied. *tongue-tied*	4. The new filing clerk in our department will probably not succeed because he is too happy go lucky.
4. The new filing clerk in our department will probably not succeed because he is too happy go lucky. *happy-go-lucky*	5. A hand to mouth existence is no fun, as those who have experienced it can tell you.
5. A hand to mouth existence is no fun, as those who have experienced it can tell you. *hand-to-mouth*	6. Madame Duval, the ex-French cooking instructor, has returned to her native land.

6. Madame Duval, the ex-French cooking instructor, has returned to her native land. *former French-cooking*

7. A five year old child could have painted a better picture than the prize winning one.

7. A five year old child could have painted a better picture than the prize winning one. *five-year-old prize-winning*

8. Benjamin Franklin, the author inventor, was a noted wit in his day.

8. Benjamin Franklin, the author inventor, was a noted wit in his day. *author-inventor*

9. The man's down at the heels appearance made Kay feel sorry for her new found friend.

9. The man's down at the heels appearance made Kay feel sorry for her new found friend. *down-at-the-heels new-found*

10. I don't know how you feel about Louise, but I have found her to be a weak kneed supporter in a no holds barred fight.

10. I don't know how you feel about Louise, but I have found her to be a weak kneed supporter in a no holds barred fight. *weak-kneed no-holds-barred*

11. Billy wanted blue tapestry on the old sofa, but Mother preferred to re-cover it in gold brocade.

11. C

12. When Dan gets that ready for anything look on his face, we all stay out of his path.

12. When Dan gets that ready for anything look on his face, we all stay out of his path. *ready-for-anything*

13. Karen's father in law is an English textbook author.

13. Karen's father in law is an English textbook author. *father-in-law English-textbook*

14. Their new apartment has tiny, celllike rooms.

14. Their new apartment has tiny, celllike rooms. *cell-like*

15. Thank-you for the beautiful silver tray you gave me.

15. Thank-you for the beautiful silver tray you gave me. *Thank you*

16. Joanne wrote Mrs. Richards a gracious thank you letter.

16. Joanne wrote Mrs. Richards a gracious thank you letter. *thank-you*

17. We're all hoping that the Blue Devils' seven game losing streak will not continue.

17. We're all hoping that the Blue Devils' seven game losing streak will not continue. *seven-game*

18. In the pre game television show the sports announcer predicted that the Los Angeles Rams would win by a ten point spread.

18. In the pre game television show the sports announcer predicted that the Los Angeles Rams would win by a ten point spread. *pre-game ten-point*

19. George's grand-father is ninety one years old; he takes a two mile walk every day.

19. George's grand-father is ninety one years old; he takes a two mile walk every day. *grandfather ninety-one two-mile*

20. That is an interesting couple; he is a romantic fiction writer, and she is a certified public accountant.

20. That is an interesting couple; he is a romantic fiction writer, and she is a certified public accountant. *romantic-fiction*

SCORE ______

Exercise 78	REVIEW OF MECHANICS

Indicate the errors in mechanics in the following sentences by underlining the words that are wrong and then writing the correct form. If a sentence is correct, write **C**.

EXAMPLE: "Put the cooler and the sleeping bags on the back seat of the car," said uncle Bob.

Uncle

	1. The eighty year old candidate for mayor was not disturbed by charges that she was too old for the job.
1. eighty year old eighty-year-old	2. "Oh," said Mary, "I have a blue raincoat just like your's."
2. your's yours	3. When we visited the U. S. air force academy, we were impressed by the beauty of the colorado landscape.
3. air force academy, colorado Air Force Academy, Colorado	4. I needed a nickel for the parking meter, and all I had was a five dollar bill.
4. five dollar five-dollar	5. Horace began his journalistic career on a small town newspaper called the Griffin Daily News.
5. Small town small-town Daily News *Daily News*	6. Those were delicious crescent rolls we had for breakfast; my french friend Pierre calls them croissants.

6. <u>french</u>, <u>croissants</u> French, *croissants*	7. "Here," thought Chris, "is a heaven sent opportunity to show Nan that I am reliable."
7. <u>heaven sent</u> heaven-sent	8. Susan has made quite a name for herself as an author illustrator.
8. <u>author illustrator</u> author-illustrator	9. My father and my mother attended the same college, but Father graduated two years ahead of Mother.
9. C	10. Everyone should learn the life saving procedure of mouth to mouth resuscitation.
10. <u>life saving</u>, <u>mouth to mouth</u> life-saving, mouth-to-mouth	11. Katie's and Bill's house has just been painted barn red.
11. <u>Katie's</u> Katie	12. The old movie fans thronged to see again that classic film Casablanca.
12. <u>old movie</u>, <u>Casablanca</u> old-movie, *Casablanca*	13. We have just heard that our cousin Steve will graduate cum laude from the university of Wisconsin.
13. <u>cum laude</u>, <u>university</u> *cum laude*, University	14. All the King's Men, a novel based on the life of Huey Long, won a pulitzer prize for it's author, Robert Penn Warren.

14. All the King's Men, pulitzer prize, it's *All the King's Men*, Pulitzer Prize, its	15. The French word fleur-de-lis means "lily" in English.
15. fleur-de-lis *fleur-de-lis*	16. Arthurs hand sewn moccasins are made of soft, smooth deerskin.
16. Arthurs, hand sewn Arthur's, hand-sewn	17. "When you see the golden gate in San Francisco," said Tommy, "you will get quite a thrill."
17. golden gate Golden Gate	18. Actually, my look alike friends are not related, but seeing them side by side, one might think that they were twins.
18. look alike look-alike	19. William, which magazine do you prefer–Newsweek or U. S. News and World Report?
19. Newsweek, U. S. News and World Report *Newsweek, U. S. News and World Report*	20. Don't get our sweaters mixed up; mine is the yellow one, and her's is the navy blue.
20. her's hers	SCORE ______

21
Use of the Dictionary

A convenient source of valuable linguistic information which is often overlooked is a standard dictionary. It is easy to use and, if used intelligently, very informative. Many people do not realize that a dictionary contains important facts far beyond simple definitions and guides to pronunciation or spelling. One of the best investments that a college student can make is the purchase and frequent use of a standard collegiate dictionary. It is a necessary step toward the development of an effective vocabulary, but more importantly it is essential to any reader's understanding of the material he encounters daily. In any college course, in the newspapers, and in regular communication with others, the alert student will read and hear unfamiliar words. A desire to learn the meaning, spelling, and pronunciation of a new word should lead him to a dictionary which can provide this information plus other facts such as the derivation of the word, its level of usage, discussions of its synonyms, and usually at least one antonym as a means to illuminate still further its precise shade of meaning.

The best dictionaries have taken years of preparation by hundreds of workers directed by the finest scholars of the time. Unabridged dictionaries are absolutely comprehensive in their explanations and descriptions of words, containing thousands more entries than the more commonly used desk dictionary. In the United States perhaps the best-known unabridged dictionary is *Webster's New International Dictionary of the English Language,* frequently called *Webster's Third* because the current issue is the third edition of the book. It was published by the G. & C. Merriam Company of Springfield, Mass., in 1961. This work, of course, though it is too bulky to be used as a casual desk dictionary (and for most purposes is not really necessary), may be found when you need it in your college library.

Any one of several extremely reliable collegiate dictionaries is the best choice for the college student. Severely abridged paperback editions of these dictionaries are a poor investment, as they do not contain the sometimes vital information which students will find necessary for any detailed or specialized assignment in their courses. Recommended by most language authorities are the following standard college dictionaries: *Webster's Seventh New*

Collegiate Dictionary, published by G. & C. Merriam Co., Springfield, Mass.; *Webster's New World Dictionary of the American Language,* Collins + World Publishing Co., Cleveland; *The American Heritage Dictionary of the English Language,* The American Heritage Publishing Co., Inc., and Houghton Mifflin Co., Boston; *The Random House Dictionary of the English Language,* Random House, New York; *Funk and Wagnall's Standard Collegiate Dictionary*, Harcourt, Brace and World, Inc., New York.

Select one of these dictionaries and buy it as soon as you get to college, and then follow the list of suggestions given below in order to familiarize yourself with the dictionary and the ways in which you can get the maximum use from this very handy and easy-to-use reference work.

1. Read all the introductory material in the front of the dictionary, because this explains what information the book has to offer. If some of it seems too scholarly for you to understand, read on, and at least find out what it is mainly concerned with and what you can expect to find in its entries.
2. Study carefully the key to pronunciation, and check it with words that you know so that you will be sure of understanding it. A need for guidance in pronunciation is one of the most common reasons for consulting a dictionary.
3. To save space, dictionaries necessarily use many abbreviations. These abbreviations are explained at the front of the book, frequently inside the front cover. You should refer often to this table of abbreviations until you know it well, so that no small bit of relevant information can escape you simply through ignorance of its meaning.
4. Examine the appendixes to learn what information is given in them. Some dictionaries list biographical and geographic information in their appendixes; others list them in the main entries in the book. Other information often found in the appendixes of a dictionary includes tables of interpretations of various specialized symbols, like those connected with mathematics, chemistry, music, chess, medicine, and pharmacy; a directory of colleges and universities; a table of weights and measures; a dictionary of English given names, etc.

One of the most important things a dictionary can tell you is the *level of usage* of a certain word. The English language, ever-changing and full of colorful informality, functions on many levels. Many young people use the expression *split* for *go* or *leave*. Politicians and reporters use the term *bottom line* to mean the end result of something. An educated adult may in ordinary conversation refer to *lots of trouble.* And an editor of a magazine may write of the *dichotomy between work and leisure classes* or, in a book review, of an *involuted search for self.* All these expressions are in a sense proper in their context. Good English is usually determined by the level on which it is used. The magazine editor would not normally write about *splitting*; the youth of today would hardly think or write using terms like *dichotomy.* Your dictionary will tell you whether the use of a word in a particular sense is slang, informal (colloquial), dialectal, archaic, obsolete, or none of these, i.e., Standard English.

Slang is the term used to describe the spontaneous, vivid, and sometimes racy inventions used frequently in the speech and writings of groups like teen-agers, gangsters, popular musicians, soldiers, and sports writers—not that these groups necessarily have anything else in common. The life of a slang expression is usually short, but sometimes, if it is striking enough and colorful enough, it may gain universal usage and become at least an informal part of the national vocabulary.

The term *informal* or *colloquial* is applied to words or expressions which are acceptable in the speech of the educated but not in formal writing. It is all right to say, "He's going to have *lots of trouble* explaining his whereabouts on the night of June third," but it is not Standard English to write this statement formally.

Dialect, another usage label, means that a word or expression is common to the speech of a particular group or geographical region. *Archaic* means that the word or term is rarely used today except in certain contexts like church ritual, but that it may be found fairly frequently in early writings. *Obsolete* means that the term is no longer used, but may be found in early writings. In addition, as a part of its usage discussion, a dictionary will inform you if a word or term is commonly considered obscene, vulgar, or profane.

To see how a dictionary presents its information, consider now the following entry from *The Random House Dictionary of the English Language*:*

bur·den[1] (bûr′dᵊn), *n.* **1.** that which is carried; load: *a horse's burden of rider and pack.* **2.** that which is borne with difficulty; obligation or trouble: *the burden of leadership.* **3.** *Naut.* **a.** the weight of a ship's cargo. **b.** the carrying capacity of a ship: *a ship of a hundred-tons burden.* **4.** *Mining.* the earth or rock to be moved by a charge of explosives. **5.** *Accounting.* overhead (def. 6). **—***v.t.* **6.** to load heavily. **7.** to load oppressively; trouble. [ME, var. of *burthen,* OE *byrthen;* akin to G *Bürde,* Goth *baurthei;* see BEAR[1]] —**bur′den·er,** *n.* —**bur′den·less,** *adj.*
—Syn. 1. See **load. 2.** weight, encumbrance, impediment.

Here we are given the correct spelling of the word *burden* and its proper division into syllables. The small numeral[1] after the entry word indicates that this is the first of two or more words which have the same spelling but which differ radically in meaning and derivation and are therefore listed separately. Next the proper pronunciation is given. It becomes clear immediately that you need to learn the significance of the signs, called diacritical marks, that are used to indicate pronunciation. In this entry the first five numbered definitions are preceded by *n* (for *noun*) and the last two by *v.t.* (for *verb, transitive*). After 3, *Naut.* (*Nautical*) means that the definitions given under 3 are special technical senses of the word as used in shipping. The same interpretation is true of definitions 4 and 5. The information in brackets gives the derivation or origin of the word. It tells that *burden* is a variant form of the older word *burthen,* which is derived from the Old English form *byrthen,* and that the word is linguistically akin to the word *bear* as described in the first *bear* entry elsewhere in the dictionary. Finally we learn that the synonyms of *burden*[1] are discussed under the entry *load.* The second entry, *burden*[2], is arranged on the same principles.

Consider now the following entry from *Webster's New World Dictionary of the American Language*:*

> **drunk** (druŋk) [ME. *dronke* < *drunken:* see DRUNKEN] *pp.* & *archaic pt. of* DRINK —*adj.* [*usually used in the predicate*] **1.** overcome by alcoholic liquor to the point of losing control over one's faculties; intoxicated **2.** overcome by any powerful emotion [*drunk* with joy] **3.** [Colloq.] *same as* DRUNKEN (sense 2) —*n.* [Slang] **1.** a drunken person **2.** a drinking spree
> ***SYN.*—drunk** is the simple, direct word, usually used in the predicate, for one who is overcome by alcoholic liquor [*he is drunk*]; **drunken,** usually used attributively, is equivalent to **drunk** but sometimes implies habitual, intemperate drinking of liquor [a *drunken* bum]; **intoxicated** and **inebriated** are euphemisms, the former often expressing slight drunkenness and the latter, a state of drunken exhilaration; there are many euphemistic and slang terms in English expressing varying degrees of drunkenness: e.g., **tipsy** (slight), **tight** (moderate, but without great loss of muscular coordination), **blind** (great), **blotto** (to the point of unconsciousness), etc. —***ANT.*** **sober**

Here we learn that the adjective *drunk*, with the specific meanings that follow, is the past participle and was formerly a past tense of the verb *to drink*. Two definitions are given: the first of these is the common one; the second is often used figuratively. The discussion of synonyms gives us the fine shades of distinction among a group of words that mean essentially the same thing. In addition, one antonym, or word of opposite meaning, is given. The final part of the entry, defining *drunk* as a noun, explains that when the word is used as a noun, meaning a person in a drunken condition, or a period of heavy drinking, the word is slang.

The kind of knowledge that a good dictionary can give you far exceeds what has been discussed here. Every good dictionary, for instance, pays special attention to biography and geography. One can learn when Beethoven died and the name of the capital of Peru. One can find the height of Mount Everest and the approximate number of islands in the Philippines. Literature, mythology, and particularly science are well covered in the modern dictionary. Finally, special appendixes sometimes include such miscellaneous information as the meanings of common Christian names, foreign words and phrases, abbreviations, and the symbols used in the preparation of copy for the printer and in proofreading. Some books even contain a dictionary of rhymes. The following exercises illustrate the variety of information one may obtain from a good dictionary.

Exercise 79 WORD ORIGINS

After each of the following words indicate the first systematically recorded language from which the word is derived and the meaning of the original source.

EXAMPLE: monologue

Greek, alone + speaking

	1. intervene
1. Latin, between + to come	2. sight
2. Old English, faculty of seeing	3. scissors
3. Latin, to cut	4. raid
4. Old English, to ride	5. report
5. Latin, back + to carry	6. scene
6. Greek, background for a dramatic performance	7. bread
7. Old English, to brew	8. epidemic

8. Greek, among + people	9. innocent
9. Latin, not + wicked	10. jurisdiction
10. Latin, law + speaking	11. dandelion
11. Middle French, lion's tooth	12. deck
12. Old High German, to cover	13. couple
13. Latin, together + to fasten	14. vapor
14. Latin, steam	15. valedictory
15. Latin, farewell + saying	16. wretch
16. Old English, outcast	17. woman
17. Old English, wife + human being	18. skill

18. Old Norse, distinction, knowledge	19. ski
19. Old Norse, stick of wood	20. library
20. Latin, books + place	21. talon
21. Latin, anklebone	22. smoke
22. Greek, to smolder	23. pantry
23. Latin, bread + place	24. plume
24. Latin, soft feather	25. perplex
25. Latin, thoroughly + to involve	26. perimeter
26. Greek, around + measure	27. waver
27. Old English, to weave, to fluctuate	28. weary

28. Greek, to faint	29. perennial
29. Latin, throughout + years	30. catapult
30. Greek, down + hurl	SCORE ______

Exercise 80 BRITISH AND AMERICAN USAGE

The following words illustrate differences between British and American usage. With the help of your dictionary, write the American equivalents of these British terms:

EXAMPLE: spanner

wrench

	1. barrister
1. legal counselor who pleads in court	2. biscuit
2. cracker or cookie	3. bonnet
3. automobile hood	4. bowler
4. derby hat	5. braces (*n.*)
5. suspenders	6. chemist
6. druggist or pharmacist	7. coach (*n.*)
7. bus	8. corn (*n.*)

8. grain	9. costermonger
9. fruit or vegetable dealer	10. croft
10. field or small farm	11. draper
11. dry goods retailer	12. dustman
12. trash collector	13. gaol
13. jail	14. geyser
14. water heater	15. ironmonger
15. hardware dealer	16. lift (*n.*)
16. elevator	17. lorry
17. truck	18. petrol

18. gasoline	19. pillarbox
19. mailbox	20. post (*v.*)
20. mail	21. pub or public house
21. saloon or bar	22. queue (*n.*)
22. a line (of persons)	23. rates
23. taxes	24. removal
24. change of residence	25. roundabout (*n.*)
25. traffic circle or merry-go-round	26. solicitor
26. lawyer	27. sweet (*n.*)
27. dessert	28. tin

28. can	29. torch
29. flashlight	30. underground or tube
30. subway	SCORE ______

Exercise 81 PLURALS

Write the plurals of the following nouns:

EXAMPLE: crisis

crises

	1. alibi
1. alibis	2. alumna
2. alumnae	3. calf
3. calves	4. cello
4. cellos	5. child
5. children	6. court-martial
6. courts-martial or court-martials	7. criterion
7. criteria or criterions	8. cupful

8. cupfuls	9. deer
9. deer	10. hoof
10. hooves	11. medium
11. media	12. monkey
12. monkeys	13. mouse
13. mice	14. ox
14. oxen	15. potato
15. potatoes	16. roof
16. roofs	17. shrimp
17. shrimp or shrimps	18. sister-in-law

18. sisters-in-law	19. tooth
19. teeth	20. woman
20. women	SCORE ______

Exercise 82 LEVELS OF USAGE

Look up the *italicized* words or expressions in the sentences below; then indicate the level of usage of each one, using the following abbreviations:

A	for archaic,	**I**	for informal or colloquial,
D	for dialectal,	**S**	for slang.

(Most standard collegiate dictionaries agree in the classification of these words. Other dictionaries may classify them differently.)

EXAMPLE: I knew that I had *goofed* when I saw my teacher's eyebrows go up.

S

	1. Living in a *dorm* makes a freshman miss his mother's home cooking.
1. I	2. *Methinks* you will get into trouble if you take that book without permission.
2. A	3. Harry's *erstwhile* roommate has moved to a fraternity house.
3. A	4. Maria says it's hard to be a *shrink*; everyone tells her his troubles.
4. S	5. Have you ever eaten boiled *goobers*, or even heard of them?
5. D	6. Heaven *forfend* that I should ever have to study organic chemistry again.
6. A	7. It was a *heavy* scene last night when I had that big argument with Joe.

7. S	8. The *jalopy* that Tom and Ralph are trying to repair will never make it to the old-car rally.
8. S	9. I've heard it said that pigs are very smart *critters.*
9. D	10. "It is my *guesstimate*," said Don, "that Sheila will be back from Sioux City before Christmas."
10. S	11. It was *chow* time, but no one seemed interested in cooking supper.
11. S	12. Roger, the *kine* in the barn should be fed some hay tonight.
12. A	13. The thug had put his loot in a burlap *poke* and was trying to escape through the bathroom window.
13. D	14. I heard on the radio that *the fuzz* have caught up with the man who has robbed five banks in the past month.
14. S	15. In his soliloquy Hamlet speaks of "the undiscovered country, from whose *bourn* no traveler returns."
15. A	16. Terry now thinks that he was a *sucker* to agree that he would be in charge of raising money for the class reunion.
16. S	17. Bill and Julia are proud to proclaim that they are Florida *Crackers.*

17. D	18. I always had a *hunch* that Marty and Charlie would get married someday.
18. I	19. I was getting *bad vibes* from the gang of bystanders, and suddenly a fight broke out.
19. S	20. When we went wading in the *branch*, the cold water kept us from staying very long.
20. D	21. After class we went to the student lounge and *gabbed* about our plans for the weekend.
21. I	22. Sue had clearly forgotten her lines, so it was up to me to *ad lib* for a while.
22. I	23. The boys decided that they would try to get dates with some *chicks* for the rock concert.
23. S	24. David says that *the going* was *pretty* rough in the debate between the rival factions.
24. I, I	25. It looks as though Earl may have been *framed* to look guilty of taking the money.
25. S	SCORE ______

Exercise 83 GENERAL INFORMATION

With the help of your collegiate dictionary fill in the information called for below:

EXAMPLE: Name of the river the Great Lakes empty into

St. Lawrence

	1. Location of the Scilly Islands
1. Off Cornwall, England	2. Meaning of the abbreviation C. O. D.
2. Collect On Delivery	3. Official name of the Common Market
3. European Economic Community	4. Animal from which mohair is obtained
4. Angora goat	5. Achievement for which Robert Fulton is best known
5. First commercially successful American steamboat	6. Altitude of the Brenner Pass, between Austria and Italy
6. 4,470 feet	7. Profession of Clarence Darrow
7. Lawyer	8. Day on which Boxing Day is annually celebrated in England

8. The first weekday after Christmas	9. Former name of Iran
9. Persia	10. River on which the city of Liverpool, England, is located
10. The River Mersey	11. Effect that lotus fruit had on those who ate it, in Greek mythology
11. They became indolent, dreamy, and forgetful	12. Birth and death years of President John Quincy Adams
12. 1767-1848	13. James Thurber's middle name
13. Grover	14. Number of sides in a trapezoid
14. Four	15. The capital of British Columbia
15. Victoria	16. How Brie cheese got its name
16. From Brie, France, where it was first made	17. Number of chessmen each player uses

17. Sixteen	18. Date of last appearance of Halley's comet
18. 1910	19. Shakespeare's play in which the character Iago is a villain
19. *Othello*	20. Characteristic of an isosceles triangle
20. It has two equal sides	21. Nickname for the state of Kansas
21. The Sunflower State	22. Name of the racetrack where the Kentucky Derby is run
22. Churchill Downs	23. The pen name of essayist Charles Lamb
23. Elia	24. Place and date of the signing of the Magna Charta
24. Runnymede, England, 1215	25. Norwegian name for Norway
25. Norge	**SCORE** ______

Exercise 84 FOREIGN EXPRESSIONS

Although the following expressions are now part of our everyday speech and writing, they are borrowed from languages other than English. Write the meaning of each, after consulting your dictionary.

	1. *gesundheit*
1. "good health," a wish for someone who has sneezed	2. *noblesse oblige*
2. nobility obligates, referring to the obligation of high-born persons to be generous and honorable	3. *en route*
3. on the way, along the way	4. *per diem*
4. by the day, frequently referring to an allowance paid to compensate for expenses incurred on business	5. *adios*
5. goodbye; farewell	6. *kimono*
6. a loose outer garment with short, wide sleeves and a sash	7. *kindergarten*

7. a school or class for young children of about four to six years of age	8. *maize*
8. a kind of grain that grows in kernels on large ears; sometimes called "Indian corn"	9. *lasagna*
9. macaroni in broad strips, often baked in a dish with ground meats and cheeses	10. *quid pro quo*
10. one thing in return for another; something equivalent	11. *kayak*
11. an Eskimo canoe made of skins stretched over a wooden frame	12. *mañana*
12. tomorrow, or at some indefinite time in the future	13. *cummerbund*
13. a sash for the waist, worn originally by men in India	14. *chic*
14. smart elegance of style and manner, referring especially to women and their clothes	15. *au gratin*

15. made with a lightly browned crust of bread crumbs or cheese	16. *par excellence*
16. in the greatest degree of excellence, beyond comparison	17. *fiesta*
17. a religious festival, gala celebration, or holiday	18. *frankfurter*
18. smoked sausage of beef and/or pork, encased in a membranous casing and formed into links a few inches long	19. *lingerie*
19. women's underwear of linen, silk, rayon, etc.	20. *kudzu*
20. a vine of Asian origin, widely used for hay, forage, and erosion control	21. *fungus*
21. a parasitic lower plant; mold, rust, mildew, smut, mushrooms, etc.	22. *ad hoc*
22. for the particular purpose or case at hand without consideration of wider application	23. *luau*

23. a Hawaiian feast, usually with entertainment	24. *bonanza*
24. a rich vein or pocket of ore; hence, any source of wealth or high profit	25. *sub rosa*
25. secretly, privately, confidentially	SCORE ______

22 Diction

Diction is one's choice of words in the expression of ideas. Because one speaks and writes on various levels of usage, the same expression may be appropriate to one level but not to another. The diction, for instance, of formal writing seems overprecise in informal conversation, and the acceptable diction of everyday speech seems out of place in serious, formal composition. But on all levels of speech and writing, faulty diction appears—in wordiness, in trite expressions, and in faulty idiom.

22a Wordiness

Wordiness is the use of too many words—more words, that is, than are necessary to express an idea correctly and clearly. Many sentences written by college students may be greatly improved by reducing the number of words. The following kind of sentence is common in student themes:

WORDY: There is a man in our neighborhood, and he has written three novels.

BETTER: A man in our neighborhood has written three novels.

A neighbor of ours has written three novels.

What is called **excessive predication** is responsible for a common type of wordiness. Usually this fault results from the too frequent use of *and* and *but*. It may usually be remedied by proper subordination:

WORDY: The test was hard, and the students were resentful, and their instructor was irritated.

BETTER: Because the students resented the hard test, their instructor was irritated.

Another kind of wordiness originates in the desire to impress but ends in pretentious nonsense. It is the language of those persons who refer to bad weather as the "inclemency of the elements," who speak of "blessed events" and "passing away" instead of birth and death. Following are further examples of this kind of wordiness:

> Due to the fact that he was enamored of Angela, Thomas comported himself in such a way as to appear ridiculous.
>
> *Because he was in love with Angela, Thomas behaved foolishly.*
>
> I regret extremely the necessity of your departure.
>
> *I am sorry you must go.*
>
> Our horse Hap has gone to the big round-up in the sky.
>
> *Our horse Hap has died.*

Sometimes, of course, expressions like these are used humorously. But do not make a habit of such usage.

Recently a new kind of wordiness has become popular, probably because it is believed to make its users appear knowledgeable. It is the jargon of government officials, social workers, educators on all levels, and others. Its basic principles seem to be these: Never use one word where two or more will do the work. Never use a concrete expression if it is possible to use an abstract one. Never be plain if you can be fancy. The clear sign of this kind of writing and speaking is seen in the repeated use of such phrases as *frame of reference, in terms of, point in time,* and compounds formed with the suffix *-wise.* The writers of this new jargon never simply look at the budget; they "consider the status budget-wise." They don't study crime among the young; they "examine social conditions in terms of juvenile delinquency." They "evaluate," they "utilize," they "expedite," and they "finalize." They speak of the "culturally deprived," the "classroom learning situation," "meaningful experiences," "togetherness," and "lifestyle." All these expressions reflect a desire to be a part of the "in group" (another example of this jargon) by picking up catchwords that seem to show a certain sophistication; what they really show is a loss of precise language and a lack of judgment.

Redundancy, or unnecessary repetition, is another common type of wordiness, due to carelessness or ignorance of the meanings of certain words. Note the following examples of redundancy:

> Repeat that again, please, [Why *again*?]
>
> His solution was equally as good as hers. [Why *equally*?]
>
> The consensus of opinion of the group was that Mrs. Jacobs will make a good mayor. [Use either *consensus of the group* or *the opinion of the group*.]
>
> This location is more preferable to that one. [The word *preferable* means "more desirable"; therefore the word *more* is unnecessary. The sentence should read *This location is preferable to that one.*]
>
> The union continues to remain at odds with factory management. [*Continues* and *remain* mean essentially the same thing. Say, *The union continues at odds with factory management* or *The union remains at odds with factory management.*]
>
> It was a dog large in size and brown in color. [*It was a large brown dog.*]
>
> Mrs. Frost rarely ever wears her fur coat. [*Mrs. Frost rarely wears her fur coat.*]

22b Vagueness

A general impression of vague thinking is given by the too frequent use of abstract words instead of concrete words. Note especially the vagueness of such common words as *asset, factor, phase, case, nature, character, line,* and *field.* All these have basic meanings and should be used cautiously in any other sense. The following examples show that the best way to treat these words is to get rid of them:

In cases where a person receives a ticket for speeding, he must pay a fine of fifty dollars. [*In cases where* can be replaced with the single word *if.*]

Industry and intelligence are important assets in business success. [Omit *assets* and the sense remains the same.]

The course is of a very difficult nature. [*The course is very difficult.*]

Jerry was aware of the fact that he was risking his savings. [*Jerry was aware that he was risking his savings.*]

Whenever you are tempted to use such words, stop and ask yourself just what you are trying to say. Then find the exact words to say it, cutting out all the "deadwood."

22c Triteness

Trite means worn. Certain phrases have been used so often that they have lost their original freshness. Oratory, sermons, newspaper headlines and captions, and pretentious writing in general are frequently marred by such diction. Expressions of this kind are often called **clichés**. The following list is merely illustrative; you can probably think of numerous ones to add to these:

upset the applecart
an ace up his sleeve
dull thud
one fell swoop
up on Cloud Nine
grim reaper
last but not least
face the music
as straight as a dye
bitter end
proud possessor
nipped in the bud
few and far between
on pins and needles
make one's blood boil
eat one's heart out
having a ball
as luck would have it
quick as a wink
gung ho

Avoid also quotation of trite phrases from literature and proverbs. Expressions like the following have already served their purpose:

a lean and hungry look
a sadder but wiser man
a rolling stone
those who live in glass houses
the best laid plans of mice and men
where angels fear to tread
love never faileth
to be or not to be

22d Euphemisms

Euphemisms are expressions used to avoid the outright statement of disagreeable ideas or to give dignity to something essentially lowly or undignified. The Victorians were notoriously euphemistic: they called their legs "limbs," and instead of the accurate and descriptive terms *sweat* and *spit*, they substituted the vague but more delicate words "perspire" and "expectorate." Unfortunately, the Victorians were not the last to use euphemisms. While we cannot admire or condone some of today's obscenely explicit language, there is little justification for the fuzzy-minded delicacy of euphemisms. There is a decided difference between the choice of an expression which offers a tactful connotation rather than a hurtful one and that of an expression which is deliberately misleading. The condition of pregnancy is euphemistically referred to as "expecting"; a garbage collector is a "sanitation engineer"; a janitor is a "superintendent," etc. *Death*, of course, has numerous euphemistic substitutes such as "passing on," "going to his reward," and many others.

Again, it should be emphasized that the laudable wish to spare the feelings of others is not to be confused with the sort of prudery or false sense of gentility that most often produces euphemisms. Unless the desire to use a euphemism is inspired by the necessity to soften a blow or avoid offensiveness, the more factual term is to be preferred. Ordinarily, avoid euphemisms—or change the subject.

22e Idiom

Construction characteristic of a language is called **idiom**. The established usage of a language, the special way in which a thing is said or a phrase is formed, must be observed if writing is to be properly idiomatic. In English the normal sentence pattern has the subject first, then the verb, and then the direct object. In French, if the direct object is a pronoun, it usually (except in the imperative) precedes the verb. In English an adjective that directly modifies a noun usually precedes it. In French the adjective usually follows the noun. In English we say, "It is hot." The French say, "It makes hot." Such differences make it hard to learn a foreign language.

Another meaning of the word *idiom* is somewhat contrary to this one. The word is also used for all those expressions that seem to defy logical grammatical practice, expressions that cannot be translated literally into another language. "Many is the day" and "You had better" are good examples. Fortunately idioms of this sort cause little trouble to native speakers.

In English, as in most modern European languages, one of the greatest difficulties lies in the idiomatic use of prepositions after certain nouns, adjectives, and verbs. Oddly enough, one agrees *with* a person but *to* a proposal, and several persons may agree *upon* a plan. One may have a desire *for* something but be desirous *of* it. One is angry *at* or *about* an act but *at* or *with* a person. These uses of prepositions may seem strange and perverse. But they are part of the idiomatic structure of English and must be learned. Good dictionaries frequently indicate correct usage in questions of this kind. Do not look up the preposition but rather the word with which it is used. The definition of this word will usually indicate the correct preposition to use with it.

22f Connotation

In selecting words that will express their thoughts accurately, careful writers pay attention to the **connotations** of certain expressions. *Connotation* is the associative meaning, or what the word suggests beyond its literal definition.

Through popular usage certain terms convey favorable or unfavorable impressions beyond their literal meanings; they frequently have emotional or evaluative qualities that are not part of their straightforward definitions. Careless use of a word with strong connotations may cause faulty communication of your ideas. On the other hand, skillful use of connotation can greatly enrich your ability to communicate accurately. For example, you would not refer to a public figure whom you admire and respect as a "politician," a term which suggests such qualities as insincerity and conniving for personal gain. The word *childish* is inappropriate when you mean "childlike"; and the adjective *thin* suggests something scanty or somehow not full enough (especially when describing a person's figure), but *slim* and *slender*, two words close to *thin* in literal meaning, imply grace and good proportion.

Again, your dictionary can provide these shades of meaning that will keep you from writing something far different from your intention and will help you develop a vocabulary you can use accurately.

GLOSSARY OF FAULTY DICTION

The following glossary should help you rid your speech and writing of many errors. The term **colloquial** means that an expression is characteristic of everyday speech. **Dialectal** means that an expression is peculiar to a particular place or class.

NOTE: Remember that colloquialisms, that is the language we use in our everyday conversations with friends and associates, are perfectly acceptable in informal writing and speech. The purpose of this Glossary of Faulty Diction is to point out expressions which should be avoided in formal writing of any kind.

Above. Avoid the use of *above* as a modifier in such phrases as *the **above** reference, the **above** names.* An exception to this rule is that the word is proper in legal documents.

Accept, Except. *To accept* is *to receive; to except* is *to make an exception of, to omit. Except* (as a preposition) means *with the exception of.*

Accidently. There is no such word. The correct form is *accidentally,* based on the adjective *accidental.*

A.D. This is an abbreviation of *Anno Domini* (in the year of our Lord). Strictly considered, it should be used only with a date: ***A.D.** 1492.* But it has recently come to mean *of the Christian era*, and expressions like *the fifth century **A.D.*** have become common. Here logic has bowed to usage.

Administrate. There is no such word. The verb is *administer*; the noun formed from it is *administration.*

Adverse, Averse. *Adverse* means *unfavorable: The weatherman forecast **adverse** conditions for the yacht race. Averse* means *opposed to: Mother was **averse** to our plans for ice skating at midnight.*

Affect, Effect. In common usage *affect* is a verb meaning *to influence, to have an effect upon* or *to like to have or use* (*He **affects** a gold-headed cane*) or *to pretend* (*She **affects** helplessness*). *Effect* is both verb and noun. *To effect* is *to produce, to bring about.* The noun *effect* is a *result*, a *consequence.*

Aggravate. Colloquial when used to mean *provoke* or *irritate. Aggravate* means to make *worse* (*The rainy weather **aggravated** his rheumatism*).

Agree to, Agree with. One agrees *to* a proposal but *with* a person. (*We **agree to** his suggestion that we go,* but *The boy did not **agree with** his father*).

Ain't. This form is occasionally defended as a contraction of *am not*, but even those who defend it do not use it in writing.

Alibi. Colloquial for *excuse*. In formal usage *alibi* has legal significance only and means a confirmation of one's absence from the scene of a crime at the time the crime was committed.

All ready, Already. *All ready* means simply that all are ready (*The players were **all ready***). *Already* means *previously* or *before now* (*He has **already** gone*).

All together, Altogether. *All together* means all of a number taken or considered together (*She invited them **all together***). *Altogether* means *entirely, completely* (*He was **altogether** wrong*).

Allusion, Illusion. An *allusion* is a reference to something that does not mention it specifically (*The quotation was an **allusion** to Shakespeare's* Macbeth). An *illusion* is a false or unreal impression of reality (*After his unkind treatment of the puppy Mildred lost her **illusions** about Arthur*).

Alright. This is not a possible alternate spelling for the words *all right*.

Alumnus, Alumna. *Alumnus* is masculine and has the plural *alumni*. *Alumna* is feminine and has the plural *alumnae.*

Among, Between. The common practice is to use *between* with two or more persons or objects (***between** a rock and a hard place*) and *among* with more than two (*The crew quarreled **among** themselves*). Exception: *The plane traveled **between*** *New York, Chicago, and Miami.* Here *among* would be absurd.

Anymore, Any more. The expression should be written as two words.

Anyone, Any One. *Anyone*, the indefinite pronoun, is one word. *Any one*, meaning any single person or any single thing, should be written as two words (***Any one** of your friends will be glad to help you.*)

Any place, No place. Dialectal corruptions of *anywhere* and *nowhere.*

Apt, Liable, Likely. *Apt* means *suitable, qualified, expert* (*an **apt** phrase, a man **apt** to succeed*). *Liable* means *exposed to something undesirable* (***liable** to be injured, **liable** for damages*). *Likely* means *credible, probable, probably* (*He had a **likely** excuse. Very **likely** it will rain*).

As far as. This expression is frequently misused when it is not followed by a clause (***As far as** her ability she is perfectly able to do the work*). It should always function as a subordinating conjunction, introducing both a subject and a verb (***As far as** her ability is concerned, she is perfectly able to do the work.*)

Asset. In its essential meaning this word is used in law and accounting (*His **assets** exceeded his liabilities*). But it seems to have established itself in the meaning of *something useful or desirable.* When used in this sense, it is frequently redundant.

Attend, Tend. *Attend* means *to be present at.* When meaning *to take care of*, it is followed by *to* (*He **attends to** his own business*). *Tend* without a preposition also means *to take care of* (*He **tends** his own garden*). *Tend to* means *to have a tendency to* (*She **tends to** become nervous when her children are noisy*).

Author, Host, Chair, Position. These nouns are frequently misused as verbs (*She has **authored** three best sellers, The Joneses plan to **host** a party for their friends, The woman who **chairs** the committee is a lawyer, Please **position** the chairs around the table.*). In these four sentences there are perfectly adequate verbs that should be used: *written, give, is* chairwoman of, and *place.*

Awful, Awfully. Either of these is colloquial when used to mean *very.*

Awhile, A While. *Awhile* is used as an adverb (*They stayed* ***awhile*** *at their friend's house*). When used after the preposition *for, while* is a noun, the object of the preposition (*I thought for* ***a while*** *that you were going to miss the plane*). The adverb is written as one word; the object of the preposition and its article are written as two.

Bad, Badly. *Bad* is an adjective, *badly* an adverb.

Balance. Except in accounting, the use of *balance* for *difference, remainder, the rest* is colloquial.

Being As. Dialectal for *since* or *because.*

Beside, Besides. *Beside* is a preposition meaning *by the side of* (*Along came a spider and sat down* ***beside*** *her*). *Besides* is a preposition meaning *except* (*He had nothing* ***besides*** *his good name*) and an adverb meaning *in addition, moreover* (*He received a medal and fifty dollars* ***besides***).

Blame On. Correct idiom calls for the use of *to blame* with *for,* not *on.* (*They* ***blamed*** *the driver* ***for*** *the accident,* not *They* ***blamed*** *the accident* ***on*** *the driver.*) *Blame on* is colloquial.

Boyfriend, Girlfriend. These two terms are colloquial, meaning *a favored male or female friend, a sweetheart.* If no other term seems appropriate, write them as two words: *boy friend, girl friend.*

Burst, Bursted, Bust. The principal parts of the verb *burst* are *burst, burst,* and *burst.* The use of *bursted* or *busted* for the past tense is incorrect. *Bust* is either sculpture or a part of the human body. Used for *failure* or as a verb for *burst* or *break*, it is slang.

But What. Use *that* or *but that* instead of *but what* (*They had no doubt* ***that*** *help would come*).

Cannot. This word is the negative form of *can*. It is written as one word.

Cannot Help But. This is a mixed construction. *Cannot help* and *cannot but* are separate expressions, either of which is correct (*He* ***cannot but*** *attempt it,* or *He* ***cannot help*** *attempting it*).

Capital, Capitol. *Capital* is a city; *capitol* is a building. *Capital* is also an adjective, usually meaning *chief, excellent.*

Case. This is a vague and unnecessary word in many of its common uses today. Avoid *case* and seek the exact word.

Calvary, Cavalry. Mistakes here are chiefly a matter of spelling, but it is important to be aware of the difference: *Calvary* is the name of the hill where Jesus was crucified; *cavalry* refers to troops trained to fight on horseback, or more recently in armored vehicles.

Chairperson. Use the terms *chairman* and *chairwoman* in preference to *chairperson,* which should be used only if it is an official title in an organization or if you are quoting directly someone who has used the term.

Claim. Do not use simply to mean *say*. In the correct use of claim some disputed right is involved (*He* ***claims*** *to be the heir of a very wealthy man*).

Complement, Compliment. In its usual sense *complement* means *something that completes* (*Her navy blue shoes and bag were a* ***complement*** *for her gray suit*). A *compliment* is an expression of courtesy or praise (*My* ***compliments*** *to the chef*).

Connotate. There is no such verb as *connotate*; the verb is *connote,* and its noun form is *connotation.*

Considerable. This word is an adjective meaning *worthy of consideration, important* (*The idea is at least* ***considerable***). When used to denote a great deal or a great many, *considerable* is colloquial or informal.

Contact. Colloquial and sometimes vague when used for *see, meet, communicate with*, as in *I must **contact** my agent.*

Continual, Continuous. *Continual* means *repeated often* (*The interruptions were **continual***). *Continuous* means *going on without interruption* (*For two days the pain was **continuous***).

Convince, Persuade. Do not use *convince* for *persuade* as in *I **convinced** him to wash the dishes. Convince* means *to overcome doubt* (*I **convinced** him of the soundness of my plan*). *Persuade* means *to win over by argument or entreaty* (*I **persuaded** him to wash the dishes*).

Couple. This word, followed by *of* is informal for *two* or *a few.*

Credible, Creditable. *Credible* mean *believable* (*His evidence was not **credible***). *Creditable* means *deserving esteem or admiration* (*The acting of the male lead was a **creditable** performance*).

Critique. This word is a noun, not a verb; it means a critical review or comment dealing with an artistic work. The verb form is *criticize.*

Cupfuls, Cupsful. The plural of cupful is *cupfuls,* not *cupsful.*

Data. *Data* is the plural of *datum, something given or known.* It usually refers to a body of facts or figures. It normally takes a plural verb (*These **data** are important*). At times, however, *data* may be considered a collective noun and used with a singular verb.

Definitely. This is frequently used to mean *very* or *quite*. It is a trite expression and should be avoided for this reason as well as for its lack of accuracy.

Different Than. Most good writers use *different from*, not *different than.*

Disinterested. Often confused with *uninterested. Disinterested* means *unbiased, impartial; uninterested* means *lacking interest in.*

Don't. A contraction of *do not.* Do not write *he, she,* or *it don't.*

Drapes. Incorrect when used as a noun to mean *curtains. Drape* is the verb; *draperies* is the correct noun form.

Due To. Do not use *due to* for *because of* as in ***Due to** a lengthy illness, he left college. Due to* is correctly used after a noun or linking verb (*His failure, **due to** laziness, was not surprising. The accident was **due to** carelessness*).

Dyeing, Dying. *Dyeing* refers to the coloring of materials with dye. Do not omit the *e*, which would confuse the word with *dying*, meaning *expiring.*

Emigrant, Immigrant. A person who moves from one place to another is both an *emigrant* and an *immigrant*, but he emigrates *from* one place and immigrates *to* the other.

Equally As. Do not use these two words together; omit either *equally* or *as*. Do not write *Water is **equally as** necessary as air*; write *Water is **as** necessary as air* or *Water and air are **equally** necessary.*

Enthuse, Enthused. These words are colloquial and always unacceptable in writing.

Etc. An abbreviation of Latin *et* (*and*) and *cetera* (*other things*). It should not be preceded by *and*, nor should it be used as a catch-all expression to avoid a clear and exact ending of an idea or a sentence.

Everyday, Every day. When written as one word (*everyday*), this expression is an adjective (*Mother's **everyday** china is ironstone*). When used adverbially to indicate how often something happens, it is written as two words (***Every day** at noon I eat an apple and drink a glass of milk*).

Exam. A colloquial abbreviation for *examination.* Compare *gym, dorm, lab,* and *prof.*

Expect. This word means *to look forward to* or *foresee.* Do not use it to mean *suspect* or *suppose.*

Fact That. This is an example of wordiness, usually amounting to redundancy. Most sentences can omit the phrase *the fact that* without changing the sense of what is said (***The fact that** he wanted a new bicycle was the reason why he stole the money* may be effectively reduced to *He stole the money because he wanted a new bicycle*). Whenever you are tempted to use this expression, try rewording the sentence without it, and you will have a more concise and a clearer statement.

Farther, Further. The two words are often confused. *Farther* means *at or to a more distant point in space or time; further* means *to a greater extent, in addition.* One says *It is **farther** to Minneapolis from Chicago than from here*, but *We will talk **further** about this tomorrow.*

Faze. Colloquial for *to disturb* to *to agitate.* Most commonly used in the negative (*Mother's angry looks didn't **faze** Jimmy*).

Feel. *Feel* means to perceive through the physical senses or through the emotions. This word should not be used as a careless equivalent of *think* or *believe,* both of which refer to mental activity.

Fellow. Colloquial when used to mean a *person.*

Fewer, Less. Use *fewer* to refer to a number, *less* to refer to amount (*Where there are **fewer** persons, there is **less** noise*).

Fine. Colloquial when used as a term of general approval.

Fix. *Fix* is a verb, meaning *to make firm or stable.* Used as a noun meaning *a bad condition* or a verb meaning *to repair,* it is colloquial.

Flaunt, flout. *Flaunt* means *to exhibit ostentatiously, to show off* (*She **flaunted** her new mink coat before her friends*). *Flout* means to show *contempt for, to scorn* (*Margaret often **flouts** the rules of good sportsmanship*).

Forego, Forgo. *Forego* means to *precede* or *go before* (*The **foregoing** data were gathered two years ago. Forgo* means *to give up, relinquish* (*I am afraid I must **forgo** the pleasure of meeting your friends today*).

Formally, Formerly. *Formally* means *in a formal manner* (*He was **formally** initiated into his fraternity last night*). *Formerly* means *at a former time* (*They **formerly** lived in Ohio*).

Gentlemen, Lady. Do not use these words as synonyms for *man* and *woman.*

Got. This is a correct past participle of the verb *to get* (*He had **got** three traffic tickets in two days*). *Gotten* is an alternative past participle of *to get*.

Guess. Colloquial when used for *suppose* or *believe.*

Guy. Slang when used for *boy* or *man.*

Hanged, Hung. *Hanged* is the correct past tense or past participle of *hang* when capital punishment is meant (*The cattle rustlers were **hanged** at daybreak*). *Hung* is the past tense and past participle in every other sense of the term (*We **hung** popcorn and cranberries on the Christmas tree*).

Hardly, Scarcely. Do not use with a negative. *I **can't hardly** see it* borders on the illiterate. Write *I **can hardly** see it* or (if you cannot see it at all) *I **can't** see it.*

Healthful, Healthy. Places are *healthful* if persons may be *healthy* living in them.

Hopefully. This word means *in a hopeful manner* (*She **hopefully** began getting ready for her blind date*). Do not use this modifer to mean *it is hoped* or *let us hope* (***Hopefully**, the new rail system for Atlanta will be completed within five years*).

If, Whether. In careful writing do not use *if* for *whether. Let me know **if** you are coming* does not mean exactly the same thing as *Let me know **whether** you are coming.* The latter leaves no doubt that a reply is expected.

Imply, Infer. *Imply* means *to suggest, to express indirectly. Infer* means *to conclude*, as on the basis of suggestion or implication. A writer *implies* to a reader; a reader *infers* from a writer.

Incidently. There is no such word. The correct form is *incidentally*, based on the adjective *incidental.*

Into, In To. *Into* is a preposition meaning *toward the inside* and is followed by an object of the preposition. Do not use the one-word form of this expression when the object of the preposition is the object of *to* only, and *in* is an adverbial modifier. Say *He went **into** the building* but *The men handed their application forms **in to** the personnel manager.*

Irregardless. No such word exists. *Regardless* is the correct word.

Its, It's. The form *its* is possessive (*Every dog has **its** day*). *It's* is a contraction of *it is* (***It's** a pity she's a bore*).

It's Me. Formal English requires *It is I. It's **me*** is informal or colloquial, perfectly acceptable in conversation but not proper fɒr written English. Compare the French idiom *C'est moi.*

Kid. Used to mean a child or young person, *kid* is slang.

Kind, Sort. These are singular forms and should be modified accordingly (*this kind, that sort*). *Kinds* and *sorts* are plural, and they, of course, have plural modifiers.

Kind Of, Sort Of. Do not use these to mean *rather* as in *He was **kind of*** (or ***sort of***) *lazy.*

Last, Latest. *Last* implies that there will be no more. *Latest* does not prevent the possibility of another appearance later. The proper sense of both is seen in the sentence *After seeing his **latest** play, we hope that it is his **last**.*

Lend, Loan. The use of *loan* as a verb is incorrect. *Loan* is a noun. The distinction between the two words may be seen in the sentence *If you will **lend** me ten dollars until Friday, I will appreciate the **loan**.*

Like, As. Confusion in the use of these two words results from using *like* as a conjunction. The preposition *like* should be followed by an object (*He ran **like** an antelope*). The conjunction *as* is followed by a clause (*He did **as** he wished, He talked **as** though he were crazy*). The incorrect use of *as* as a preposition is a kind of reaction against the use of *like* as a conjunction. Consider the sentence: *Many species of oaks, **as** the red oak, the white oak, the water oak, are found in the Southeast.* Here the correct word is *like*, not *as.*

Literally. The word means *faithfully, to the letter, letter for letter, exactly.* Do not use in the sense of *completely*, or *in effect.* A sentence may be copied *literally*; but one never, except under extraordinary circumstances, ***literally** devours a book.* Frequently, the word *virtually*, meaning *in effect or essence, though not in fact,* is the correct word.

Lot, Lots. Colloquial or informal when used to mean *many* or *much.*

Mad. The essential meaning of *mad* is *insane.* When used to mean *angry,* it is informal.

May Be, Maybe. *May be* is a verb phrase (*It **may be** that you are right*). *Maybe* used as an an adverb means *perhaps* (***Maybe** you are right*).

Mean. Used for disagreeable (*He has a **mean** disposition, He is **mean** to me*), the word is informal or colloquial.

Media. *Media* is the plural of *medium, a means, agency,* or *instrumentality.* It is often incorrectly used in the plural as though it were singular, as in *The **media** is playing an important role in political races this year.*

Midnight, Noon. Neither of these words needs the word *twelve* before it. They themselves refer to specific times, so *twelve* is redundant.

Most. Do not use for *almost.* ***Almost** all of them are here* or ***Most** of them are here* is correct. ***Most all** of them are here* is incorrect.

Muchly. There is no such word as *muchly. Much* is both adjective and adverb (***Much** water has flowed over the dam, Thank you very **much***). Compare *thusly.*

Mutual. The use of *mutual* for *common* is usually avoided by careful writers. ***Common** knowledge, **common** property, **common** dislikes* are things shared by two or more persons. ***Mutual** admiration* means *admiration of each for the other.*

Myself. Colloquial when used as a substitute for *I* or *me*, as in *He and **myself*** were there. It is correctly used intensively (*I **myself** shall do it*) and reflexively (*I blame only **myself***).

Nice. *Nice* is a catch-all word that has lost its force because it has no clearcut, specific meaning as a modifier. When writing in praise of something, select an adjective that conveys more specific information than *nice* does.

Of. Unnecessary after such prepositions as *off, inside, outside* (not *He fell **off of** the cliff* but *He fell **off** the cliff*).

On Account Of. Do not use as a conjunction; the phrase should be followed by an object of the preposition *of* (***on account of** his illness*). *He was absent **on account of** he was sick* is bad grammar.

Oral, Verbal, Written. Use *oral* to refer to spoken words (*An **oral** examination is sometimes nerve-wracking for a student*); use *verbal* to contrast a communication in words to some other kind of communication (*His scowl told me more than any **verbal** message could*); use *written* when referring to anything put on paper.

Orientate. There is no such word. The verb is *orient*, meaning *to cause to become familiar with or adjusted to facts or a situation* (*He **oriented** himself by finding the North Star*). The noun is *orientation.*

Over With. The *with* in unnecessary in such expression as *The game was **over with** by five o'clock.*

Party. Colloquial when used to mean *a person.* Properly used in legal documents (***party** of the first part*).

Peeve. Either as a verb or noun, *peeve* is informal diction.

Personally. This word is often redundant and is a hackneyed, sometimes irritating expression, as in ***Personally**, I think you are making a big mistake.*

Plan On. Omit *on*. In standard practice idiom calls for an infinitive or a direct object after *plan. They **planned** to go* or *They **planned** a reception* are both correct usage.

Plenty. This word is a noun, not an adverb. Do not write *He was **plenty** worried.*

Pore, Pour. *Pore,* meaning *to meditate* or *to study intently and with steady application,* is a verb used with the preposition *over*. (*She **pored over** her chemistry assignment for several hours.*) It should not be confused with *pour*, meaning *to set a liquid flowing or falling.* (*They **poured** the tea into fragile china cups*.)

Principal, Principle. *Principal* is both adjective and noun (***principal** parts, **principal** of the school, **principal** and interest*). *Principle* is a noun only (***principles** of philosophy, a man of **principle***).

Pupil, Student. School children in the elementary grades are called *pupils*; in grades nine through twelve *student* or *pupil* is correct; for college the term must always be *student.*

Quite. The word means *altogether, entirely* (*He was **quite** exhausted from his exertion*). It is colloquial when used for *moderately* or *very* and in expressions like ***quite** a few, **quite** a number.*

Quote, Quotation. *Quote* is a verb and should not be used as a noun, as in *The **quote** you gave is from Shakespeare, not the Bible.*

Real. Do not use for *really. Real* is an adjective; *really* is an adverb (*The **real** gems are **really** beautiful*).

Reason Is Because. This is not idiomatic English. The subject-linking verb construction calls for a predicate nominative, but *because* is a subordinating conjunction that introduces an adverbial clause. Write *The **reason** I was late **is that** I had an accident,* not *The **reason** I was late **is because** I had an accident.*

Respectfully, Respectively. *Respectfully* means *with respect*, as in *The young used to act **respectfully** toward their elders. Respectively* is a word seldom needed; it means *in the order designated*, as in *The men and women took their seats on the right and left **respectively**.*

Reverend. This word, like *Honorable,* is not a noun, but an honorific adjective. It is not a title like *doctor* or *president.* It is properly used preceding *Mr.* or the given name or initials, as in *the **Reverend** Mr. Gilbreath, the **Reverend** Earl Gilbreath, the **Reverend** J. E. Gilbreath.* To use the word as a title as in ***Reverend**, will you lead us in prayer*? or *Is there a **Reverend** in the house*? is plainly absurd. ***Reverend** Gilbreath* instead of *the **Reverend** Mr. Gilbreath* is almost as bad.

Right. In the sense of *very* or *extremely, right* is colloquial. Do not write (or say) *I'm **right** glad to know you.*

Same. The word is an adjective, not a pronoun. Do not use it as in *We received your order and will give **same** immediate attention.* Substitute *it* for *same.*

Savings. This word is frequently misused in the plural when the singular is the correct form. It is particularly puzzling that many people use this plural with a singular article, as in *The ten per cent discount gives you a **savings** of nine dollars. A saving* is the proper usage here. Another common error occurs in reference to *Daylight **Saving** Time*; the right form again is *Saving*, not *Savings.*

Shape. In formal writing do not use *shape* for *condition* as in *He played badly because he was in poor **shape**.* In this sense *shape* is informal.

Situation. This is another catch-all term, frequently used redundantly, as in *It was a fourth down **situation**.* Fourth down *is* a situation, so the word itself is repetitious. This vague term can usually be omitted or replaced with a more specific word.

Should Of, Would Of. Do not use these terms for *should have, would have.*

So, Such. Avoid the use of *so* and *such* for *very,* as in *Thank you **so** much; you are **such** a darling.* These words are subordinating conjunctions, calling for a dependent clause expressing result, as in *He was **so** late **that** the others left without him*, or *Her hair was **such** a mess **that** she could not go to the party.*

Some. Do not use for *somewhat,* as in *She is **some** better after her illness.*

Species. This word is both singular and plural. One may speak of *one species* or *three species.* The word usually refers to a kind of plant or animal.

Sprightly, Spritely. *Sprightly* means *animated, vivacious, lively.* There is no such word as *spritely,* but many people use this term, probably because it suggests the word *sprite,* an *elf* or *fairy.* Do not write *her **spritely** conversation was fascinating.*

Stationary, Stationery. *Stationary* means *fixed, not moving.* Remember that *stationery,* which is paper for writing letters, is sold by a *stationer.*

Statue, Stature, Statute. A *statue* is a piece of sculpture. *Stature* is bodily height, often used figuratively to mean *level of achievement, status,* or *importance.* A *statute* is a law or regulation.

Strata. This is the plural of the Latin *stratum.* One speaks of *a stratum* of rock but of *several strata.*

Super, Fantastic, Incredible, etc. When used to describe something exciting or marvelous, these overworked words actually add little to our everyday conversation because they have lost their original force. At any rate, they must never be a part of written formal English, as they are simply slang, and trite slang at that.

Suppose, Supposed. Many people incorrectly use the first form *suppose* before an infinitive when the second form *supposed* is needed, as in *Am I **suppose** to meet you at five o'clock?* The past participle *supposed* must go along with the auxiliary verb *am* to form the passive voice. This error almost certainly arises from an inability to hear the final *d* when it precedes the *t* in the *to* of the infinitive. The correct form is *Am I **supposed** to meet you at five o'clock?*

Sure, Surely. Do not use the adjective *sure* for the adverb *surely. I am **sure** that you are right* and *I am **surely** glad to be here* are correct.

Trustee, Trusty. The word *trustee* means *a person elected or appointed to direct funds or policy* for a person or an institution, as in *Mr. Higginbotham is a **trustee** on the bank's board of directors.* A *trusty*, on the other hand, is a prisoner granted special privileges because he is believed trustworthy, as in *Although he was a **trusty**, Harris escaped from prison early today.*

Too. *Too* means *in addition,* or *excessively.* It is incorrect to use the word to mean *very* or *very much*, as in *I was not **too** impressed with her latest book* or *I'm afraid I don't know him **too** well.*

Toward, Towards. The first form is greatly preferred over the second.

Try And. Use *try to*, not *try and*, in such expressions as ***Try to** get here on time* (not ***Try and** get here on time*).

Type. Colloquial in expressions like *this **type** book;* write *this **type of** book.*

Undoubtably, Undoubtedly. There is no such word as *undoubtably.* The correct word is *undoubtedly.*

Unique. If referring to something as the only one of its kind, you may correctly use *unique.* (*The Grand Canyon is a **unique** geological formation.*) The word does not mean *rare, strange,* or *remarkable,* and there are no degrees of *uniqueness*; to say that something is *the **most unique** thing one has ever seen* is faulty diction.

Use (Used) To Could. Do not use for *once could* or *used to be able to.*

Very. Do not use as a modifier of a past participle, as in ***very** broken.* English idiom calls for ***badly** broken* or ***very badly** broken.*

Wait For, Wait On. To *wait for* means *to look forward to, to expect* (*For two hours I have **waited for** you*). *To wait on* means *to serve* (*The butler and two maids **waited on** the guests at dinner*).

Want In, Want Off, Want Out. These forms are dialectal. Do not use them for *want to come in, want to get off, want to get out.*

Way. Colloquial when used for *away* as in ***Way** down upon the Swanee River.*

Ways. Colloquial when used for *way* as in *a long **ways** to go.*

Whose, Who's. The possesive form is *whose* (***Whose** book is this*?). *Who's* is a contraction of *who is* (***Who's** at the door*?). The use of *whose* as a neuter possessive is confirmed by the history of the word and the practice of good writers. *The house **whose** roof is leaking* is more natural and less clumsy than *the house the roof **of which** is leaking.*

Your, You're. The possessive form is *your* (*Tell me **your** name*). *You're* is a contraction of *you are.*

Exercise 85 DICTION

Rewrite the following sentences, reducing wordiness as much as possible.

EXAMPLE: In terms of his intelligence it is my opinion that Sam quite probably believes himself to be far superior in mentality than he actually is.

I think that Sam probably considers himself to be more intelligent than he is.

(Note that only one correct version of each sentence is given in the answer section.)

Answers	Sentences
	1. If you will repeat that poem again, Mary, I will be able to recall it to my memory and recite it for the whole entire class tomorrow.
1. If you will repeat that poem, Mary, I will be able to recite it for the entire class tomorrow.	2. Her pants suit, which is purple in color with pink trim adorning the jacket, is absolutely the ugliest outfit I have ever seen in all the days of my life without a doubt.
2. Her purple pants suit with pink trim on the jacket is undoubtedly the ugliest outfit I have ever seen.	3. Tom and Suzanne went to the grocery store, and then they went to the drug store for cough drops, and then they drove home by way of Aunt Annie's house.
3. After going to the grocery store, Tom and Suzanne picked up cough drops at the drugstore and drove home by Aunt Annie's house.	4. Although both authors are regional writers concerned with the South, the fictional works of William Faulkner and Thomas Wolfe are quite different from each other in the case of their structure, their subject matter, and their style.

4. Although both authors are concerned with the South, the fiction of William Faulkner and that of Thomas Wolfe are different in structure, subject and style.

5. In Martha's case her normal voice is perfectly audible to my ears, but she insists upon shouting loudly when she speaks.

5. Although Martha's normal voice is audible to me, she insists upon shouting.

6. I ate very little when I was at dinner because of the fact that I had had a great deal to eat at lunchtime.

6. I ate very little dinner because I had had a large lunch.

7. Mark was given the choice of selecting a blue blazer or a brown one, and he said that the situation was really a dilemma.

7. Mark said that having to choose between a blue blazer and a brown one presented a dilemma.

8. As a rule we usually go swimming about nine a.m. every morning, but in my judgment I think we should go earlier.

8. We usually go swimming about nine every morning, but I think we should go earlier.

9. The fundamental principles on which this country of ours was founded are frequently ignored in this modern world of today.

9. The principles on which our country was founded are frequently ignored today.

10. The man's heroic courage has been an important factor in his extreme popularity with people.

10. The man's courage has been a factor in his popularity.

SCORE ______

Exercise 86 DICTION

Rewrite the following sentences, reducing wordiness as much as possible.

EXAMPLE: In most cases people are usually sympathetic and feel sorry for poor people who are financially distressed.

Most people are sympathetic with the poor.

(Note that only one correct version of each sentence is given in the answer section.)

	1. In order to create a meaningful classroom situation, a teacher must use every possible means available to see that in all circumstances her students are aware of the fact that she is in control.
1. An effective teacher must show her students that she controls the classroom.	2. One important essential factor in the matter of highway accidents is the drinking done by drunk drivers.
2. An essential factor in highway accidents is drunk drivers.	3. Reference was made by the speaker to the present-day modern trend of popular musicians to revert back to the beginning origins of jazz for much of their music.
3. The speaker mentioned the present-day trend of popular musicians to revert to the origins of jazz for their music.	4. It is said that Dr. Samuel Johnson was a man physically large in frame and that his intellect was equally as large as his body.

4. Reportedly, Dr. Samuel Johnson was a man equally large in body and intellect.	5. In considering all the circumstances of your situation, George, I am taking into account all aspects of your predicament, and I am evaluating the whole affair objectively and without bias.
5. George, I am considering all aspects of your predicament in order to evaluate it objectively.	6. We have concluded that in the event that Helen is unable to sit with the baby, the decision will be made to take him to accompany us to the drive-in movie.
6. If Helen cannot sit with the baby, we will take him with us to the drive-in movie.	7. Dr. Johnstone is a well-known and famous expert in the field of horticulture, and he will be a valuable asset to our faculty.
7. Dr. Johnstone, a famous horticulturalist, will be valuable to our faculty.	8. Billy thought that it was far more preferable to be honest and forthright than to win the praise and acclaim of his friends through trickery.
8. Billy preferred being honest to winning his friends' praise through trickery.	9. Thad and Sue wanted to return back to the town where they had seen the motel, but Frank and Ginny thought it better to forge ahead by pushing forward.

9. Although Thad and Sue wanted to return to the town where they had seen the motel, Frank and Ginny preferred to push ahead.	10. The crowd was so large in number that it took several police officers to control the situation, but in time they eventually calmed things down.
10. Several police officers were needed to control the large crowd and eventually calm things down.	SCORE ______

Exercise 87 DICTION

The following sentences contain one or more trite expressions (**T**) or euphemisms (**E**). Underline the offending phrases and write **T** and/or **E** after each sentence.

EXAMPLE: Mr. Franklin introduced us to his better half, who he says wears the pants in the family.

Mr. Franklin introduced us to his better half, who he says wears the pants in the family. **T, T**

1. The sight-seeing bus took us through an area of sub-standard housing, where we saw many individuals who were obviously down on their luck.

---

1. The sight-seeing bus took us through an area of sub-standard housing, where we saw many individuals who were obviously down on their luck. E, T

2. As jealousy reared its ugly head, dissension between the two factions grew by leaps and bounds.

---

2. As jealousy reared its ugly head, dissension between the two factions grew by leaps and bounds. T, T

3. Tim has been deviating from the truth; I am shocked that he would pull the wool over my eyes.

---

3. Tim has been deviating from the truth; I am shocked that he would pull the wool over my eyes. E, T

4. Foster said that the pizza and strawberry ice cream that he ate last night gave him a pain in his tummy.

---

4. Foster said that the pizza and strawberry ice cream that he ate last night gave him a pain in his tummy. E

5. The powers that be gave Maria notice that they would ask for her resignation if she continues to use the phone during business hours.

---

5. The powers that be gave Maria notice that they would ask for her resignation if she continues to use the phone during business hours. T, E

6. Far be it from me to criticize, Dorothy, but it is a crying shame that you refuse to answer when opportunity knocks.

6. Far be it from me to criticize, Dorothy, but it is a crying shame that you refuse to answer when opportunity knocks. T, T, T	7. Both of Lucile's parents have passed away within the last year; they are gone but not forgotten.
7. Both of Lucile's parents have passed away within the last year; they are gone but not forgotten. E, T	8. Her son's teacher said that the boy is an under-achiever who lacks adequate motivation.
8. Her son's teacher said that the boy is an under-achiever who lacks adequate motivation. E, E	9. That lecture last night was as dull as dishwater, but all was not lost; I met a girl who is as pretty as a picture.
9. That lecture last night was as dull as dishwater, but all was not lost; I met a girl who is as pretty as a picture. T, T, T	10. The young man's advanced state of inebriation did not escape the eagle eye of his date's father.
10. The young man's advanced state of inebriation did not escape the eagle eye of his date's father. E, T	11. The pompous news secretary replied to the reporters that last week's statement was inoperative.
11. The pompous news secretary replied to the reporters that last week's statement was inoperative. E	12. Henry has always been Fran's ardent admirer, and he is on cloud nine since she has consented to be his blushing bride.
12. Henry has always been Fran's ardent admirer, and he is on cloud nine since she has consented to be his blushing bride. T, T, T	13. There is going to be a blessed event in the Garrett household next spring; it goes without saying that the whole family will be delighted to welcome the little stranger.
13. There is going to be a blessed event in the Garrett household next spring; it goes without saying that the whole family will be delighted to welcome the little stranger. E, T, T,	14. After the fire the building superintendent worked like a beaver to clean up the mess, but, let's face it, Rome was not built in a day.

14. After the fire the building super-intendent worked like a beaver to clean up the mess, but, let's face it, Rome was not built in a day. E, T, T, T	15. There was a breathless silence as everyone waited for the woman to reveal her deep, dark secret, but we were doomed to disappointment when she suddenly beat a hasty retreat.
15. There was a breathless silence as everyone waited for the woman to reveal her deep, dark secret, but we were doomed to disappointment when she suddenly beat a hasty retreat. T, T, T, T	SCORE ______

Exercise 88	DICTION

The following sentences contain unidiomatic uses of prepositions. Underline each preposition that is incorrectly used and write the correct form.

EXAMPLE: Marcus finally prevailed with Louise to go to the hockey match.

Marcus finally prevailed with Louise to go to the hockey match. *on*

	1. Father has repeatedly told Frank not to aim the gun to anyone.
1. Father has repeatedly told Frank not to aim the gun to anyone. *toward* or *at*	2. Nell walked in the house and sat down wearily into the big wing chair.
2. Nell walked in the house and sat down wearily into the big wing chair. *into, in*	3. Katy has been listening at that same BeeGees recording for forty-five minutes.
3. Katy has been listening at that same BeeGees recording for forty-five minutes. *to*	4. I know it is hard, Melissa, but I think that you must comply to your mother's wishes.
4. I know it is hard, Melissa, but I think that you must comply to your mother's wishes. *with*	5. Walter expects around a hundred people to attend his party.
5. Walter expects around a hundred people to attend his party. *about*	6. Come and sit besides me and tell me about your trip along the Appalachian Trail.
6. Come and sit besides me and tell me about your trip along the Appalachian Trail. *beside*	7. Almost every citizen in town is complaining at the litter on the downtown streets.

7. Almost every citizen in town is complaining at the litter on the downtown streets. *about*	8. Tony asked whether everyone was aware about the change in plans for the dedication ceremony.
8. Tony asked whether everyone was aware about the change in plans for the dedication ceremony. *of*	9. Apart to all his other problems Sonny has failed chemistry again.
9. Apart to all his other problems Sonny has failed chemistry again. *from*	10. I was surprised that Frederick was guilty in being ungentlemanly.
10. I was surprised that Frederick was guilty in being ungentlemanly. *of*	SCORE ______

Exercise 89 DICTION

The following exercises are based on the Glossary of Faulty Diction. Underline all errors and colloquialisms (informal expressions) and write first the original form and then the correct form for formal writing.

EXAMPLE: Most people are enthused about new civic projects irregardless of the costs until their taxes are raised.

enthused *enthusiastic*
irregardless *regardless*

	1. Joanne's jogging program has had a wonderful affect on her health.
1. affect *effect*	2. Flannery O'Connor authored a great many short stories but only two novels.
2. authored *wrote*	3. It was awfully hot at the football game; I know the players couldn't hardly stand the heat.
3. awfully *very* or *quite* couldn't hardly *could hardly*	4. I was ready to leave school a couple of months ago, but now that I am doing good in calculus, I plan to complete the year's work.
4. a couple of *two* good *well*	5. The recipe calls for two cupsful of flour, which I had to run next door to borrow from Myra.
5. cupsful *cupfuls*	6. My wife and I feel that the speed limit of fifty-five miles per hour is a muchly needed way of preventing accidents.

6. feel *think* or *believe* muchly *much*	7. Lucy and myself had planned on spending at least two hours shopping, so we were aggravated when Mother said we had to be home by four.
7. myself *I* planned on spending *planned to spend* aggravated *irritated* or *annoyed*	8. The principle of our high school will be the principal speaker at the two-day conference on public education.
8. principle *principal*	9. I personally prefer white stationary to green.
9. personally omit as redundant after *I* stationary *stationery*	10. Many people think that the media is responsible for increased crime in the streets; the last report on the subject provides convincing data.
10. media is *media are* last *latest*	11. The reason that I trade with Scott's grocery store is because it offers a big savings in canned goods.
11. The reason . . . is because *The reason . . . is that* a savings *a saving*	12. It is hard to tell whose going to win the election; I sure wouldn't want to bet on the outcome.
12. whose *who's* sure *surely*	13. Mother wasn't too pleased with the way her waffles turned out, but no one made an averse comment about them.
13. too *very* averse *adverse*	14. Annie doesn't live here anymore; were you formally her friend?

14. anymore *any more* formally *formerly*	15. The old house sat in it's desolate grounds, undoubtably ready to tumble down before long.
15. it's *its* undoubtably *undoubtedly*	SCORE ______

Exercise 90 DICTION

Underline all errors and colloquialisms in the following sentences and write first the original form and then the correct or preferred form.

EXAMPLE: Ted finished last in the race on account of he had sprained his ankle on the second lap.

on account of *because*

	1. I was suppose to meet Sara Jane at twelve noon, incidently, but she was thirty minutes late.
1. suppose *supposed* twelve noon omit *twelve* as redundant (*noon* is a specific time) incidently *incidentally*	2. Even as a kid, William used to pour over books about astronauts and space travel.
2. kid *child* pour *pore*	3. Hopefully, you will not have to forego your plans to visit Istanbul next spring.
3. Hopefully *I hope that* forego *forgo*	4. She tried to persuade me that she is going to study harder, but I am sort of doubtful that she will.
4. persuade *convince* sort of *rather*	5. Marcia isn't sure if she can meet us at the restaurant; it may take her too long to select the new drapes.
5. if *whether* drapes *draperies*	6. The man has flaunted the rules of ethical conduct; he is literally a beast.

6. flaunted *flouted* literally *virtually* or *essentially*	7. You are likely to be criticized if you blame all your misfortunes on other people.
7. likely *liable* blame . . . people *blame other people for your misfortunes*	8. Her bright green shoes made an interesting compliment to her navy dress; I expect she was the best dressed person there.
8. compliment *complement* expect *suppose* or *believe*	9. Far less people are smoking now than several years ago; most everyone I know has stopped.
9. less *fewer* most *almost*	10. When the service was over with, Reverend Slope greeted everyone at the church door; he is a right friendly man.
10. over with *over* Reverend Slope *the Reverend Mr. Slope* right *very* or *quite*	11. The gentleman who delivers our newspaper is the brother of the lady who works at the bakery.
11. gentleman *man* lady *woman*	12. It is a long ways to you're house, isn't it, Margaret?
12. ways *way* you're *your*	13. The plane was in a holding situation over Denver, and the guy sitting next to me was growing more and more nervous.

13. in a holding situation omit in a . . . situation and say, *The plane was holding* guy *man*	14. Whoever forgot to put the roast in the refrigerator ought to be hung at sunrise; I cannot help but think that it was Joe.
14. hung *hanged* help but think *help thinking*	15. Since Mrs. Reginald Pettibone was elected chairperson of the program committee, she has become all together insufferable.
15. chairperson *chairwoman* all together *altogether*	16. As far as being healthy, the climate of Arizona is definitely the best to be found.
16. As far as *As far as . . . is concerned,* healthy *healthful* definitely *quite*	17. The two sisters quarreled among themselves because of the fact that Jennie would not loan Henrietta her pink blouse.
17. among *between* because of the fact that *because* loan *lend*	18. Is it alright with you if I stay after class for awhile to ask you about conjugation, Mrs. Hardy?
18. alright *all right* awhile *a while*	19. Being as you claim that you saw them talking together, I guess they must have resolved their differences.
19. Being as *Since* claim *say* guess *suppose*	20. Frost's illusion in his poem to a passage from Shakespeare infers a certain attitude towards death.
20. illusion *allusion* infers *implies*	**SCORE** ______

Exercise 91	DICTION

Underline all errors, colloquialisms, and trite expressions in the following sentences; write first the original form and then the correct or preferred form.

EXAMPLE: Rob was green with envy when he saw my new plaid slacks, so he will probably try and get some like them.

green with envy *envious*
try and *try to*

	1. Slowly but surely it dawned on us that the contest would prove the survival of the fittest.
1. Slowly but surely *Finally* or *Eventually* it dawned on us *we realized* survival of the fittest *that the strongest competitor wins*	2. I used to could jog five miles a day when I was in shape, but now I'm as limp as a dishrag after two miles.
2. used to could *once could* or *used to be able to* in shape *in good physical condition* limp as a dishrag *tired and weak*	3. Liz is a very unique person; she is certainly off the beaten track in her attitudes toward politics and religion.
3. very unique *unique* off the beaten track *different from most people*	4. We received Uncle Charlie's package yesterday, and I immediately wrote a letter to thank him for same.
4. same *it*	5. Lily May plays poker like she has been playing all her life, but she vows she is a real babe in the woods.

5. like *as though* babe in the woods *inexperienced*	6. Lots of times James goes farther than he should in telling it like it is.
6. Lots of *many* farther *further* telling it like it is *being forthright*	7. No one was the worse for wear after the frightening experience, but I have a sneaking suspicion that from now on Charlotte will tend to her own business.
7. was the worse for wear *suffered any ill effects* have a sneaking suspicion *secretly suspect* tend to *tend* or *mind*	8. The McPhersons hosted a wonderful gathering in their home last night, and a good time was had by all.
8. hosted *were hosts at* a good time was had by all *everyone greatly enjoyed it*	9. In Tallahassee, Florida, the capital building is a handsome one.
9. capital *capitol*	10. Frank is an alumni of Duke University; in fact, he is the proud possessor of a degree in accounting from there.
10. alumni *alumnus* is the proud possessor *has*	11. Her alibi for being late is that she accidently lost her car keys.

11. alibi *excuse* accidently *acci-dentally*	12. To make a long story short, Fred, we cannot except your resignation at this point in time because we have no one to replace you.
12. To make a long story short *To be brief* or *To put it briefly* except *accept* at this point in time *now*	13. You are apt to end in the depths of despair, Susie, if you won't agree with the suggestion your father has made.
13. apt *liable* the depths of despair *despair* agree with *agree to*	14. Harry bursted into the room, yelling bloody murder, and we couldn't make heads or tails of what he was trying to say.
14. bursted *burst* bloody murder *hysterically* make heads or tails of *understand* or *figure out*	15. Uncle Andrew is a colonel in the calvary, but in this modern day and age the calvary uses mechanized vehicles instead of horses.
15. calvary *cavalry* in this modern day and age *nowadays*	16. As we positioned the benches around the table, there was considerable grumbling about the lack of comfortable chairs.
16. positioned *placed* considerable *a great deal of*	17. The word *home* usually connotates warmth, security, and love.

17. connotates *connotes*

18. Ralph really stirred up a hornet's nest when he remarked that he is disinterested in finishing college.

18. stirred up a hornet's nest *caused great consternation*
disinterested *uninterested*

19. Due to my bad attack of asthma I discontinued my trumpet lessons for two weeks.

19. Due to *Because of*

20. The spritely dance music was fantastic, so we all had a super time until about twelve midnight.

20. spritely *sprightly*
fantastic *unusually good*
super *delightful*
twelve midnight omit *twelve* as redundant (*midnight* specifically means *twelve*)

SCORE ______

Exercise 92	DICTION

Underline all errors and colloquialisms in the following sentences and write first the original form and then the correct or preferred form.

EXAMPLE: It was getting kind of late, but we were having a real good time and hated to break up the party.

kind of *rather*
real *very*

	1. Your going to be sorry, Pam, that you didn't study like you promised.
1. Your *You're* like *as*	2. Is that quote from the Old Testament or the New Testament?
2. quote *quotation*	3. Elise says that she was plenty concerned about the outcome of that English exam, and may be she was.
3. plenty *quite* or *very* exam *examination* may be *maybe*	4. Some say that the basis of Audrey and Augusta's friendship is their mutual dislike of Alfred.
4. mutual *common*	5. To make good biscuits, mix the ingredients well and then roll the dough out thusly on a smooth, flat surface.

5. thusly *thus*	6. Those kind of errors will certainly cause a college pupil to fail.
6. Those kind *That kind* or *Those kinds* pupil *student*	7. My two sisters are alumni of St. Mary's College in Raleigh, and I don't doubt but what they will send their daughters there.
7. alumni *alumnae* but what *that*	8. Timothy hasn't many allusions left after being in the business world for a year; I expect he has become somewhat cynical.
8. allusions *illusions* expect *suppose*	9. You should have been more careful, Laura; Mother will be peeved that you fell off of the dock and ruined your clothes.
9. peeved *angry* off of *off*	10. The party that called you on the telephone wanted to know when you would be in, and he inferred that the call was important.
10. party *person* that *who* inferred *implied*	11. I was literally exhausted, but the long, miserable day hadn't fazed Mike.

11. literally *virtually* fazed *bothered*	12. Mr. Spalding is in poor condition; he has a busted leg and a sprained wrist.
12. busted *broken*	13. I understand that the professor will critique our reports in class tomorrow; I hope that the data in mine is satisfactory.
13. critique *review* or *criticize* data . . . is *data . . . are*	14. The lady who washed my windows also polished the silver, ironed the tablecloth, and dusted the furniture.
14. lady *woman* etc. *and did several other things*	15. Miriam's chocolate pound cake is equally as good as mine, but Miriam's recipe is different than mine.
15. equally as *as* different than *different from*	16. The story he tells is creditable, I guess, although it may not persuade the judge that he is innocent.
16. creditable *credible* guess *suppose* persuade *convince*	17. The Jensens emigrated to the United States in 1951, and everyone here considers the family to be an asset to our community.

17. emigrated *immigrated* an asset to *valuable* *members of*	18. If you wish to chair the committee, Mr. Franklin, please hand your name into the club president.
18. chair *be chairman of* into *in to*	19. It takes a great deal of tact and stamina to administrate the affairs of a large university; I don't scarcely see how one man can handle the job.
19. administrate *administer* don't scarcely *scarcely*	20. The continuous cheers that broke out from the crowd gave evidence of how enthused everyone was about the victory.
20. continuous *continual* enthused *enthusiastic*	SCORE ______

23
Building a Vocabulary

As you know from your own experience, one of your greatest needs for successful composition is to improve your vocabulary. One of the best ways to build a vocabulary, of course, is always to look up in a dictionary the meanings of unfamiliar words which you hear spoken or come across in your reading. This chapter on vocabulary will provide you with a minimal body of information concerning word formation and the derivations of the various words which comprise the English language. For a more intensified study of all aspects of this fascinating subject, including ways to strengthen your own vocabulary, consult and use frequently a book devoted exclusively to this purpose.

Learning the derivation of a word will fix in your mind the meaning and spelling of that word. Since the largest part of our English vocabulary comes from three main sources–the Anglo-Saxon, the Greek, and the Latin languages–a knowledge of commonly used prefixes, roots, and suffixes from these languages will prove very useful.

A **prefix** is a short element, a syllable or syllables, that comes before the main part of the word, which is the **root**. A **suffix** is added to the end of the word. Thus the word *hypodermic* has *hypo-*, meaning "under," as its *prefix*; *derm*, meaning "skin," as its *root*; and *-ic*, meaning "having to do with," as its *suffix*. You see that the *prefix* and *suffix* of a word modify the meaning of the *root*. The word, then, *hypodermic,* when used as an adjective, means "having to do with something under the skin."

So basic is Anglo-Saxon that, though the words of classical origin outnumber those from Anglo-Saxon, we use most commonly in our speech words of Anglo-Saxon origin. For instance, the Anglo-Saxon prefixes *un-* (not) and *for-* (from) are found in many of our words, such as *unfair* and *forbid.* The Anglo-Saxon root word *hlaf* (loaf) gives us the word *lord*, a lord being a loafkeeper or warden (*hlaf-weard*). The root word *god* (God) gives us *goodbye*, a contraction of *God be with ye.* Anglo-Saxon suffixes such as *-ish* (having the qualities of) and *-ly* (like) are seen in many words such as *foolish* and *courtly*.

If you combine the Greeek root *tele*, meaning "at a distance," with *graph* (writing), *phone* (sound), *scope* (seeing), *pathy* (feeling), you have *telegraph* (writing at a distance), *telephone* (sound at a distance), *telescope* (seeing at a distance), *telepathy* (feeling at a distance).

The Latin root *duc* is seen in such words as *adduce, aqueduct, conduce, conduct, induce, produce, reduce, seduce, conductor, ducal,* and *ductile.* If you know that *duc* means "to lead," and if you know the meanings of the prefixes and suffixes combined with it, you can make out the meanings of most of these words.

Each prefix, root, and suffix that you learn may lead to a knowledge of many new words or give a clearer understanding of many you already know. Therefore, a list of some of the most common prefixes, roots, and suffixes is given below. Look up others in your dictionary, or as suggested earlier, get a good vocabulary text book and use it often.

23a Prefixes

Prefixes Showing Number or Amount

BI– (*bis–*) two	*(bi)*annual, *(bis)*sextile
CENT– (*centi–*) hundred	*(cent)*enarian, *(centi)*pede
DEC– (*deca–*) ten	*(dec)*ade, *(Deca)*logue
HEMI– half	*(hemi)*sphere, *(hemi)*stich
MILLI– (*mille–*) thousand	*(milli)*on, *(mille)*nnium
MULTI– many, much	*(multi)*form, *(multi)*graph
MON– (*mono–*) one	*(mono)*gyny, *(mono)*tone
OCTA– (*octo–*) eight	*(octa)*ve, *(octo)*pus
PAN– all	*(pan)*acea, *(pan)*demonium, *(pan)*orama
PENTA– five	*(penta)*gon, *(Penta)*teuch
POLY– much, many	*(poly)*glot, *(poly)*chrome
PROT– (*proto–*) first	*(prot)*agonist, *(proto)*type
SEMI– half	*(semi)*circle, *(semi)*final
TRI– three	*(tri)*angle, *(tri)*ad
UNI– one	*(uni)*fy, *(uni)*cameral

Prefixes Showing Relationship in Place and Time

AB– (*a–, abs–*) from, away from	*(a)*vert, *(ab)*sent, *(abs)*tract
AD– (*ac–, af–, al–, ag–, an–, ap–, ar–, as–, at–*) to, at	*(ad)*mit, *(ac)*cede, *(af)*fect, *(al)*lude, *(ag)*gregate, *(an)*nounce, *(ap)*pear, *(ar)*rive, *(as)*sume, *(at)*tain
AMB– (*ambi–*) around, both	*(ambi)*dextrous, *(ambi)*guous
ANTE– before	*(ante)*cedent, *(ante)*date
ANTI– (*ant–*) against	*(anti)*thesis, *(ant)*agonist
CATA– away, against, down	*(cata)*clysm, *(cata)*strophe
CIRCUM– around, about	*(circum)*scribe, *(circum)*stance
CON– (*com–, col–, cor–*) with, together, at the same time	*(con)*tract, *(com)*pete, *(col)*league, *(cor)*relate
CONTRA– (*counter–*) opposite, against	*(contra)*dict, *(counter)*mand
DE– from, away from, down	*(de)*pend, *(de)*form, *(de)*tract
DIA– through, across	*(dia)*gram, *(dia)*meter
DIS– (*di, dif–*) off, away from	*(dis)*tract, *(di)*verge, *(dif)*fuse
EN– (*em–, in-*) in, into	*(en)*counter, *(em)*brace, *(in)*duct
EPI– on, over, among, outside	*(epi)*dermis, *(epi)*demic
EX– (*e–, ec–, ef–*) out of, from	*(ex)*pel, *(e)*lect, *(ec)*centric, *(ef)*face

EXTRA–(*extro*–) outside, beyond	(*extra*)mural, (*extro*)vert
HYPO– under	(*hypo*)dermic, (*hypo*)crite
INTER– among, between, within	(*inter*)fere, (*inter*)rupt
INTRO– (*intra*–) within	(*intro*)spection, (*intra*)mural
OB– (*oc*–, *of*–, *op*–) against, to, before toward	(*ob*)ject, (*oc*)casion, (*of*)fer, (*op*)press
PER– through, by	(*per*)ceiver, (*per*)ennial
PERI– around, about	(*peri*)meter, (*peri*)odical
POST– after	(*post*)script, (*post*)erity
PRE– before	(*pre*)cedent, (*pre*)decessor
PRO– before in time or position	(*pro*)logue, (*pro*)bate
RETRO– back, backward	(*retro*)gress, (*retro*)spect
SE– aside, apart	(*se*)clude, (*se*)duce
SUB– (*suc*–, *suf*–, *sug*–, *sum*–, *sup*–, *sus*–) under, below	(*sub*)scribe, (*suc*)cumb, (*suf*)fer, (*sug*)gest, (*sum*)mon, (*sup*)pose, (*sus*)pect
SUPER– (*sur*–) above, over	(*super*)sede, (*super*)b, (*sur*)pass
TRANS– (*tra*–, *traf*–, *tres*–) across	(*trans*)port, (*tra*)vesty, (*traf*)fic, (*tres*)pass
ULTRA– beyond	(*ultra*)marine, (*ultra*)modern

Prefixes Showing Negation

A– (*an*–) without	(*an*)onymous, (*a*)theist
IN– (*ig*–, *im*–, *il*–, *ir*–) not	(*in*)accurate, (*ig*)nore, (*im*)pair, (*il*)legal, (*ir*)responsible
NON– not	(*non*)essential, (*non*)entity
UN– not	(*un*)tidy, (*un*)happy

23b Greek Roots

ARCH	chief, rule	(*arch*)bishop, an(*archy*), mon(*archy*)
AUTO	self	(*auto*)graph, (*auto*)mobile, (*auto*)matic
BIO	life	(*bio*)logy, (*bio*)graphy, (*bio*)chemistry
CAU(S)T	burn	(*caust*)ic, holo(*caust*), (*caut*)erize
CHRON(O)	time	(*chron*)icle, (*chron*)ic, (*chrono*)logy
COSM(O)	order, arrangement	(*cosm*)os, (*cosm*)ic, (*cosmo*)graphy
CRIT	judge, discern	(*crit*)ic, (*crit*)erion
DEM(O)	people	(*demo*)crat, (*demo*)cracy, (*dem*)agogue
DERM	skin	epi(*dermis*), (*derm*)a, pachy(*derm*), (*derm*)ophobe
DYN(A) (M)	power	(*dynam*)ic, (*dynam*)o, (*dyn*)asty
GRAPH	write	auto(*graph*), (*graph*)ic, geo(*graphy*)
HIPPO	horse	(*hippo*)potamus, (*hippo*)drome
HYDR(O)	water	(*hydr*)ant, (*hydr*)a, (*hydro*)gen
LOG(Y), LOGUE	saying, science	(*log*)ic, bio(*logy*), eu(*logy*), dia(*logue*)
MET(E)R	measure	thermo(*meter*), speedo(*meter*), (*metr*)ic
MICRO	small	(*micro*)be, (*micro*)scope, (*micro*)cosm
MOR(O)	fool	(*moro*)n, sopho(*more*)
NYM	name	ano(*nym*)ous, pseudo(*nym*)
PATH	experience, suffer	a(*path*)y, sym(*path*)y, (*path*)os

PED	child	*(ped)*agogue, *(ped)*ant, *(ped)*iatrician
PHIL	love	*(phil)*antrophy, *(phil)*osophy, *(phil)*ander
PHON(O)	sound	*(phono)*graph, *(phon)*etic, *(phono)*gram
PSYCH(O)	mind, soul	*(psycho)*logy, *(psych)*ic, *(Psych)*e
SOPH	wisdom	philo*(sopher)*, *(soph)*ist, *(soph)*istication
THEO	God	*(theo)*logy, *(theo)*sophy, *(theo)*cratic
THERM	heat	*(therm)*ostat, *(therm)*ometer, *(therm)*os

23c Latin Roots

AM	love	*(am)*ity, *(am)*orist, *(am)*orous
ANIM	breath, soul, spirit	*(anim)*al, *(anim)*ate, un*(anim)*ous
AQU(A)	water	*(aqu)*educt, *(aqua)*tic, *(aqua)*rium
AUD	hear	*(aud)*itor, *(aud)*ience, *(aud)*itorium
CAPIT	head	*(capit)*al, *(capit)*ate, *(capit)*alize
CAP(T), CEP(T), CIP(T)	take	*(cap)*tive, pre*(cept)*, pre*(cip)*itate
CED, CESS	go, yield	ante*(ced)*ent, con*(cede)*, ex*(cess)*ive
CENT	hundred	*(cent)*ury, *(cent)*urion, per*(cent)*(age)
CER(N), CRI(M,T), CRE(M,T)	separate, judge, choose	dis*(cern)*, *(crim)*inal, dis*(crete)*
CRED	believe, trust	*(cred)*it, in*(cred)*ible, *(cred)*ulity
CLAR	clear, bright	*(clar)*ity, *(clar)*ify, de*(clar)*ation
CORD	heart	dis*(cord)*, con*(cord)*, *(cord)*ial
CORP(OR)	body, substance	*(corpor)*al, *(corp)*se, *(corp)*ulent
DON	give	*(don)*or, *(don)*ate
DOM(IN)	tame, subdue	*(domin)*ant, *(domin)*ate, *(domin)*ion
DORM	sleep	*(dorm)*ant, *(dorm)*itory, *(dorm)*ient
DUC	lead	con*(duc)*t, *(duc)*tile, aque*(duc)*t
FER	bear	in*(fer)*ence, *(fer)*tile, re*(fer)*
FORT	strong	*(fort)*ress, *(fort)*e, *(fort)*itude
FRAG, FRING FRACT	break	*(frag)*ile, in*(fring)*e, *(fract)*ure
GEN	beget, origin	en*(gen)*der, con*(gen)*ital, *(gen)*-eration
JAC(T), JEC(T)	cast	e*(jac)*ulate, pro*(ject)*, e*(ject)*
LATE	carry	col*(late)*, vacil*(late)*, re*(late)*
MI(SS,T)	send	dis*(miss)*, *(miss)*ionary, re*(mit)*
NOMIN, NOMEN	name	*(nomin)*ate, *(nomen)*clature
NOV	new	*(nov)*el, *(nov)*ice, in*(nov)*ation
PED	foot	*(ped)*al, centi*(pede)*, *(ped)*estrian
PLEN, PLET	full	*(plen)*ty, *(plen)*itude, re*(plete)*
PORT	bear	*(port)*er, de*(port)*, im*(port)*ance
POTENT	able, powerful	*(potent)*, *(potent)*ial, *(potent)*ate
SECT	cut	dis*(sect)*, in*(sect)*, *(sect)*ion

23d Suffixes

NOUN SUFFIXES

1. *Suffixes Denoting an Agent*

–ANT (*–ent*) one who, that which	ten(*ant*), ag(*ent*)
–AR (*–er*) one who	schol(*ar*), farm(*er*)
–ARD (*–art*) one who (often deprecative)	cow(*ard*), bragg(*art*)
–EER one who	privat(*eer*), auction(*eer*)
–ESS a woman who	waitr(*ess*), seamstr(*ess*)
–IER (*–yer*) one who	cash(*ier*), law(*yer*)
–IST one who	novel(*ist*), Commun(*ist*)
–OR one who, that which	act(*or*), tract(*or*)
–STER one who, that which	young(*ster*), road(*ster*)

2. *Suffix Denoting the Receiver of an Action*

–EE one who is the object of some action	appoint(*ee*), divorc(*ee*)

3. *Suffixes Denoting Smallness or Diminutiveness*

–CULE (*–cle*)	mole(*cule*), ventri(*cle*)
–ETTE	din(*ette*), cigar(*ette*)
–LET	ring(*let*), brace(*let*)
–LING	duck(*ling*), prince(*ling*)

4. *Suffixes Denoting Place*

–ARY indicating location or repository	diction(*ary*), api(*ary*)
–ERY place or establishment	bak(*ery*), nunn(*ery*)
–ORY (*–arium, –orium*) place for, concerned with	dormit(*ory*), audit(*orium*)

5. *Suffixes Denoting Act, State, Quality, or Condition*

–ACY denoting quality, state	accur(*acy*), delic(*acy*)
–AL pertaining to action	refus(*al*), deni(*al*)
–ANCE (*–ancy*) denoting action or state	brilli(*ance*), buoy(*ancy*)
–ATION denoting result	migr(*ation*), el(*ation*)
–DOM denoting a general condition	wis(*dom*), bore(*dom*)
–ENCE (*–ency*) state, quality of	abstin(*ence*), consist(*ency*)
–ERY denoting quality, action	fool(*ery*), prud(*ery*)
–HOOD state, quality	knight(*hood*), false(*hood*)
–ICE condition or quality	serv(*ice*), just(*ice*)
–ION (*–sion*) state or condition	un(*ion*), ten(*sion*)
–ISM denoting action, state, or condition	bapt(*ism*), plagiar(*ism*)
–ITY (*–ety*) action, state, or condition	joll(*ity*), gai(*ety*)
–MENT action or state resulting from	punish(*ment*), frag(*ment*)

–NESS quality, state of	good*(ness)*, prepared*(ness)*
–OR denoting action, state, or quality	hon*(or)*, lab*(or)*
–TH pertaining to condition, state, or action	warm*(th)*, steal*(th)*
–URE denoting action, result, or instrument	legislat*(ure)*, pleas*(ure)*

ADJECTIVES SUFFIXES

–ABLE (*–ible, –ile*) capable of being	lov*(able)*, ed*(ible)*, contract*(ile)*
–AC relating to, like	elegi*(ac)*, cardi*(ac)*
–ACIOUS inclined to	pugn*(acious)*, aud*(acious)*
–AL pertaining to	radic*(al)*, cordi*(al)*
–AN pertaining to	sylv*(an)*, urb*(an)*
–ANT (*–ent*) inclined to	pleas*(ant)*, converg*(ent)*
–AR pertaining to	sol*(ar)*, regul*(ar)*
–ARY pertaining to	contr*(ary)*, revolution*(ary)*
–ATIVE inclined to	demonstr*(ative)*, talk*(ative)*
–FUL full of	joy*(ful)*, pain*(ful)*
–IC (*–ical*) pertaining to	volcan*(ic)*, angel*(ical)*
–ISH like, relating to, being	devil*(ish)*, boy*(ish)*
–IVE inclined to, having the nature of	elus*(ive)*, nat*(ive)*
–LESS without, unable to be	piti*(less)*, resist*(less)*
–OSE full of	bellic*(ose)*, mor*(ose)*
–OUS full of	pi*(ous)*, fam*(ous)*
–ULENT (*–olent*) full of	fraud*(ulent)*, vi*(olent)*

VERB SUFFIXES

The following verb suffixes usually mean "to make" (to become, to increase, etc.).

–ATE	toler*(ate)*, vener*(ate)*
–EN	madd*(en)*, wid*(en)*
–FY	magni*(fy)*, beauti*(fy)*
–IZE (*–ise*)	colon*(ize)*, exerc*(ise)*

Exercise 93 WORD ANALYSIS: PREFIXES

Break the following English words into their parts and give the literal meaning of each part as derived from its source. Consult the list of **prefixes** and **roots** given on the previous pages. After **P**, write the prefix and its literal meaning; after **R**, write the root and its literal meaning; and after **M**, write the meaning of the whole word. Use your dictionary if you encounter a part that is not listed in this book. Be able to use each word in a sentence.

EXAMPLE: *amoral*

P *a*, without
R *moral*, principles of conduct
M without principles of conduct

Answers	Exercise
	1. abnormal P R M
1. P *ab*, away, from, off, down R *normal*, average, natural, standard, regular M irregular, unnatural	2. antecedent P R M
2. P *ante*, before R *cedent*, going M going before, prior, previous	3. antisocial P R M
3 P *anti*, against, hostile to R *social*, companionable, having to do with human beings living together M unsociable, against the basic principles of society	4. bibliography P R M

4. P *biblio*, book; of books R *graphy*, something written M study or list of editions, dates, authors, etc., of books and other writings	5. bicentennial P R M
5. P *bi*, two R *centennial*, hundred years M happening once in a period of two hundred years, lasting for two hundred years	6. contact P R M
6. P *con* (or *com*), with, together R *tact*, to touch M the act of touching, meeting, or being in association with	7. dismiss P R M
7. P *dis*, separation, negation, or reversal; away or apart from R *miss*, to send M to send away	8. exclude P R M
8. P *ex*, out, from R *clude*, to shut M to shut out	9. extraordinary P R M
9. P *extra*, outside of, beyond, beyond the scope of R *ordinary*, usual, usual order of things M beyond the usual	10. hemisphere P R M

10. P *hemi*, half R *sphere*, globe M any half of the celestial globe or of the earth	11. hypertension P R M
11. P *hyper*, over, above, more than the normal, excessive R *tension*, stretched M abnormally high tension or abnormally high blood pressure	12. international P R M
12. P *inter*, between, among R *national*, pertaining to a nation or country M between or among nations	13. misplace P R M
13. P *mis*, wrong, bad R *place*, to put in a particular spot or condition M to put in the wrong place, to mislay	14. monopoly P R M
14. P *mono*, one R *poly*, sale, or right to sell M exclusive control of a commodity or service in a given market	15. multiply P R M
15. P *multi*, many, much R *ply*, to fold M to cause to increase in number, amount, extent, or degree; to make manifold	16. nonresident P R M

16. P *non*, not R *resident*, living or staying in a particular place M not residing in a specified place	17. perforate P R M
17. P *per*, through, by R *forate*, to bore M to make a hole or holes through, by boring, piercing, punching	18. perimeter P R M
18. P *peri*, around, about R *meter*, measure M the outer boundary of an area of a figure	19. prevent P R M
19. P *pre*, before R *vent*, to come M to anticipate, to stop or keep from happening by prior action	20. submerge P R M
20. P *sub*, under, below R *merge*, to plunge M to place under (as water), to cover over, suppress	21. synonym P R M
21. P *syn*(o), together R *nym*, a name M a word having the same or nearly the same meaning as another in the same language	22. telepathy P R M

22. P *tele*, far off R *pathy*, feeling, suffering M transference of thought or feeling	23. transform P R M
23. P *trans*, across, over R *form*, a shape, figure, or image M to change the form or outward appearance of	24. tricycle P R M
24. P *tri*, three R *cycle*, wheel M a three-wheeled vehicle, usually for children, operated by pedals	25. unemployed P R M
25. P *un*, not R *employed*, engaged, made use of M not employed; without work	SCORE ______

Exercise 94 WORD ANALYSIS: SUFFIXES

Break the following English words into their parts and give the literal meaning of each part as derived from its source. Consult the list of *suffixes* given on the previous pages and consult your dictionary for the *roots* contained in the words, or for any suffixes not listed in this book. After **R**, write the root and its literal meaning; after **S**, write the suffix and its literal meaning; and after **M**, write the meaning of the whole word. Be able to use each word in a sentence.

EXAMPLE: *freedom*

R *free*, at liberty
S *dom*, general condition
M the condition of being at liberty

	1. activist R S M
1. R *activ(e)*, acting; functioning; working; moving S *ist*, one who M one who acts, works, moves, etc., especially one who adopts the policy of moving or acting with force and decision	2. alienate R S M
2. R *alien*, an outsider S *ate*, to make M to make an outsider; to make unfriendly	3. broaden R S M
3. R *broad*, wide; of large extent from side to side S *en*, to make M to widen or to make larger from side to side	4. cemetery R S M

4. R *cemet*, to put to sleep S *ery*, place or establishment M place where people are "put to sleep, laid to rest," etc.; place for burial of the dead	5. commendable R S M
5. R *commend*, to mention as worthy of regard S *able*, capable of being M deserving to be commended; praiseworthy	6. communism R S M
6. R *commune(e)*, to make common; share S *ism*, action; state; condition M an economic theory or system of ownership of all property by the community as a whole	7. corpulent R S M
7. R *corp*, body S *ulent*, full of M fat; fleshy; stout; obese	8. defendant R S M
8. R *defend*, to guard from attack; to ward off S *ant*, one who M the defending person; in law, the person charged or accused	9. deference R S M

9. R *defer*, to submit or yield with courtesy; to be respectful S *ence*, state or quality of M a yielding; courteous regard or respect	10. dictatorship R S M
10. R *dictator*, a ruler with absolute power or authority S *ship*, quality, condition, or state of M state ruled by a dictator; a dictatorial government	11. gosling R S M
11. R *gos (goose)*, a web-footed, long-necked wild or domestic bird, like a duck but larger S *ling*, small or young M a young goose	12. kindness R S M
12. R *kind*, sympathetic; friendly; gentle; tender-hearted S *ness*, quality or state of M the quality or habit of being kind	13. literal R S M
13. R *lïter*, letter S *al*, pertaining to M word for word; following the exact words of the original; habitually interpreting statements according to their actual meaning	14. magnetize R S M

14. R *magnet*, a piece of iron or steel that has the property of attracting iron or steel S *ize*, to make or become M to make into a magnet; give magnetic qualities to; attract or charm (a person)	15. management R S M
15. R *manage*, to control; guide; work S *ment*, action or state resulting from M act, art, or manner of controlling, handling, directing	16. mannish R S M
16. R *man*, an adult male human being S *(n)ish*, like, relating to M characteristic of, like, or imitating a man	17. merciless R S M
17. R *merc(i)(y)*, refraining from harming or punishing offenders S *less*, without, unable to be M without mercy; having, feeling, or showing no mercy; cruel	18. monotonous R S M
18. R *monoton(e)*, sameness of tone, style, manner, color, etc. S *ous*, full of M going on in the same tone without variation; unvarying; tiresome because unvarying	19. motherhood R S M

19. R *mother*, a female parent; a woman who has borne a child S *hood*, state or quality of M the state of being a mother; mothers collectively	20. nominee R S M
20. R *nomin*, to name or appoint S *ee*, one who is the object of some action M a person who is nominated (usually as a candidate for election)	21. pollster R S M
21. R *poll*, canvassing of people to discover public opinion on some subject S *ster*, one who M a person who conducts polls	22. residence R S M
22. R *resid(e)*, to dwell for a long time S *ence*, state or quality of M the place in which a person or thing resides; dwelling place; abode	23. rivulet R S M
23. R *rivu(le)*, stream S *let*, small M small stream	24. roguery R S M

24. R *rogu(e)*, wandering beggar; tramp; rascal; scoundrel S *ery*, behavior or act of M behavior of a rogue; specifically, trickery, cheating, or playful mischief	25. satisfy R S M
25. R *satis*, enough S *fy*, to make M to fulfill the needs, expectations, wishes, or desires of	26. secretive R S M
26. R *secret*, kept from public knowledge or the knowledge of certain persons S *ive*, inclined to; having the nature of M tending to conceal one's thoughts, feelings, affairs from others; not frank or open; reticent	27. sensation R S M
27. R *sens(e)*, the power of physical feeling S *ation*, result M an immediate reaction to external stimulation of a sense organ; conscious feeling or sense impression, as a *sensation of cold*	28. solitary R S M
28. R *soli(t)*, alone S *ary*, pertaining to M living or being alone; without others; single	29. spiteful R S M

29. R *spite*, a mean or evil feeling toward another S *ful*, full of M full of or showing spite	30. student R S M
30. R *stud(y)*, the act or process of applying one's mind in order to acquire knowledge S *ent*, one who M one who studies	31. teacher R S M
31. R *teach*, to show how to do something; give instructions; train S *er*, one who M one who teaches, gives instructions, or trains	32. wisdom R S M
32. R *wis(e)*, wise; having or showing good judgment S *dom*, general condition M the quality of being wise; the power of judging rightly	SCORE ______

Exercise 95 WORD ANALYSIS: ROOTS

For each root listed below write the meaning and at least three words containing the root. Do not use the same word under two roots. Be able to explain the meaning of the root as related to the word. Use your dictionary for this exercise.

EXAMPLE: *clar-* clear, bright

clarify, clear, clarinet

	1. *anim-*
1. *anim-* to make alive; to fill with breath animated, animal, animosity	2. *cent-*
2. *cent-* sharp point, point around which a circle is described center, central, centrifugal, concentric, concentrate	3. *cert-*
3. *cert-* determined, fixed, settled certain, certify, certitude, ascertain	4. *germ-*
4. *germ-* sprig, sprout, offshoot, bud, embryo germ, germinate, germane	5. *habit-*
5. *habit-* condition, appearance, dress habit, habitat, habituate	6. *jus-, jud-*

6. *jus-, jud-* law judge, justice, judicial, just	7. *lex-, legis-*
7. *lex-, legis-* law legislation, legitimate, legal, lexicon	8. *man-*
8. *man-* hand manipulate, manicure, manufacture, manuscript, manage, manner, manual	9. *mot-, mov-*
9. *mot-, mov-* to move motion, motivate, move, motor, commotion, promote, emotion	10. *pass-*
10. *pass-* a step pass, passage, passenger	11. *pono, posit-*
11. *pono, posit-* to place position, positive, post, poster, posture, impose, expose, suppose	12. *quer-, quest-*
12. *quer-, quest-* to ask; seek; inquire quest, question, query, bequest, inquest, request	13. *rect-*
13. *rect-* right, straight rectitude, rectify, rectangle, erect, direct, correct	14. *simil-*

14. *simil-* like similar, simulate, simultaneous, simile, same, seem	15. *spec-*
15. *spec-* to look, behold spectacle, spectrum, spectator, inspect, respect, circumspect	16. *stat-*
16. *stat-* position, standing, to stand status, statement, static, station	17. *tract-*
17. *tract-* to drag; to haul; to draw along traction, trace, track, tractable, tractor	18. *verb-*
18. *verb-* word verb, verbose, verbatim	19. *veri-*
19. *veri-* true very, verify, verity, veritable, veracity	20. *vis-*
20. *vis-* to see vision, visit, visible, vista	SCORE ______

Exercise 96 VOCABULARY: PREFIXES AND SUFFIXES

A. Underline the prefix for each of the following words, give its meaning, and use the word in a sentence.

EXAMPLE: prepare, before

Eleanor will prepare supper for fourteen tonight.

	1. universal
1. universal, one Hope for world peace is universal.	2. anticlimax
2. anticlimax, against After "Staying Alive" the rest of the BeeGees' concert was anticlimax.	3. circumference
3. circumference, around; about The circumference of Lake Sequoyah is approximately two miles.	4. semiannual
4. semiannual, half The company pays its stockholders a semiannual dividend.	5. controversy
5. controversy, against The mayor knew that his action would cause controversy.	6. mispronounce

6. mispronounce, wrong; bad; wrongly; badly If Henry mispronounces *congratulations* again, I will scream.	7. postpone
7. postpone, after Margaret and Rob have postponed their wedding until after graduation.	8. impossible
8. impossible, not It is impossible for me to hear when you all speak at once.	9. hyperbole
9. hyperbole, over; above; more than normal; excessive Hyperbole, or exaggeration, is sometimes an effective way to get the attention of an audience.	10. multimillionaire
10. multimillionaire, many; much Tom tells me that Mrs. Landers is a multimillionaire.	

B. Underline the suffix in each of the following words, give its meaning, and use the word in a sentence.

EXAMPLE: commendable, capable of; worthy of

Jane, your handling of the emergency was commendable.

	1. laggard

1. laggard, one who (usually with unfavorable connotation) All the children marched quickly along, and there were few laggards.	2. brotherhood
2. brotherhood, state; quality The brotherhood of man is an ideal that everyone should strive for.	3. religion
3. religion, state; condition Freedom of religion is promised all Americans by the United States Constitution.	4. brooklet
4. brooklet, small The brooklet in our woods makes a tiny pool at one point in its path.	5. neatness
5. neatness, quality; state of Mother hopes that I will acquire the habit of neatness from my new roommate.	6. confident
6. confident, inclined to Leslie seems confident of winning the tournament, and I hope that she is right.	7. mischievous
7. mischievous, full of Those mischievous girls put fiddler crabs into the boys' beds.	8. wealth
8. wealth, condition; state; action She receives pleasure from her wealth by using it to help others.	9. sanity

9. sanity, action; state; condition It became apparent that the murderer's sanity was questionable.	10. exonerate
10. exonerate, to make We believe that the judge will exonerate Frank after hearing the true story.	SCORE ______

Exercise 97 EXERCISES USING LATIN AND GREEK ROOTS

A. With the help of your collegiate dictionary, use the derivatives of **vers, vert**, meaning "to turn," necessary to complete the statements below. *Remember that this root and others in the exercise may have prefixes.*

	1. A sensation of dizziness or giddiness is called ________________.
1. vertigo	2. One who is competent in many things, able to turn easily from one occupation to another, is frequently described as ________________.
2. versatile	3. An account or report showing one point of view may be defined as a ________________.
3. version	4. To go back in action, thought, or speech is to ________________.
4. revert	5. When one changes or transforms something, he ________________ it.
5. converts	

B. Use the derivatives of **path**, meaning "to experience or suffer," necessary to complete the sentences below.

	1. Something that arouses pity, sorrow, or compassion is described as ________________.
1. pathetic	2. A sameness of feeling or an affinity between two persons is ________________.

2. sympathy	3. The projection of one's own personality into the personality of another in order to understand him better is called ______.
3. empathy	4. Persons suffering from certain mental disorders are often characterized by the adjective ______.
4. psychopathic	5. The branch of medicine that deals with the nature of disease, especially with the structural and functional changes caused by disease, is known as ______.
5. pathology	

C. Use the derivatives of **auto**, meaning "self," necessary to complete the statements below.

	1. The story of one's life, written by oneself, is called an ______.
1. autobiography	2. If a machine moves, operates, or regulates itself, it is ______.
2. automatic	3. An ______ is a ruler with supreme power over his people.
3. autocrat	4. A person's signature in his own handwriting is his ______.
4. autograph	5. A state or nation which is self-governing is said to have ______.

<table>
<tr><td>5. autonomy</td><td></td></tr>
<tr><td colspan="2">D. Use the derivatives of fer, meaning "to bear or carry," necessary to complete the statements below.</td></tr>
<tr><td></td><td>1. Land that is rich in resources, fruitful, and prolific is said to be ________________.</td></tr>
<tr><td>1. fertile</td><td>2. A boat used for carrying people or goods across a narrow body of water is called a ________________.</td></tr>
<tr><td>2. ferry</td><td>3. To convey, carry, remove, or send something from one place or person to another is to ____________ _____ it.</td></tr>
<tr><td>3. transfer</td><td>4. To draw a conclusion by reasoning from knowledge or assumption is to make an ________________.</td></tr>
<tr><td>4. inference</td><td>5. A ________________ is a tree or shrub that bears cones.</td></tr>
<tr><td>5. conifer</td><td>SCORE ______</td></tr>
</table>

24
Spelling

Spelling is an important aspect of written communication. Instructors seldom have the opportunity, however, to spend adequate classroom time on the subject. The responsibility for the mastery of spelling, therefore, rests almost solely on the individual student.

Here are a few practical suggestions on how to approach the problem of spelling:

1. Always use the dictionary when you are in doubt about the spelling of a word.
2. If there is a rule applicable to the type of words which you misspell, learn that rule.
3. Employ any "tricks" which might assist you in remembering the spelling of particular words that give you trouble. If, for example, you confuse the meaning and hence the spelling of *statue* and *stature*, remember that the longer word refers to bodily "longness." Certain troublesome words can be spelled correctly if you will remember their prefixes (as in *dis/appoint*) or their suffixes (as in *cool/ly*). Also it might help you to remember that there are only three *-ceed* words: *exceed, proceed,* and *succeed.*
4. Keep a list of the words which you misspell. In writing down these words, observe their syllabication and any peculiarities of construction. Try to "see" – that is, to have a mental picture of – these words.
5. Practice the correct pronunciation of troublesome words. Misspelling is often the result of mispronunciation.

Of the many rules governing spelling four are particularly useful since they are widely applicable. Study these four rules carefully.

24a Final *e*

Drop the final ***e*** before a suffix beginning with a vowel (*-ing, -ous,* etc.) but retain the final ***e*** before a suffix beginning with a consonant (*-ment, -ly,* etc.):

Final *e* dropped: come + ing = coming
fame + ous = famous

	love + able = lovable
	guide + ance = guidance
Final *e* retained:	move + ment = movement
	fate + ful = fateful
	sole + ly = solely

EXCEPTIONS: Acknowledge, acknowledgment; abridge, abridgment; judge, judgment; dye, dyeing; singe, singeing; hoe, hoeing; mile, mileage; due, duly; awe, awful; whole, wholly. The final **e** is retained after **c** or **g** when the suffix begins with **a** or **o**: peace, peaceable; courage, courageous.

24b Final Consonant

Double a final consonant before a suffix beginning with a vowel if (1) the word is of one syllable or is accented on the last syllable and (2) the final consonant is preceded by a single vowel:

Word of one syllable: stop + ed = stopped

Word in which the accent falls on the last syllable: occur + ence = occurrence

Word in which the accent does not fall on the last syllable: differ + ence = difference

24c *ei* and *ie*

When **ei** and **ie** have the long **ee** sound (as in *keep*), use **i** before **e** except after **c**. (The word *lice* will aid you in remembering this rule; **i** follows **l** and all other consonants except **c**, while **e** follows **c**.)

ie	***ei*** (after ***c***)
chief	ceiling
field	receive
niece	deceive
siege	conceit

EXCEPTIONS (grouped to form a sentence): Neither financier seized either species of weird leisure.

24d Final *y*

In words ending in ***y*** preceded by a consonant, change the ***y*** to ***i*** before any suffix except one beginning with ***i***.

Suffix beginning with a letter other than *i*:

fly + es = flies
ally + es = allies
easy + ly = easily
mercy + ful = merciful
study + ous = studious

Suffix beginning with *i*:

fly + ing = flying
study + ing = studying

24e Spelling List

The following list is made up of approximately 450 frequently misspelled words. Since these are commonly used words, you should learn to spell all of them after you have mastered the words on your individual list.

absence
academic
accept
accidentally
accommodate
accumulate
accustomed
acknowledge
acquaintance
across
address
advantage
aggravate
allege
all right
altogether
always
amateur
among
amount
analysis
angel
anonymous
anxiety
any more
apology
apparatus
apparent
appearance
appreciate
appropriate
arctic
argument
arithmetic
around
arrangement
ascend
assassin
association
athletics
attendance
attractive

audience
autumn
auxiliary
awkward
bankruptcy
barbarous
becoming
beginning
believe
beneficial
benefited
brilliant
Britain
buoyant
bureau
business
cafeteria
calendar
camouflage
candidate
captain
carburetor
carriage
cavalry
ceiling
cemetery
certain
changeable
characteristic
chauffeur
choose
chosen
clothes
colloquial
colonel
column
coming
commission
committee
comparative
compel
compelled

competent
competition
complement
completely
compliment
compulsory
confident
congratulate
connoisseur
conqueror
conscience
conscientious
conscious
contemptible
continuous
convenient
coolly
council
counsel
courteous
criticism
curiosity
curriculum
dealt
deceit
decide
defendant
definite
dependent
descend
descent
describe
description
desert
desirable
despair
desperate
dessert
dictionary
dietitian
difference
dilapidated

dining
diphtheria
disappear
disappoint
disastrous
discipline
discussion
disease
dissatisfied
dissipate
distribute
divine
division
dormitories
drudgery
dual
duchess
duel
dyeing
dying
ecstasy
efficiency
eighth
eligible
eliminate
embarrassed
eminent
emphasize
enthusiastic
environment
equipped
equivalent
erroneous
especially
exaggerate
excellent
except
exercise
exhaust
exhilaration
existence
expel

expelled
experience
explanation
extraordinary
familiar
fascinate
February
finally
financial
financier
forehead
foreign
foreword
forfeit
formally
formerly
forth
forty
fourth
fraternity
friend
fulfill
fundamental
futile
furniture
gauge
generally
genius
government
grammar
granddaughter
grandeur
grievance
guarantee
handkerchief
harass
having
height
hindrance
hitchhike
hoping
hygiene
hypocrisy
illusion
imaginary
imitation

immediately
incidentally
independence
indispensable
inevitable
infinite
influential
innocence
instance
instant
intellectual
intelligence
intentionally
interested
irrevelant
irresistible
its
it's
judgment
kindergarten
knowledge
laboratory
led
legitimate
leisure
library
likable
literature
livelihood
loose
lose
lovable
magazine
maintain
maintenance
maneuver
manual
manufacture
mathematics
meant
medicine
mediocre
miniature
mirror
mischievous
misspell

momentous
morale
mortgage
murmur
muscle
mysterious
naturally
necessary
nevertheless
nickel
niece
ninety
ninth
noticeable
notoriety
nowadays
nucleus
obedience
obstacle
occasion
occasionally
occurrence
o'clock
off
omission
omitted
operate
opinion
opportunity
optimism
organization
original
outrageous
overrun
paid
pamphlet
parallel
paralysis
paralyzed
parliament
particularly
partner
passed
past
pastime
perform

permanent
permissible
perseverance
persistent
personal
personnel
perspiration
persuade
physically
physician
picnicking
piece
pleasant
politician
politics
politicking
possession
possible
practically
precede
preference
preferred
prejudice
preparation
prevalent
principal
principle
privilege
probably
procedure
professor
prominent
pronunciation
propaganda
psychology
publicly
purchase
pursue
quantity
quarter
questionnaire
quiet
quite
quiz
quizzes
realize

really
recognize
recommend
region
reign
relevant
religious
remembrance
repetition
representative
resistance
respectfully
respectively
restaurant
rhetoric
rheumatism
ridiculous
sacrifice
sacrilegious
salable
salary
sandwich
schedule
science
secretary

seize
sense
sentence
separate
sergeant
severely
sheriff
shining
shriek
siege
significant
similar
sincerely
sophomore
source
speak
specimen
speech
stationary
stationery
statue
stature
statute
strength
strenuous

stretch
studying
superintendent
supersede
surprise
susceptible
syllable
symmetry
temperature
tendency
their
thorough
too
tournament
tragedy
transferred
tremendous
truly
Tuesday
twelfth
tying
tyranny
unanimous
undoubtedly
universally

unnecessary
until
unusual
using
usually
vaccine
vacuum
valuable
vegetable
vengeance
vigilance
vigorous
village
villain
weather
Wednesday
weird
whether
who's
whose
women
writing
written

Exercise 98 SPELLING

A. Combine the specified suffix with each of the following words and write the correct form in the blank space.

EXAMPLE: ally + ance

alliance

	1. kindly + ness
1. kindliness	2. dine + ing
2. dining	3. benefit + ed
3. benefited	4. dispense + able
4. dispensable	5. distribute + ion
5. distribution	6. disaster + ous
6. disastrous	7. special + ly
7. specially	8. please + ant

8. pleasant	9. grieve + ance
9. grievance	10. ordinary + ly
10. ordinarily	11. calamity + ous
11. calamitous	12. usual + ly
12. usually	13. comfortable + ly
13. comfortably	14. transfer + ed
14. transferred	15. sacrifice + al
15. sacrificial	16. remember + ance
16. remembrance	17. manage + able
17. manageable	18. document + ary

18. documentary	19. satisfy + ed
19. satisfied	20. drive + ing
20. driving	21. critic + ism
21. criticism	22. bet + ing
22. betting	23. drop + ed
23. dropped	24. editorial + ly
24. editorially	25. monotone + ous
25. monotonous	26. impel + ed
26. impelled	27. tie + ing
27. tying	28. glad + en

28. gladden	29. wise + dom
29. wisdom	30. waiter + ess
30. waitress	

B. Supply either **ie** or **ei** in each of the following words:

EXAMPLE: gr____f

grief

	1. r____gn
1. reign	2. conc____t
2. conceit	3. misch____f
3. mischief	4. c____ling
4. ceiling	5. f____gn
5. feign	6. p____dmont
6. piedmont	7. h____ght
7. height	8. dec____ve

8. deceive	9. p_____rce
9. pierce	10. n_____ce
10. niece	11. r_____ndeer
11. reindeer	12. p_____r
12. pier	13. s_____ve
13. sieve	14. n_____ghbor
14. neighbor	15. l_____sure
15. leisure	16. p_____ce
16. piece	17. n_____ther
17. neither	18. h_____fer
18. heifer	19. w_____ght
19. weight	20. h_____ress
20. heiress	**SCORE** ______

Exercise 99 SPELLING

For each line of five words, choose the word that is misspelled and write it correctly in the space provided. If all five words in a line are spelled correctly, write **C**.

EXAMPLE: mathematics, parliament, mispell, original, coming

misspell

	1. confident, courteous, exellent, difference, especially
1. excellent	2. contemptable, eighth, division, writing, sophomore
2. contemptible	3. secretary, niece, morgage, infinite, maintain
3. mortgage	4. grandeur, manufacture, chauffeur, dispair, except
4. despair	5. eliminate, deceit, calendar, unanimous, schedule
5. C	6. strenuous, preference, studing, opinion, professor
6. studying	7. grandaughter, prominent, occasion, murmur, piece
7. granddaughter	8. forty, innocence, payed, independence, noticeable

8. paid	9. maintenance, precede, forfeit, priviledge, definite
9. privilege	10. cemetery, coolly, dissipate, bankruptcy, ninty
10. ninety	11. paralyzed, strength, irresistible, mirrow, finally
11. mirror	12. sincerely, relevant, persistent, restaraunt, government
12. restaurant	13. seize, undoubtedly, weird, whether, incidentally
13. C	14. franticly, statute, stationery, nowadays, immediately
14. frantically	15. schedule, questionnaire, harrass, grammar, friend
15. harass	16. sacrilegious, pursue, intellectual, publically, guarantee
16. publicly	17. psychology, literature, meant, quanity, mysterious

17. quantity	18. picnicking, predjudiced, operate, nevertheless, lovable
18. prejudiced	19. permanant, pamphlet, opportunity, diphtheria, awkward
19. permanent	20. congratulate, conscience, discipline, alright, exhaust
20. all right	21. divine, acquaintance, atheletics, tyranny, writing
21. athletics	22. personnel, vacuum, unecessary, judgment, laboratory
22. unnecessary	23. hankerchief, library, perseverance, forehead, February
23. handkerchief	24. indispensable, fullfil, parallel, pastime, nickel
24. fulfill	25. momentous, fundamental, fascinate, expelled, nineth
25. ninth	SCORE ______

Exercise 100 SPELLING

For each sentence write the correct form of any misspelled word. Write **C** if all the words in a sentence are spelled correctly.

EXAMPLE: Mrs. Locke says that the sucess of our choral concert depends upon its apeal to everyone in town.

success, appeal

	1. Many people believe that a year of kindergarden is a good transition for pre-school children.
1. kindergarten	2. Nell maintains that their is undoubtly something wrong with her carburator.
2. there, undoubtedly, carburetor	3. When it was time for desert, some people had already left the dinning room.
3. dessert, dining	4. Although the calendar says that it is Febuary, the weather feels more like May.
4. February	5. Mathmatics is Jack's weakest subject, but nowadays its an indispensable skill.
5. Mathematics, it's	6. Don't you think it is unecessary, Bill, to exercise as strenuously as you formally did?

6. unnecessary, formerly

7. Father imediately forbade Earl and Harry to hitchike to New York, so they have cancelled their plans.

7. immediately, hitchhike

8. Mr. Blalock's eroneous pronunciation embarassed his wife, but she has often made similiar mistakes.

8. erroneous, embarrassed, similar

9. We all enjoyed the delicious vegtable soup we had for lunch; Ty, who is a connoisser, pronounced it the best he had ever eaten.

9. vegetable, connoisseur

10. I don't know whose going to drive the car pool today, but I was disatisfied with the route we took yesterday.

10. who's, dissatisfied

11. Joe is such a likeable boy that I can't believe he would intentionally harrass his little brother.

11. likable, harass

12. I am to exausted to feed the dogs tonight, Jill; will you give them there supper?

12. too, exhausted, their

13. The police officer reported that Jimmy past him going seventy miles per hour; to my knowledge this is Jimmy's forth traffic ticket.

13. passed, fourth	14. Uncle John gave Cissy a nickle for an ice cream cone, but she told him that she wasn't particuly hungry.
14. nickel, particularly	15. My principle reason for calling the sherriff was to report the anonymous letter I had received.
15. principal, sheriff	16. Mr. Canfield is a man of statue and principal; he would not be guilty of deciet.
16. stature, principle, deceit	17. The alledged assasin has a competant lawyer, I understand.
17. alleged, assassin, competent	18. Mark coolly stated that the superintendent's criticism was unjust and that the curriculum was anything but mediocre.
18. C	19. It was the first time that I had met a real dutchess, and I was facinated by her extrordinary intelligence.
19. duchess, fascinated, extraordinary	20. Whose the villian that scheduled my first class for eight o'clock?

20. Who's, villain	21. My rememberance of the ocassion is that Sidney announced publically that he would start politicking for you at once.
21. remembrance, occasion, publicly	22. I didn't want to loose my allusions, but it was almost imposible not to after seeing the corruption prevelant in their goverment.
22. lose, illusions, impossible, prevalent, government	23. The minature clock that my freind gave me is an all together satisfactory timepiece.
23. miniature, friend, altogether	24. Everyone crowded around Wesley to congradulate him on his exellent speech.
24. congratulate, excellent	25. It was definately an exageration to say that the report was outrageous; in my judgment it was merely irrelevant.
25. definitely, exaggeration	**SCORE** ______

NAME ______________________________ SCORE ________

TEST ON LESSONS 1-7

A. In each of the following sentences underline the subject once and the verb twice, then circle the complement (or complements). On the first line at the right tell whether the verb is transitive active (**TA**), transitive passive (**TP**), or intransitive (**I**). On the second line tell whether the complement is a direct object (**DO**), an indirect object (**IO**), a predicate nominative (**PN**), a predicate adjective (**PA**), an objective complement (**OC**), or a retained object (**RO**).

1. Dr. Friedman and his daughter will spend Christmas in Colorado. ________ ________
2. The recent heavy rains ruined my garden. ________ ________
3. That young man is our public relations officer. ________ ________
4. Truth is not always obvious. ________ ________
5. Jane remained very calm during the crisis. ________ ________
6. Henry's promise of brevity reminds me of Polonius's promise. ________ ________
7. For which team will you be cheering? ________ ________
8. Charles always seems happy and cheerful. ________ ________
9. We were all embarrassed by his foolish actions. ________ ________
10. Why, I did not give her cause for alarm. ________ ________

B. What part of speech is each of the following underscored words?

1. <u>and</u> in the first sentence above ________________
2. <u>recent</u> in the second sentence above ________________
3. <u>That</u> in the third sentence above ________________
4. <u>not</u> in the fourth sentence above ________________
5. <u>during</u> in the fifth sentence above ________________
6. <u>brevity</u> in the sixth sentence above ________________
7. <u>which</u> in the seventh sentence above ________________
8. <u>always</u> in the eighth sentence above ________________
9. <u>foolish</u> in the ninth sentence above ________________
10. <u>Why</u> in the tenth sentence above ________________

C. In each of the sentences below identify the *italicized* expression by writing one of the following numbers in the space at the right:

- 1 if it is a prepositional phrase,
- 2 if it is a participial phrase,
- 3 if it is a gerund phrase,
- 4 if it is an infinitive phrase,
- 5 if it is an appositive phrase,
- 6 if it is an absolute phrase,
- 7 if it is a noun clause,
- 8 if it is an adjective clause,
- 9 if it is an adverbial clause.

1. Please bring me the stack of books *on the table.* ______
2. *If you will wash the car*, I will vacuum the inside. ______
3. I think *that I'll finish this book tonight.* ______
4. "The Necklace," *one of my favorite short stories*, often appears in anthologies. ______
5. The novel *Arrowsmith, which deals with the medical profession*, was written by Sinclair Lewis. ______
6. *Having wiped the mud off her shoes*, Terri went into the house for lunch. ______
7. *The fire alarm having sounded*, we all rushed out of the building. ______
8. Angie was eager *to attend the reception for the ambassador.* ______
9. *Serving as the hostess for the Tour of Homes* is quite an honor. ______
10. Of course, winning the play-offs means everything *to the coach and the team.* ______

D. Underline the dependent clause (or clauses) in each of the following sentences. In the first space at the right tell whether the clause is a noun clause (**N**), an adjective clause (**Adj**), or an adverbial clause (**Adv**). In the second space tell how the noun clause is used (that is, whether it is a *subject*, *direct object*, etc.), or what the adjective or adverbial clause modifies.

1. After I had explained my problem, Jeff offered to help. ______ ______
2. Will you explain why this class was cancelled? ______ ______
3. Let us return to the place where the accident occurred. ______ ______
4. While I am in Europe, forward all my mail to my parents. ______ ______
5. When the project can be financed has not been decided. ______ ______
6. Unless both parties are willing to compromise, there can never be a settlement. ______ ______
7. Penny, who is an accounting major, wants to work for her brother's firm this summer. ______ ______
8. The fact is that Leon can never finish a crossword puzzle on his own. ______ ______
9. Because her lectures are short but informative, the students can understand her points. ______ ______
10. In order to get the position which she wanted, Betsy prepared herself well. ______ ______

E. In the following sentences insert all necessary commas and semicolons. Rewrite sentence fragments in such a way as to make complete sentences. If a sentence is correct, mark it C.

1. Reading children's literature is sometimes enjoyable for adults.

2. My mobile home although it is small is a very comfortable place to live.

3. If you would remember all that we have done for you.

4. After driving from Raleigh to Norfolk in the rain I was too tired even to watch television.

5. Penny McPherson is a designer of women's sport clothes and she is very successful.

6. Flannery O'Connor like William Faulkner lived in the South both wrote about its people.

7. Having practiced medicine for forty years Dr. Franklin decided to retire.

8. John Appleby a professor at the College of William and Mary is a champion marathon runner.

9. I enjoy visiting the Harrises occasionally however I usually don't stay more than a day or two.

10. Janet Sims and Ted Davis the student government president and the treasurer attending a conference in Houston.

NAME ______________________________ SCORE ________

TEST ON LESSONS 8-18

Correct all errors in the following sentences. Errors may be crossed out and corrections written above the sentence. A misplaced element may be underscored and its proper place in the sentence indicated by a caret (^). In some cases the entire sentence will have to be rewritten. If a sentence is correct, write **C**.

1. After failing to find Norfolk St., a map of the city solved my problem.

2. Lois is clever, creative, and enjoys needlework.

3. Lawton not only plans to visit the exhibition at the art gallery but also to see the film at the library.

4. Following the truck filled with cabbages, I found my way to Market Square.

5. Fay wants to open a book shop because she has always enjoyed them.

6. To find their way through the mountain pass, a careful study of the map was necessary.

7. I stopped at the drug store, and I had a prescription filled, and I arrived home at five o'clock.

8. Every afternoon she turned on her television set to watch the game show, which is in her kitchen.

9. While Richard is in Salt Lake City, either Stella or I are going to pick up his mail.

10. My roommate Norman has sold more tickets to the spring concert than any student on our hall.

11. I believe that I lain the mail on the table in the hall.

12. Everyone has their own version of the train wreck.

13. Sadie has a clearer understanding of backgammon than me.

14. Whom do you think should be given the award for the year's best editorial?

15. Mexico has a large supply of oil, which is encouraging to motorists in the United States.

16. Although he is an expert airplane pilot, he does not own one.

17. Olive took off her hat and coat, hung them up, and then she plugged in the coffeepot.

18. Because the Bears won a berth in the play-off games delighted the Chicago fans.

19. The old prospector wore a wide-brimmed hat, ragged coat, and a pair of stout boots.

20. Having caught the express train, only thirty minutes was required to reach Nathans's office.

21. We sure did enjoy the new production of *Mourning Becomes Electra.*

22. That handsome table was designed by Baker sitting in the bank lobby.

23. Last year Francis hoped to have completed his science requirements.

24. Belle can play the organ as well if not better than her father.

25. *Business Week* reported that it was him who was responsible for the company's recent success.

26. I was surprised that the traffic on the expressway how heavy it is at midnight.

27. Geraldine is one of those grocery shoppers who regularly clips coupons.

28. The temperature is below freezing, which is the reason I am looking for my gloves and scarf.

29. Warren has made the punch, and he thinks that it tastes splendid, and he wants you to sample it.

30. The reason that I could not meet you at the Collegiate Grill was because I had not completed my art project.

31. The child gathered up her belongings: a blanket, a doll, and a small suitcase.

32. If I was you, I would paint the wicker chairs white.

33. Friday afternoon Mr. Steuben as well as his pupils are to visit the radio station.

34. Is it them who are to bring the chili?

35. On the street below, the police officer's whistle sounded sharply and clearly.

36. I never seem to recognize Mary Boswell: I often take Lottie to be she.

37. My father's job requires more traveling than Uncle Morris.

38. Because of the extreme heat, Stan only jogged a dozen blocks this morning.

39. To please me, his clothes were always picked up before he left for class.

40. Louisa does not know if her plane stops in Washington.

41. Who do you think is the subject of this Whistler painting?

42. John feels as badly as anyone about missing the extra point.

43. Every one of the pedestrians know that they should use the crosswalk.

44. When decorating a Christmas tree, the lights should be put on first.

45. I sure am afraid that I have lost the key to my front door.

46. Neither you nor Theodore is able to carry this chest up three flights of stairs.

47. This year's snowfall is heavier than last year.

48. To completely restore this house will be a major undertaking.

49. I neither plan to have an early morning class nor one in the afternoon.

50. Why do you think that most of us loves a parade?

NAME ______________________________ SCORE ________

TEST ON LESSONS 19–24

A. In the following sentences insert all necessary punctuation marks, and correct all errors of mechanics.

1. I believe Ted that this jacket is your's mine is the green one on the chair.

2. Theres an article in this weeks Saturday Review that I think you will enjoy reading it is called Heroes In Literature.

3. Holly's and Jim's apartment overlooks a beautiful public garden in Geneva Switzerland.

4. My Grandmother came originally from the east, and she says that she cannot get used to the informality of California.

5. I want more than anything to spend a traditional christmas in Williamsburg said Aunt Louisa. Dont you think that would be grand?

6. The walllike cliff was so high that the boys decided not to attempt a climb to the top.

7. Its good news that doctors are on the verge of finding a treatment for the dread disease leukemia.

8. I would like to know who's raincoat that is in my hall closet it has been there for three weeks.

9. Never have I known such a holier than thou individual; she is like Mrs. Proudie in Trollopes book Barchester Towers.

10. Department stores should teach their sales clerks how to pronounce the french word lingerie.

11. Longfellows popular poem A Psalm Of Life is full of platitudes.

12. Nell tiptoed into the baby's room turned on the night light covered the baby with a blanket and quietly returned to her bedroom.

13. Letty I expected you to turn in some original work on that report not just a cut and dried excerpt from an encyclopedia.

14. Remember that there are two ps and only one s in the word disappointed.

15. My Sister says that she always does two things before starting to study washes her hair and turns on her record player.

B. After each of the following groups of words indicate the level of usage of the *italicized* word(s), using the following abbreviations: **A** for archaic, **I** for informal (colloquial), and **S** for slang. Use your dictionary for this test.

1. Erle Stanley Gardner wrote *whodunits.* ________
2. She's a *stick-in-the-mud.* ________
3. That's a *nifty* car. ________
4. "It is He that *hath* made us . . . ." ________
5. He pulled a *boner.* ________
6. Todd is a *square shooter.* ________
7. The defendant says that he was *framed.* ________
8. *Ofttimes* I wonder where she is now. ________
9. What's your *gripe*? ________
10. Mac and Greg usually *hang around* together. ________

C. The following section of the test is based on the Glossary of Faulty Diction. Cross out all the errors or colloquialisms and write the preferred forms above each sentence.

1. Mr. Walker has affected a remarkable improvement in the efficiency of his department.

2. Lillian was aggravated when Dan kept her waiting in the cold for thirty minutes.

3. I feel alright now; I hope I won't have that toothache anymore.

4. Among the two versions of the story I can see very little difference.

5. The judge's seat was positioned so that he could follow the proceedings personally.

6. Due to my demanding job, I am not able to jog everyday.

7. Hopefully we will have a pretty day for the football game Saturday; all the guys are planning on going.

8. A couple of you fellows help me with this tennis net; I would muchly appreciate your help.

9. Billy wants me to loan him my boat when he goes to the lake; after his last escapade I wonder if I should.

10. Lots of people have trouble in becoming orientated in this big city, but others act like they have lived here all their lives.

11. Betty and myself walked over to Janet's house, irregardless of the snow; we were literally frozen when we arrived.

12. The reason I wanted to talk with Reverend Sims is because I am real sorry that I missed church last Sunday.

13. I hear your right uneasy about the big test tomorrow; you should of studied for it.

14. Our college has less pupils now than it had ten years ago.

15. Bob was enthused about the fact that he would not have to forego his skiing trip; he had finally convinced his employer to give him the time off.

D. Give the meaning of each of the following prefixes or roots. Then write two words containing each prefix or root.

1. *multi-* ______________________

(1)______________________ (2)______________________

2. *derm* ______________________

(1)______________________ (2)______________________

3. *circum-* ______________________

(1)______________________ (2)______________________

4. *ob-* ______________________

(1)______________________ (2)______________________

5. *pre-* ______________________

(1)______________________ (2)______________________

6. *graph* ______________________

(1)______________________ (2)______________________

7. *poly-* ______________________

(1)______________________ (2)______________________

8. *phil* ______________________

(1)______________________ (2)______________________

9. *aud* ____________________

(1)____________________ (2)____________________

10. *epi-* ____________________

(1)____________________ (2)____________________

E. If there is a misspelled word in any line of five words given below, write it correctly in the space at the right. If all five words are correctly spelled, write **C** in the space.

1. definite, exaggerate, calander, describe, especially. ____________________
2. emphasize, dying, dissipate, writing, ecstacy ____________________
3. strenuous, pronounciation, propaganda, sophomore, forty ____________________
4. purchase, quarter, optimism, quanity, omitted ____________________
5. particularly, original, pardner, strength, likable ____________________
6. manufacture, mediocre, restaurant, tyranny, pamplet ____________________
7. livelihood, grandure, laboratory, irrelevant, gauge ____________________
8. magazine, niece, prominent, symmetry, vaccine ____________________
9. tradgedy, vengeance, villain, superintendent, murmur ____________________
10. overrun, manuever, paid, literature, occurrence ____________________
11. prejudice, futile, knowledge, innocence, priviledge ____________________
12. handkerchief, judgment, grammar, persistant, pursue ____________________
13. paralell, truly, shining, seize, descent ____________________
14. dilapidated, curriculum, buoyant, disatisfied, colonel ____________________
15. anonymous, captain, benefitted, courteous, column ____________________

NAME ______________________________ SCORE ________

ACHIEVEMENT TEST

In the following sentences identify the part of speech of each *italicized* word by writing one of of the following numbers in the space at the right:

1	if it is a noun,	5	if it is an adverb,
2	if it is a pronoun,	6	if it is a preposition,
3	if it is a verb,	7	if it is a conjunction,
4	if it is an adjective,	8	if it is an interjection.

1. *Toni* made a large asparagus casserole for her dinner party. ________
2. The mountains in the distance were a smoky shade *of* blue. ________
3. Ty's father wanted *him* to be a lawyer. ________
4. *When* he was young, Mr. Abbott played drums in a dance band. ________
5. Go ahead and begin the climb, *and* I will be just behind you. ________
6. Everyone *but* Molly ordered lemon pie for dessert. ________
7. Joan and Bill first *met* on a blind date. ________
8. Peter was always *small* for his age. ________
9. Mother was *especially* glad to see Uncle Martin after all these years. ________
10. I will be happy to drive you home *or* to let you spend the night here. ________
11. Miriam, who is *always* late, came dragging in at ten o'clock. ________
12. Unless you are prepared to wait in line for tickets, I would *not* plan to go to *A Chorus Line* tonight. ________
13. *Oh*, I wish that you would tell me the truth. ________
14. We have neither seen nor heard from Ted *since* last February. ________
15. *Only* Margaret is unwilling to join in the plans for a bake sale. ________
16. Johnson's is having a half-price sale of shoes *today*. ________
17. *Whoever* left the door open is responsible for the cat's disappearance. ________
18. Mother's new *hairdo* is reminiscent of the Twenties. ________
19. Our *grandfather* clock has a beautiful chime. ________
20. Jean sprained *her* ankle while skiing at Sugar Valley. ________
21. *Horrors!* I have spilled tomato soup on your new white carpet. ________
22. *Either* of those men is qualified for the job of manager. ________
23. Todd was driving much too *fast* on the way home last night. ________
24. *Neither* you *nor* I can predict the outcome of this tournament. ________
25. Mimi *was taken* by surprise when Elliott came through the door. ________

Each of the following sentences either contains an error or is correct. Indicate the error or the correctness by writing one of the following numbers in the space at the right:

1 if the case of the pronoun is incorrect,
2 if the subject and the verb do not agree,
3 if a pronoun and its antecedent do not agree,
4 if an adjective or an adverb is used incorrectly,
5 if the sentence is correct.

26. I cannot understand you leaving for the airport without me. ______
27. There is a ham sandwich and two cupcakes left over from the picnic. ______
28. Harriet thinks that she did good on her algebra test. ______
29. I believe that that is the man who I saw lurking in the bushes. ______
30. If everyone would come on time, they could easily get a seat on the bus. ______
31. I, who am usually suspicious, was completely taken in by her sad story. ______
32. Every one of those pears are overripe. ______
33. The judges said that whomever is selected for the scholarship will be notified tomorrow. ______
34. Each of the twins has their own bicycle. ______
35. Whomever responds to the invitation should be sent a copy of the conference program. ______
36. The finance committee have submitted the annual report. ______
37. A prospective customer should look carefully at a used car. ______
38. Seeming as happily as ever, the couple looked forward to their fiftieth wedding anniversary. ______
39. Tony as well as his sister are invited to the party on New Year's Eve. ______
40. Do you remember the time that Charles tried to teach Father and I to ski? ______
41. If you want to see a real good movie, come with me to Eastgate Drive-in. ______
42. Why should I, who is unable to carry a tune, offer to sing in the choir? ______
43. Neither jogging nor playing tennis are Martha's idea of interesting exercise. ______
44. Every one of us will have to bring their skates. ______
45. Between you and I no one should be allowed to keep the book for two weeks. ______
46. The loaves of bread sitting on the kitchen counter still felt warmly. ______
47. On the balcony was a small table, a pair of chairs, and three or four geraniums. ______
48. Everybody is planning to buy their own ticket. ______
49. Ginger is one of those persons who really enjoy hot tamales. ______
50. You suggesting that we stay at home tonight pleased Mother. ______

Each of the following sentences either contains an error in sentence structure or is correct. Indicate the error or correctness by writing one of the following numbers in the space at the right:

1 if the sentence contains a dangling modifier,
2 if the sentence contains a misplaced modifier,
3 if the sentence contains a faulty reference of a pronoun,
4 if the sentence contains faulty parallelism,
5 if the sentence is correct.

51. Exhausted by my work in the yard, the glass of lemonade was refreshing. ________
52. The car skidded across the road, struck the guard rail, and then it climbed the embankment. ________
53. This year I have only sent a dozen Christmas cards. ________
54. Carol explained to Nell that she has a long trip ahead of her. ________
55. He is an excellent athlete and who gives his best effort in every game. ________
56. Looking into the rear-view mirror, the huge truck was bearing down on me. ________
57. Richard called to ask me to go to the dance this morning. ________
58. Because she has nearly lost five pounds, Catherine is delighted with her diet. ________
59. Generally speaking, a crowd will support the underdog. ________
60. We not only enjoy shopping at the mall in the suburb, but we also look forward to an occasional trip downtown. ________
61. In reporting the tornado warnings, the media fulfilled its responsibility to the public. ________
62. When riding to town on the bus, the zoo was a regular stop. ________
63. I hope to successfully complete my research paper before spring holidays. ________
64. The statue is the work of a well-known sculptor dominating the entrance to the gardens. ________
65. The view from your roof is as clear if not clearer than any in the entire city. ________
66. "If one wants to eat, you have to cook" is an old political saying. ________
67. If anyone wants to enter the bowling tournament, you must turn in your entry form before Friday. ________
68. When Marty told Julie the joke about a talking gorilla, she couldn't stop laughing. ________
69. I have just read a fascinating article about Charles Lamb's essays in last month's *Harper's*. ________
70. I had a long talk with a man who is in the Secret Service, and I have decided to be one. ________

71. In trying to repair the flat tire, the car suddenly fell off the jack. ________

72. Not only is Hilda a fine musician but also a wonderful dancer. ________

73. If I have only one life to live, I would certainly rather be a redhead than a blonde. ________

74. The people who attend the clinic frequently must walk there and then back home again. ________

75. Mother stared at the vase that had been broken with her hands clenched. ________

Each of the following sentences contains an error in punctuation or mechanics, or is correct. Indicate the error or correctness by writing one of the following numbers in the space at the right:

1 if a comma has been omitted,
2 if a semicolon has been omitted,
3 if an apostrophe has been omitted,
4 if quotation marks have been omitted,
5 if the sentence is correct.

76. Jim has just played Linda Ronstadt's Blue Bayou for the tenth time today. ______
77. Toward Linda Ellis felt no animosity. ______
78. The woman wearing the blue stain blouse is a police officer. ______
79. Trying not to smile I watched the two children wearing their mother's high-heeled shoes. ______
80. I remember that on January 14, 1975 I got my driver's license. ______
81. My new tennis coach Ms. Rogers has helped me develop my backhand. ______
82. Ernie Flowers says that his brother Sam has joined the Marines. ______
83. I used to like television now I am bored with it. ______
84. Don't bother to wait, said Corinne; I will join you in about an hour. ______
85. Olin was cooking the Thanksgiving turkey and Bobbie was preparing oyster dressing and cranberry sauce. ______
86. Trying to save fifty dollars a month Lucile often went without lunch. ______
87. Above the plane sputtered and lost altitude rapidly. ______
88. At first I thought that my carburetor was flooded then I realized that I was out of gas. ______
89. Wanting desperately to win the division title the boys were very tense. ______
90. Jacks going to be surprised when we tell him about Marcia's wedding plans. ______
91. Just before the starting gun, the star swimmer an Australian girl fainted dead away. ______
92. My mother used to love Rudyard Kipling's poem L'Envoi. ______
93. I refused to tell Bobby what his Christmas present would be for I wanted to surprise him. ______
94. Jerry walked away in disgust and never mentioned the matter again. ______
95. A highlight of our Nova Scotia trip was the tasty seafood we enjoyed there I have never had such delicious scallops. ______
96. Bob said to Madeleine, I am sure that two can live as cheaply as one. ______
97. Well all be ready for bed by the time we drive the twenty-five miles home. ______

98. Frazier and Mike our friends from Mississippi are coming to spend the Christmas holidays with us. ________

99. Katie begins her classes on Monday so she will have to leave for Phoenix on Sunday. ________

100. Generally speaking it is warm here in Athens until the middle of October. ________

Index

6 7 8 9 10